ADOPTED BY COUNTRY

An Artist from China in Aboriginal Australia

ZHOU Xiaoping

From the late 1980s, the artist Zhou Xiaoping has lived, travelled and painted in Aboriginal communities across northern Australia. To his impressive body of art, we now have a sharply observed account of his unique experiences in this compelling and very readable memoir.

David Walker
Inaugural BHP Chair of Australian Studies
Peking University

Some thirty-seven years ago now, a young Chinese artist found himself living in the camps of Arnhem Land and the desert, as one with the mobs. Ever since, Xiaoping has made Aboriginal people, their art and culture the central theme of his life's work. It is a touching story from the heart, of deep friendships in life, art and cultural connection, offering unique insights. But the outside world views such closeness between Chinese and Aboriginal people with suspicion, provoking a form of protectionist racism. This book is truth telling at its best.

Adj. Professor Margo Ngawa Neale
Emeritus Curatorial Fellow: First Nations
National Museum of Australia

ADOPTED
BY COUNTRY

An Artist from China in Aboriginal Australia

ZHOU Xiaoping

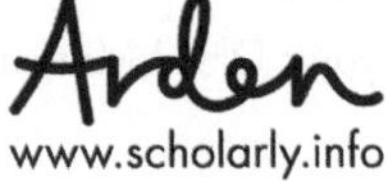

First published 2025 by Arden
the international general books' imprint of
Australian Scholarly Publishing Pty Ltd
7 Lt Lothian St Nth, North Melbourne, Vic 3051
Tel: 03 9329 6963
contact@scholarly.info / www.scholarly.info

ISBN 978-1-923267-53-4

Cover design: Zhou Xiaoping, David Morgan
Cover illustration: *How He Sees Me*, by Zhou Xiaoping
Image Layout: David Morgan

Foreword

Zhou Xiaoping arrived in Australia with an unbridled curiosity about our lands and peoples. After a few chance encounters, he quickly immersed himself in learning from our elders, from the country and their cultural traditions. He found treasures, enticing legendary heroes from their resting places to animate our world through his brushes and ink. Ancestral heroes and stories came alive through the brush of a Chinese artist.

For over three decades, Xiaoping has journeyed between two worlds – his adopted home of Melbourne and the remote Aboriginal communities of Arnhem Land and the Central Desert. With remarkable persistence and sensitivity, he has forged close relationships with Indigenous artists and elders, learning their stories, customs and artistic traditions. This book chronicles Xiaoping's extraordinary odyssey as he is gradually adopted into Aboriginal kinship systems and granted permission to participate in artistic practices and ceremonies that are usually closed to outsiders.

Xiaoping brings a unique perspective as a Chinese immigrant artist encountering Indigenous Australian culture. His exquisite ink paintings blend traditional Chinese techniques with Aboriginal motifs and stories, creating a compelling visual dialogue between two ancient civilisations. But more than just an artistic collaboration, this book offers profound insights into cross-cultural understanding and reconciliation.

Through vivid, often poignant anecdotes, Xiaoping reveals the deep kinship connections Aboriginal people maintain with their land and ancestors. He grapples honestly with the ethical dilemmas of an outsider representing Indigenous culture, facing criticism from both Aboriginal and non-Aboriginal Australians. Yet he persevered, driven by genuine respect and a desire to build bridges between cultures.

Adopted by Country is a deeply personal story of transformation. Xiaoping's journey from bewildered newcomer to trusted friend and artistic collaborator mirrors Australia's own evolving relationship with its First Peoples. His experiences offer hope that through patience, humility and genuine engagement, divides between cultures can be bridged. This remarkable book stands as a testament to the power of art to foster mutual understanding in our increasingly interconnected world.

Professor Marcia Langton AO
The University of Melbourne

Contents

Part One

In the Desert

If you look down and see footprints in the Australian desert sand, you would assume that they had been left by Aboriginal people. You would not expect the footprints of a Chinese artist also to be there. Why did hc walk into this desert?

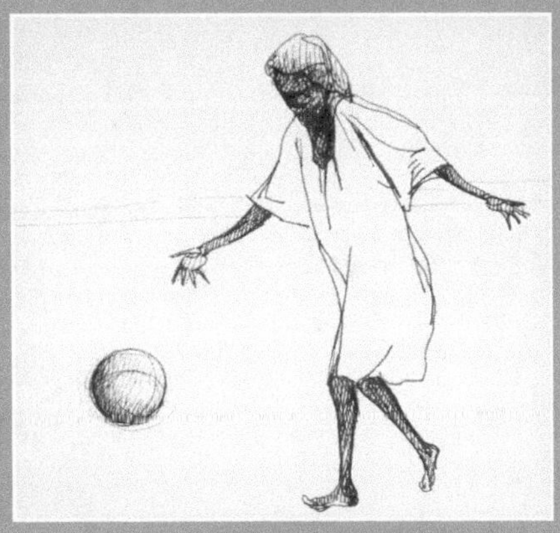

Children enjoy playing sports.

1

A Chinese Artist Meets Australian Aborigines

In October 1988, I took a bus from Melbourne to Alice Springs, a small town in central Australia. My map showed that this was the only town in this desert area, and looking around, I felt as if I had arrived in a place as barren as the Gobi/Gebi Desert in China's Great Northwest frontier. The only difference was the weather. Under the translucent sky, rolling waves of heat churned over me. With only the little money I had earned from selling paintings at an exhibition in Melbourne, I had embarked on this journey around Australia, naively thinking it would allow me to become a real artist able to support myself by selling my work. Young people have the advantage of daring to dream. As I looked out through the bus window, the landscape of Australia's wilderness passed before my eyes, like a long scroll without an end. A large area of golden grass resembling a piece of silk floating on the ground undulated in the wind, while patches of scorched earth stood out like the translucent black ink of a Chinese painting. This endless landscape was rich in iron ore, and in the blazing sun it looked like red-hot iron. I was curious: such a desolate virgin land must contain huge resources of energy and so many unknown mysteries. I was grateful and excited to have the opportunity to see all this. The word 'opportunity' conjures up memories of the person associated with the first major turning point in my life. This story took place in Huangshan, the Yellow Mountains in China.

Huangshan is famous for its strange and peculiar peaks with tall, century-old pine trees clinging to them. Cloaked in a mighty sea of clouds, the extraordinary vistas to be seen have led many artists to praise and portray them. The tallest mountain, Lianhua Peak, is 1,864 metres above sea level. The area has many microclimates and the scenery changes dramatically throughout the year. During the day, as the weather changes quickly, the clouds lift to reveal breathtaking views. Since my youth, I have lived from time to time in these mountains and, like so many other artists, have been deeply attracted to the beautiful landscape.

One autumn while I was painting there on the mountain, groups of tourists, climbers and artists began to arrive to enjoy the scenery. One of the passing visitors, a young lady, stopped to watch me paint. I gave her a smile, which she politely returned. A smile like this often allows conversation between two strangers. Her name was Helen Huang, and she was holidaying in China. She told me that she was a student at the Royal Melbourne Institute of Technology in Australia. When our chat came to an end, she asked if she could buy my painting. I was very happy, and said, 'Please take it as a gift'. At that time, Chinese artists were not aware of the value of art as a commodity. In return, Helen left me her contact details, and said to come and see her if I ever visited Australia. Just like that, my landscape painting drifted across the ocean to hang in Miss Helen's living room.

About a year later, a letter arrived from Miss Helen in Australia. She said that her friends really liked my painting and that she wanted to arrange an exhibition for me in Melbourne. I couldn't believe it, and read and reread the letter, until I was sure that the Chinese characters standing there clearly in black and white were not lying to me. In one bound, I had reached the moon: I had the opportunity to hold a solo exhibition in a foreign country. At that time, for artists, especially young artists who were often considered mere painters, it was almost impossible to hold an exhibition in China. They always lived in the shadow of established artists or masters. China's art world emphasised inheriting traditional artistic style and form, and the master–student relationship. In this restrictive academic atmosphere that was under heavy government control, it was impossible for young artists to develop new ideas and to innovate. When Western contemporary art was introduced to China, it caused a huge stir, and offered a chance to get rid of these restrictions.

My exhibition included traditional Chinese landscapes and flower and bird paintings, because these were the subjects that I had been trained to paint. In the 1980s and 1990s, Australian interest and understanding of Chinese culture was somewhat like my own uncertain knowledge of Aboriginal culture. Australians knew only some basic Chinese greetings and about lion dances. Even so, it was clear that Australians were quite tolerant, and aware that there was a nation in the Far East whose culture was ancient, rich and splendid.

Luckily my Melbourne exhibition allowed me to sell some of my work. I needed some cash to make a trip around Australia before my visa expired. This trip proved to be another important turning point in my life as an artist, even though it was completely unplanned, an impulsive trip from which no feelings of apprehension would hold me back. I was like a young deer full of restless curiosity, impatient to bound off into the unknown.

On the way to Alice Springs, the bus made a few short stops, including one in Adelaide, to pick up and drop off passengers. Most of the passengers were tourists from all over the world. I wasn't sure if their motivations were like my own, but I quickly noticed that none of them was Chinese. I assumed that most other Chinese were back in Sydney or Melbourne, working desperately hard to make some money and to improve their socio-economic prospects. The thought made me feel uneasy, and caused me to question my own aims and ambitions. What would I do after my trip? Go back home. But then what? What about my future? Like most young people, I had little idea of what I wanted to do.

After thirty hours of travelling, I finally arrived at Alice Springs. When I got off the bus, I was shocked by what I saw. What was going on? Dishevelled, dark-skinned people were walking on the streets in small groups. In the distance, two men were arguing fiercely, as if they would soon come to blows. Who were they? I had never heard that there were many black people in Australia. Mixed with them on the street were white people walking around with cameras hanging from their necks. The contrast was stark. As I stared blankly at them, I remembered that the bus driver had told me that there used to be only black people here, until one day some white people discovered the giant rock here and everything has since changed. Ayers Rock (Uluru) had become a tourist attraction as the largest monolithic rock in the world. Like me, most of the white people on the street were tourists who had come to explore Uluru's secrets. Watching the passers-by, I noticed that wherever there were groups of black people, there were no white people. The white people kept their distance from the black people, avoiding them. The bus driver had warned passengers not to stare at the black people or to photograph them. It could cause trouble and we might be attacked. I found it hard to believe that these black people would really be so fierce. The gulf between blacks and whites in this town came as a big surprise to me.

I spotted an unkempt man, his upper body bare, exposing several very prominent scars, each about 30 centimetres long on his chest and stomach. He was wearing ill-fitting, oil-stained suit pants, while walking barefoot along the broken steps of a driveway. His hands were clasped behind, and his back was very straight. Nearby on the roadside was a Coca-Cola advertisement, its familiar bright colours contrasting sharply with the man's appearance. A Toyota drove by, throwing up the dust and disturbing his long hair. He didn't seem to notice, and kept walking slowly ahead, gazing at nothing. Forgetting the bus driver's warning, I quickly raised my camera and took his photo from about 10 metres away. At the 'click' of the shutter, he quickly turned and walked straight towards me. I looked at his muddy eyes and the dust collected in the wrinkles on his face. The smell of his body grew stronger. As I murmured a quick 'Thank you', he stretched out his palm, his face expressionless. I stepped back in panic, not knowing what he wanted. He kept staring at me silently as if he couldn't be bothered speaking, looking past me, his eyes not quite meeting mine, but fixed shyly off to one side. After a few moments, I realised that he wanted me to pay him for the photograph. Finding a handful of coins, I placed them in his hand. Expressionless, he turned and walked away. As I watched his retreating back, I felt a strange unease: why did this man look so utterly despondent? For a young artist like myself, who had grown up in Hefei, the capital of Anhui province, China, and who was now standing in a strange country with many beautiful illusions about Western civilisation in my head, what I had just experienced shocked me deeply.

I have not only kept this image in my photo album since that time, but have also drawn upon it in many of my paintings. It is engraved in my memory as the first time that I had come into close contact with an Aboriginal Australian.

———— ≈ ————

I decided to stay in town for a few more days. Alice Springs was a tourist town. In addition to backpacker and mid-range motels, several coffee shops, and bars, there were many shops selling tourist items: mostly T-shirts, hats, boomerangs, and daily necessities printed with various Aboriginal patterns. What especially caught my attention was the paintings, composed almost entirely of small dots. At first glance, they seemed incomprehensible, but I soon saw that these were significant cultural symbols. After seeing more of them, I gradually began to like them. They condensed the natural landscape into countless small dots with a panoramic view of the earth. When I was told that these Aboriginal artists had never had any art training, I was most surprised, as they had achieved such a professional level in the use of colour and expression. They had learned this from their elders, just as I had learned from Chinese masters, not in a formal art school. Art academies are not necessarily the only effective way for nurturing artists. The unique vision and way of thinking of these Aboriginal artists really attracted me and planted the seeds for my later cross-cultural artistic work.

Over the next few days, I explored the town, seeking out Aboriginal people. Before long, people were talking about me. Everyone in town knew about the Chinese artist who walked among the Aboriginal people with a sketchbook and a camera. Later, friends would ask me how I had developed a 'relationship' with Aboriginal people in such a short period of time. The answer was very simple: I showed respect. What else establishes good and lasting relationships between people? Of course, at first, I also had some other strategies to use in these encounters. Whenever I approached a circle of Aboriginal people, I would hold out a packet of tobacco. We then joked, chatted, and painted while rolling cigarettes together. Gradually, I learned some words of their languages, and sometimes taught them a few words of Chinese. They enjoyed looking through my sketchbook. This was usually the first time that they had seen life drawing, where the subject looked real on paper. After passing around each sketch, it was inevitable that they would leave dirty fingerprints. Later, when I wanted to exhibit these drawings, the gallery curator would complain that they were too dirty and wouldn't show them. But I didn't think there was a problem. For me, these fingerprints were like Chinese seals, confirming the origins of the drawings and their appraisal by 'experts'. They were a record of the warm friendships and stories behind these special drawings, important testimonies for me and my work.

———≈———

The Alice had a strong effect on the people living there: both long-term residents and visiting tourists. In these hot outback conditions, people forgot their city ways and let their hair down. They became much more casual and sometimes even unruly. The monotony of daily life here was relieved only by the bar, where everyone liked to gather. It was a good place to make new friends, relax and meet girls. On weekends, two beautiful blonde girls would shuffle through the crowds with trays of wine, clad only in mini-skirts. As they approached topless with their breasts swaying, the men gladly grabbed their drinks. Chatting and cooling off, this was a great place for them to be.

One day, I met two guys who were around my own age. Soon we started talking, and to my surprise, one of them said that he had heard about me: the Chinese artist who mixed with Aboriginals. He said that in this small place, whatever happened would attract everyone's attention. From our conversation, I gathered that the two men had been university classmates. Five years ago, after finishing a law degree, they came to Alice for a holiday and stayed to work part-time when they ran out of money. Later, the bearded man – who looked very fit and had resolute, confident eyes – decided to stay, practising law while working part-time as a musician. His fair-skinned friend – who was meticulously well groomed, a typically 'well-maintained' man, despite his casual outfit – eventually returned to live in Sydney. I had assumed that someone like him would have worked out his future life while at university. Having received a good education, he would begin an enviable career with a high salary, respectability, high social standing, and all the things sought for by elites. If he had inherited a bit of restlessness in his make-up, his ambition would be even higher, like that of this bearded man's friend who said that he was going to join one of the major political parties. He had everything mapped out.

'I like the Aboriginal people here', the bearded man said. His friend demurred that he didn't like them drinking. 'But we're drinking', the bearded man replied. 'You might even get drunk tonight yourself, right? It's not a good thing, but it can happen to anyone. We should understand these problems without exaggerating them. The main reason I've stayed here is because once you really get close to Aboriginal people, you can truly start to understand and appreciate their culture.' His friend remained unconvinced. 'Well, you always were a weird bloke', he joked. The bearded man turned to me, curious. 'How come a Chinese artist is attracted to this town and these Aboriginal people, while my mate here can't see the point in it?', he asked. 'Why, is that?'

I shrugged; I really didn't know why either. 'Errr…' I struggled to find the right words to say in my limited English. Not to embarrass me, he continued, 'Well, man, no matter what the reason, it seems that everyone here has accepted you. And that's not easy.'

'Aren't Aboriginal people easy to get to know?', I asked.

'What do you think?', he replied, 'Surely, you've noticed the tense atmosphere in this town?' While his words confirmed the feelings I had about the place, he seemed hesitant to continue any further with the subject, but finally he concluded, 'If you are really interested in Aboriginal people, I suggest you go to Arnhem Land, where traditional Aboriginal culture continues. But it is not certain that you'll be able to actually get into these areas.'

'Where is it? How do I get there?', I asked.

'Oh, do you want to walk there?', he joked.

'I don't know, is it really far away?'

'Maybe you can try', he said with a smirk. 'Have you heard of Darwin? It's only a day's drive away from there.'

I'd heard about the city of Darwin, which is located at the northernmost tip of Australia. It was also the place where I wanted to go next. 'Okay, I'll remember it', I said.

'However, I have never been there.' Reaching out his hand, he said goodbye: 'Wish you good luck, man'.

The very next day, I approached the local Aboriginal Land Council, asking for help, and met Bob. Shaking my hand enthusiastically, he said, 'Everyone's talking about this Chinese artist in town, who sits down with Aboriginal people'. The bearded man in the bar was right: the Chinese artist had certainly attracted attention. I briefly introduced myself, hoping that through Bob I could meet more local Aboriginal people, especially the elders. He listened to me attentively, but with doubt showing on his face. Why would Aboriginal people want to have anything to do with a Chinese?

Bob said very little but simply told me to come back the next morning, because there was somewhere he wanted to take me. Perhaps this would be a place where I could find some answers? I gave him a quick but grateful hug, surprising us both, because Chinese people are usually quite reserved about such physical contact.

The next day, Bob took me to a river outside town. It was almost completely dry: water ran in just one small ditch about a metre wide. Yet the riverbanks were about 15 metres across, indicating that there had once been ample water here. Cans, dirty clothes and all sorts of other garbage were scattered everywhere. It was strange to see a riverbed in this dry desert, the banks overgrown with weeds and sparse trees. Why had Bob brought me here? I looked at him, puzzled, but he just stood in the grass, not responding to my confusion. He yelled a few words in native language that I didn't understand. What was he up to? Who was he calling? I thought, if this was happening at night, I would be getting out of here fast. Bob yelled a few more times, until finally there was some movement in the grass, and a noise that sounded like a snort. Immediately alert, I looked in the direction of the sound. With a 'hum, hum', an Aboriginal man emerged from the bushes. Rubbing his eyes, he said something I didn't understand. Was he cross about being woken up?

Bob introduced us in Aboriginal language. This was the first time that I had heard a non-English Aboriginal name. It felt strange, but natural. The man also had an English name, Henry. Later, I discovered that many Aboriginal people also had English names – names that white people found easier to remember. This happens as well to Chinese students. One of the first things that Australian teachers do in class is to give their Chinese students an English name. But our names were carefully chosen for us by our parents, so why should we change them for the convenience of anyone else?

I shook Henry's hand that was soft like a woman's. Muttering something to Bob, he retreated into the bushes. Bob motioned to me not to move, and I heard someone peeing. Looking around, I noticed a plastic sheet hung between two trees. Alongside were blankets and dirty clothes, a few empty bottles and piles of rubbish everywhere. Bob looked across at me again, shrugged, and curled his lips. I could see the state of things, so there was nothing he needed to say.

More coughing came from the bushes, followed by spitting and whispering. Several heads appeared above the grass, looking around then slinking back. An Aboriginal man got up and walked past me. 'Morning', I said softly but got no answer. Perhaps we had woken him up, too? Then more and more Aboriginal people appeared, both men and women. They started walking silently towards the town, avoiding me as much as possible. The gentle sunlight shone on them, casting shadows. In the crowd I spotted an old hunchbacked man who I had seen at the bar, still wearing his red check shirt, and carrying his stick. In the bar, the old man had managed to quickly calm down a rather tense atmosphere caused by a drunk man's behaviour, with little more than the strong aura of majesty which surrounded him. The incident had left a deep impression on me.

I became thoughtful as I watched him go, and remembered how Aboriginal people in town had asked me for money when I took pictures. As the group moved away from me now, I felt as though they all had eyes in their backs, looking at me. I followed, walking slowly towards the town. Another day had begun.

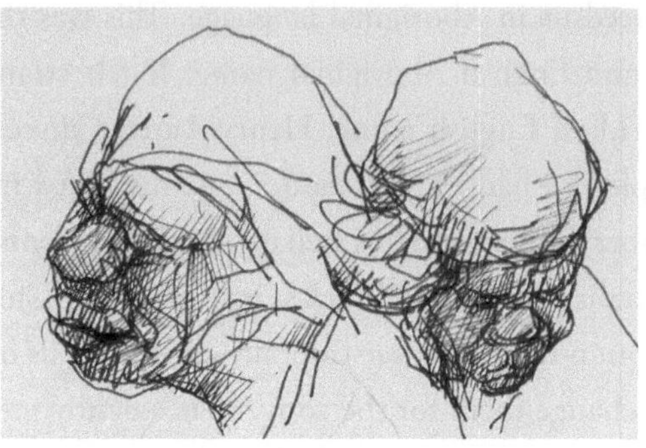

Sketch, from my early years in Alice Springs.

2

Lost in the Desert

All the tourists in Alice Springs were there to see Uluru. From Alice, you had to catch a bus to the foot of the monolith, where you could truly marvel at this huge rock that attracted worldwide attention.

The manager at the Backpacker's Inn said, 'Oh, Uluru is not far, it's right near here'. And I, a novice lacking travel experience, believed him. But for a poor artist like me, even a short trip required careful planning. It seemed that my best option was to hitch a ride. Luckily, if I chipped in for petrol, the two charming and vivacious young girls – university students from France and Germany – who were sharing the room with me, were happy to take me with them. It would be an economical, freewheeling and romantic travel plan.

'Why did you come to Australia?', they asked.

'I'm an artist, and I came here to hold an exhibition of my works.'

'Okay… and then what?'

'Then, I wanted to take the chance to look around before returning to China. I also hope to do some new paintings. That's it.' My reasoning was simple but important for me. I knew that this might be my only chance to see anything of the Western world. Unlike most other Chinese students coming to Melbourne at the time, I was not thinking of staying long-term, as perhaps I should have been. I was still rather young and naive.

On 9 September 1976, Chairman Mao Zedong had died. For the Chinese people, it was an unforgettable day, an event that shocked the country. While everyone was deeply concerned about the fate of China and the Chinese people, some heard the news with mixed feelings, feeling thankful that this day had arrived at last. It meant that the decade-long Cultural Revolution would finally end. As the era of Deng Xiaoping began, people slowly awakened from a decade of diabolical political oppression and were able at last to leave the country through the slowly opening door to see what the rest of the world looked like.

Many Chinese people at the time were eager to leave their homeland. Those who were overseas suppressed complaints and hardships in their hearts, and sent back only positive messages and accounts of the good money that they were making. As a result, many Chinese flocked to the United States, Canada, Japan and Australia in order 'to study abroad'. Between 1986 and the early 1990s, around 40,000 students came to Australia from China.

They were not the first Chinese to come to the country. A case can be made, I believe, that Chinese had been coming to Australia for nearly three hundred years. Since the eighteenth century, Chinese workers followed the Macassans to the coast of Northern Australia to fish for sea cucumber, and following those early arrivals, small numbers of Chinese continued to arrive in Australia. Then, from the early 1850s, Australia's gold attracted a large influx of Chinese peasants. In just two years, the number of Chinese immigrants reached 30,000. There are striking similarities between the wave of Chinese immigration in the 1850s and the wave that occurred in the 1980s and 1990s. In both cases, people were leaving their homeland to escape dire poverty, hoping to make a better life for themselves and their families in succeeding generations. I wasn't thinking that far ahead. I had little real idea of what the world outside China was like until I came to Melbourne.

My first impression of Melbourne was one of a large, untouched canvas. This country had a population of only 17 million people and in physical space was not much smaller than China, where the population was 1.3 billion. I saw garden-fronted houses scattered alongside the road from the airport to the centre of Melbourne city, but barely any pedestrians at all. Where were the people hiding?

Over my first few days in Melbourne, my feelings went from curiosity to excitement, then from excitement to serenity. Australians lived in such a beautiful, idyllic environment – conditions that people the world over yearned for. The comfort, tranquillity and simplicity of this lifestyle was infectious. Yet even so, I experienced a sense of helplessness, loss and insecurity without the support of the community I had abruptly left. It was difficult to know how I would find the creative passion to work 'freelance' in this place. I had been introduced to this wonderful life too quickly to be able to adapt properly to it.

A friend suggested that I should get out of Melbourne, to seek inspiration in some place like Uluru in the desert. The word 'desert' immediately conjured up images of sand and dust marked by footprints and dunes. But what I saw when I got there was a magnificent – flat but desolate – landscape stretching out in front of me in barbecue-like heat. Our car sped across the desert along a straight highway with no speed limits. I could feel the energy emanating from this uncultivated land. For me, this was the best place in the country. This place is certain to contain unique natural resources and a profound culture. The desert land was Australia's real treasure.

The French girl told me how much she liked Aboriginal dot paintings. For her, the colours were so harmonious and the works possessed such a strong vitality. I told her to buy one otherwise she might never have the chance again.

'Sure', she said. 'But… when I see these dot paintings everywhere, how would I know if it is art or just a tourist souvenir?' She hesitated, 'Different standards lead to different budgets and quality'.

I had indeed noticed that every corner of the Alice was full of dot paintings, an ubiquitous tourist product. I heard that many of these paintings were bought by art dealers very cheaply, and then sold on at five times the price. The French girl wondered whether these decorative works were in fact good art and worth the price.

With a characteristic gesture of her hand, she explained, 'Yesterday, I saw a painting I really liked, but the asking price was too high at $500. I can't afford it.' I told myself that buying such art was something I couldn't even think about, but at least this girl had a desire to collect a dot painting.

'Poor artist', she added. I thought she had read my thoughts from my expression, but she was referring to the Aboriginal painters. 'I found out that the gallery owner had given one woman artist only two $50 dollar notes for her painting', she said.

'Really? That's outrageous. But maybe, she was just taking a deposit.'

'At first, I thought so too. But afterwards, I met her on the street, and the woman confirmed that it was a one-off deal.'

At this, the conversation in the car lapsed into silence. A strong wind blew in through the window.

I was speechless, although everyone knows that the life of an artist was very difficult. For most people, the word 'artist' is invariably associated with poverty, conjuring up images of people filled with unrealistic dreams. Yet $100 would only just cover the cost of buying canvas and paint.

'Does this kind of thing happen only to Aboriginal painters?', I asked. 'Or …?' The French girl admitted that she had been thinking along these lines too.

'Are other artists also treated like this?'

To me, it didn't sound right, but I only knew about what it was like to be an artist in China. There, the status of artists has been on a roller-coaster, up and down entirely under the control of the government, especially during the Cultural Revolution (1966–76) when artists fell to the bottom of the heap overnight. In the 1980s, Deng Xiaoping's Reform and Opening Up Movement revived the social standing of artists. But rather than returning to traditional forms of art, they turned to Western art forms and concepts, including ideas for the commercialisation of art. Previously, artworks either expressed political ideas or were made purely for enjoyment: no one ever thought that their works could be sold for cash. This was the difference between working in a socialist versus a capitalist system. Under Chinese socialism, the social status of traditional artists reached unprecedented heights. As a result, there came about a strange phenomenon: the bigger the artist's name, the greater the price for his or her artworks. Although some artists chose to become 'freelancers', they were still symbolically attached to institutions such as universities. However, very few were able to make a successful living by selling their works. Most earned very little and lived a frugal life, but with their ideals.

Soon after I began dealing with galleries in both Australia and China, I realised that the relationship between an artist and a gallery depends on whether the artist is considered important, and how important. When unknown artists ask a gallery to sell their work, they must abide by the conditions laid down by the gallery. However, when a gallery shows works by a famous artist, it is the gallery that must accommodate the requirements of the famous artist. The relationship between artist and gallery is always carefully negotiated. So, finding a good gallery is not an easy task.

Laughing and chatting as the car tore down the highway, I suddenly began to feel dizzy as I sat there leafing through my sketchbook. I looked out the window. A huge, lone boulder appeared far away on the horizon. It must be Uluru. I pressed my lips together tightly, trying to suppress the rumbling in my stomach, as I told myself we would get there soon. But not long after, I had to ask, 'Can you stop the car?'

The French girl turned to me, concerned. 'What's wrong? You don't look good.' My pale and pained face must have frightened her.

'Car sick', I muttered.

The car quickly pulled off the road and before I knew it, I was vomiting violently, feeling very embarrassed. Handing me a bottle of water, the girls gently patted my back.

'I'm so sorry', I said.

'Oh, no, no, no. We can rest here for a while', the French girl replied.

When the girls thought we should get going, the French girl told her friend to drive more slowly. 'There is still enough time to arrive at Yulara before dark', she said. But another unexpected challenge awaited us. The car wouldn't start. We were all anxious but had no idea what to do. Getting out of the car, the German girl looked up at the sky and drew a cross on her chest, 'Oh, help me, God!' Then turning to the car for a while, she began kicking the tyre and swearing in German. She knew what it meant to break down in the desert. Seeing her so angry, I felt sorry about having caused so much trouble. We began waiting to flag down a passing car. But after a long time waiting, there was still no car to be seen.

The sun shone down fiercely with a vengeance. It must have been over 40 degrees. Opening all the car doors, we leaned back in our seats, chatting quietly while wondering what to do next. Even if we saw passing cars, we still might not be able to leave, so what should we do? Time passed slowly, my eyes closing, still troubled by the discomfort caused by the swaying. I tried to empty my mind to calm myself down and I gradually fell asleep, until a sudden shout from the German girl woke me.

'Hey, what's that?'

A black dot on the horizon, towards Alice Springs, was slowly growing larger.

'Thank you, God! I knew you wouldn't leave us to suffer in this heat', the German girl called out. She again made the sign of the cross on her chest. No matter whatever happened, this vivacious German girl always retained her good spirits, and was forever repeatedly chanting and thanking God. Clearly, she thought that God had sent his messenger to help us, but all the same, God did not provide us with a perfect ending. None of us could fix the car, and the new car could only carry two extra persons and all their luggage. In the end, we decided that the two girls would leave with our rescuers, and I would wait for God to send another messenger. I was just able to see Uluru, and thought, it shouldn't be too long before another car comes past. If worst came to worst, I could just walk to the rock. At the time, I did not realise how dangerous this idea really was. Looking back, I think what happened next really was God's will. Some magic must have transpired, and I would be led on to a path of no return.

Stepping up to me, the French girl hugged me, saying, 'We'll be waiting for you at Uluru'.

'Yes, wait for me', I replied, as two hands with thumbs up stretched out through opposite windows. Smiling as I hoisted up my backpack, I returned their thumbs-up sign, and began walking in the direction of Uluru.

Deserted countryside. Weeds swayed slowly in the heat. Metre-high anthills dotted the landscape everywhere. The scorching sun bore down, sapping the energy from my body with currents of hot air. Still, I would rather walk on slowly than sit in the scorching sun waiting.

The landscape here had little charm and in fact was rather boring. Perhaps the road to Uluru would continue like this? Perhaps it would be better if I took a shortcut? As my feet gradually deviated from the road, my mind wandered as I thought about all the things that had happened over the past few days. But after pondering hard about the matter, I asked myself: what does all this have to do with me as a Chinese artist, just staying temporarily in Australia? After three months, I'll leave and everything here will stay the same. Yet somehow my heart was touched by emotions that couldn't be put into words, and a profound feeling that I would rarely encounter again.

Quietly, the sun had set, and the wilderness turned from a scorched yellow to an orange red. The rays of the sun crossing the transparent sky turned the clouds into a variety of different scenes, like some beautiful oil painting. The vast wilderness began to reveal its majesty, comforting me as twilight descended. This moving scene remains in my mind as a source of inspiration for my art.

After all this thinking and walking, I felt a headache coming on. I was drained of energy, and I suddenly felt inexplicably agitated. My lips were parched, and my skin was dry and hot. I took a sip of water, and let it slowly run down my throat. Now I realised how important water was to the people who lived on this land. Uluru looked as if it were right in front of me, but to get there would take a long time. If I couldn't get to Yulara before dark, where the two girls were waiting, I would have to sleep here alone in the wilderness. I had never experienced this before, and really couldn't imagine what would happen next.

A strange rustling sound, 'sa… sa…', suddenly came from the grass. Holding my breath, I looked anxiously around for a sign of any movement. Was I just imagining things? I started to stride out towards Uluru, but again came this strange sound. Mustering all my faculties, I scanned the grass around and finally found a huge goanna hiding there. Instinctively, I got down on my haunches and picked up a lump of dried mud. I wondered if I could catch this giant goanna, and if it would hurt me. This was the first time I had ever seen a goanna that was some 1.5 metres long. For a time, it remained motionless, but as I moved slowly forward, it raised its head and stared back at me. This stalemate lasted for about fifteen seconds or so before the goanna fled suddenly into the grass. Scanning all around, I could find no further sign of it but, looking down, I noticed that the jagged weeds had scratched my legs and hands and I was bleeding.

A gentle breeze sprung up and took away the heat from my body. It was strangely quiet, and I could hear nothing but the rhythmic pounding of my feet as I began to run. I had no idea how far I had gone, but after some time my legs began to shake, probably because I was dehydrated. I stopped to catch my breath, and suddenly there was that 'sa… sa…' sound again. It had to be a goanna, as there was nothing else out there. But my instincts warned that something was behind me. Turning abruptly, I saw three black faces staring at me through the bushes. Terrified, we stole glances speechlessly. I looked around them but found nothing unusual.

Standing before me were three bare-chested children, who looked to be around six or seven years old. One of them was holding a stick and observing me with a serious expression. I wasn't sure whether it was due to my nervous behaviour, or because they were seeing a stranger appear where none should have been. What was truly remarkable was those huge round eyes on their small dark faces: they were alert and attentive.

'Hi!', one of them greeted me.

'Hi!', I replied softly.

There was a moment's silence.

'What you doing here?'

'I'm lost.'

'How come?', they asked with a faint smile. While exchanging glances, one of the kids started laughing, and the sound immediately dissolved the tension.

'What do you mean, "how come?" I'm lost', I replied.

'You can go back follow your foot tracks.'

'What foot tracks?' Looking at the ground, I couldn't see anything.

'Oh, never mind. Where you want to go?'

'There', I replied pointing to the big rock far in the distance.

'Oh… What's your name?'

'Xiaoping', I told them. Until now, only one of the children had spoken. Gathering the other two kids to him, he began whispering in their language. Then he approached me.

'What's your name?', I asked.

'Justin', he said. Then pointing to another boy, 'He's Sandy'. They didn't give me the name of the third boy, a small kid with long curly hair. From his behaviour, I guessed he was older than he appeared. His friends just called him 'Curly Boy'.

'Why are you here?', I asked, but immediately regretted my silly question. This was their territory, perhaps their home was just nearby.

They didn't answer. 'You got a lighter?', Justin asked.

'No', I replied, subconsciously patting my pocket. Later I learned that people walking in the desert should always carry a lighter and a knife. Turning his head, Justin muttered something to the two other kids as they all set off in different directions. But then, just a moment later, back came Justin dragging a goanna. Seeing how surprised I was, Justin explained that they had gone out to play when they saw a stranger's footprints. While tracking me, they managed to catch this goanna.

Again, looking hard at the ground, I asked, 'What footprints?'

'If you bushman, you know.' Justin casually waved his hand, to show that he couldn't be bothered trying to explain. Many years later, I too learned this skill from the Aboriginal artist, Jimmy Pike.

Curly Boy returned with a bundle of branches.

Grabbing a handful of dry grass, Justin rubbed it in his hands for a while, then put it in a small heap on a nearby rock. He cut a hole in the middle of a stick with his knife and placed it carefully on top of the grass. He then asked me to hold each end of the stick, while he positioned another sharp stick into the hole and began rubbing it back and forth. It reminded me of the ancient Chinese practice of drilling wood to make fire. Unexpectedly, at the end of the twentieth century, deep in the Australian wilderness, I was seeing this ancient art of making fire. Survival skills seem to be similar for all human beings, although now we usually only see this fire-making art pictured in museums.

'We don't often do this to make fires', Justin explained as he continued rubbing the two sticks together. A smart boy, he always seemed to understand what I was thinking. As he rubbed the sticks together faster and faster, I could at last smell burning as a line of faint smoke snaked up from the pile of grass. Arching his neck forward, Curly Boy blew gently on the grass. The smoke became thicker, and following a few crackles, flames appeared.

Sandy picked up the goanna by the tail with both hands and threw it on to the fire. Before long, the goanna's skin began to char. Curly Boy threw on a few more branches and the flames crackled louder. Looking at these three boys, I thought how different their childhood was to my own. I admired their bush knowledge and survival skills.

Justin dragged the goanna out of the fire, thrust the knife deep into its neck and pulled down, tearing out the internal organs, then he threw the goanna back on to the fire. It seemed that they were going to cook and eat it right there. While I was curious to taste the meat, I was more worried about getting out of there.

'How long will it take to cook it?', I asked.

'You in a hurry?', Justin asked. Then adding, 'Just follow us, okay?'

I had no choice, I had to stay, but Justin's tone reassured me that they wouldn't be leaving me all alone.

While the boys were busy, I took out my sketchbook to draw, although I remained anxious and worried.

Coming up behind me, Curly Boy yelled out to his mates, 'Hey, look!' Sandy snatched my sketchbook and handed it to Justin, who took the book in his blood-stained hands and flipped through my drawings.

'Hey, hey!', he laughed, then pointing to Curly Boy, said, 'Draw him!'

'Yes, draw him, draw him!', Sandy shouted.

'No, no!', shouted Curly Boy as Sandy grabbed him. He twisted and struggled desperately, refusing to give in. When Justin also joined in, it was futile to resist. Four hands soon overpowered the boy's skinny body. He covered his eyes with his hands and cried. I couldn't bear to see him being bullied, so I pulled him towards me, grabbed my sketchbook and, pointing at Justin, I said, 'I want to draw you'.

Sandy hesitated, then laughed in agreement, 'Yes. Draw him!' Joining in his laughter, I skipped over the pages to find one without dirty fingerprints. Turning towards Justin, I told him sharply, 'Don't move!' Caught off guard by my change of tone, he stood stock still.

'Yes, just like that. Bend that leg and sit on that boulder and look at me.' While he sat quietly, I quickly sketched the outlines of his face and his skinny body.

Sandy and Curly Boy stood nearby watching me draw. I asked if they could draw.

'No', Curly Boy replied as he wiped his snot-covered hands on my trouser leg. 'But when I grow up, Old Man will teach me.'

'Who is Old Man?', I asked, thinking that he must be referring to the tribal elder.

'Old Man is Old Man', Curly Boy replied.

'All right.' I had to accept this for now, knowing I would find out when the time was right.

After all the fuss, the boys changed their cooking plan. 'Let's go back and bake the goanna there', Justin said decisively. When he asked me if I wanted to come with them, I at last began to feel more at ease.

Walking in the wilderness with these children, we went among bushes, past piles of rocks. The bushes were full of thorns and soon my legs were scratched all over. The boys were all barefoot, walking as if they were in iron-clad shoes. I was surprised that I could keep up with them so well, and did not feel tired at all although my skin was scorched from the sun.

'Where do you live?', I asked, wanting some conversation to entertain us on our walk.

'There', said Justin pointing off into the distance. I realised then how hard it was to describe locations in such a large desert. 'There' could have been under a mountain. I tried to imagine what 'there' would look like. Why were these kids here? Why weren't they living in cities like other Australians? Had the passing of time left no marks of change on them?

I looked back at the boy. 'You haven't told me your name', I said.

'I don't have a name', he replied hesitantly.

'You must have a name. Everyone's got a name.'

He shook his head. Then he explained that his name was the same as someone who had recently died, so according to Aboriginal custom, he could not be called by this name until some time had passed.

'What do people call you, then?'

'No name.'

'No name?', I repeated. 'Then "No Name" is your name.'

He lowered his head and, with a smile, agreed. We continued chatting and, before long, arrived at a small patch of trees. A few scrawny dogs sprang from behind some bushes, rushing frantically up to me.

'Sha!'

I heard loud shouts to frighten off the fierce dogs. These shouts came from Aboriginal adults who were sitting or lying about and looking at me in a puzzled way. I felt very confused having descended upon them so suddenly and unexpectedly. Everything I had seen and experienced out here in the desert had a big impact on me.

We had reached 'there', the place where the three boys lived, a place regarded by many as mysterious, dangerous and forbidden.

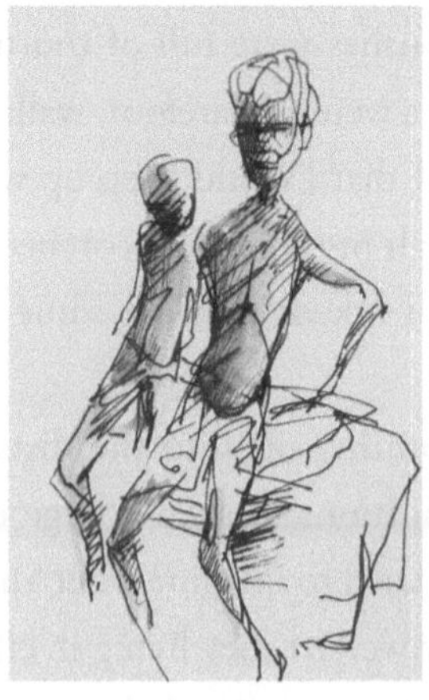

The first time I met Aboriginal children, 1988.

3

A Night at the Aboriginal Campfire

The campsite was very flat and very clean. There were no weeds on this piece of red earth, only a few clusters of tall bushes that looked as if they had been carefully trimmed. Between the bushes, there were several shelters built from bundles of branches with leaves. Used jars and bottles, together with clothes, blankets and other daily necessities lay scattered around. Everyone was sitting on the ground or lying on blankets. Curly Boy told me that they were not staying here long.

Justin took me up to see an older man. I guessed this was the 'Old Man' the boys had spoken about. He was sitting in an interesting posture: one hand supported his head, which was placed on a pillow that had long since lost its original colour, and his other hand was stretched out holding a long pipe. This pipe immediately caught my attention because it reminded me of pipes smoked by many old men in Chinese villages. How had such a pipe come into the hands of an Aboriginal man? I was itching to ask him but held myself back. Although the stem of the pipe was clamped in his mouth, no smoke emerged. Seeing this, I felt sorry.

He knocked the pipe against a rock. As I looked questioningly at Justin, the man motioned for me to sit down. I carefully removed my backpack, paying close attention to every movement of the old man. I was waiting for his questions to begin, but they never came. It almost seemed that I had been forgotten or had faded into the background. Whatever the reason, his silence made me nervous. The old man had a face that looked like that of many other Aboriginal people I had met: a big flat nose, protruding forehead, lowered eyebrows, and sunken eyes. He had grey-black curly hair that looked quite different from his big grey-yellow beard. He had deep scars on his chest and abdomen. Although I had seen these on other Aboriginal people, I had never seen anyone with scars so numerous and so long. The old man's eyes were closed as he nonchalantly continued tapping his pipe. The other people standing or sitting around seemed listless, no one appeared to be puzzled or interested in my sudden appearance. Silently, I took out a pouch of tobacco, placed a small piece of cigarette paper to my lips and taking a small pinch of tobacco in one hand, I began to roll a cigarette. Then, as my anxiety increased, I threw the pouch on the ground in a small ritual gesture that I hoped might start a conversation. I had learned this by watching tourists in Alice. I was not a heavy smoker.

The old man glanced at me, grabbed the tobacco, and filled his pipe. The young man sitting next to him lit it for him. Once this young man began rolling a cigarette for himself, another soon followed suit. Some sort of unspoken understanding developed. I lit my cigarette in the dying embers of the campfire, inhaled, and felt my embarrassment and tension melt away. I had no idea what to do or say next. It was a difficult situation. Would the old man let me stay? If he sent me away, where could I go?

After a long while, the old man murmured something, nudging the large woman next to him. Her breasts hung heavily on her chest, hanging almost down to her crossed legs. She grabbed a piece of cloth and threw it over her shoulders, then began muttering while moving her hands, as if looking for something to do.

'What's your name?', the old man finally asked me.

After I told him, he repeated it to himself several times, as if it were strange and awkward to say. I heard someone laughing in the background.

'Where you from? Why you here?'

I was unsure how best to reply. 'From Melbourne, err… China. I am Chinese. I want to go to Uluru, but I got lost.'

'Yeah', he snorted and raised an eyebrow while studying me carefully. My anxiety grew when I noticed his forehead furrowing tighter and tighter. His murky eyes bore into mine, judging me. Would he let me stay or ask me to leave? But there was also something else in his expression. Was it doubt, sadness, or resentment? I wasn't sure but his thoughts seemed very heavy. A certain majesty was hidden deep in those murky eyes. Would he be able to see that I, a Chinese man, although light-skinned like other 'whites' was not his 'enemy'?

I wanted to know his name. I assumed he would have an English name, as the others did. But I didn't dare ask him directly. In my culture, to do this would be very rude. In the meantime, I just thought of him as 'Grandpa'. I was accustomed to using honorifics like 'Uncle' or 'Grandpa' when I spoke with older Chinese, although sometimes, I might add a person's surname, as in 'Grandpa Wang'.

While observing this Aboriginal grandpa, I had a sudden urge to draw him. I boldly asked, 'Can I draw you?'

'What?' He was surprised. Evidently, he had been thinking a lot about me, but it would never have occurred to him that I would make such a request. I had even surprised myself with my recklessness. Perhaps it was because of my profession as an artist. Confronted by such a powerful image, my timidity had totally vanished. I couldn't let such a rare opportunity pass me by.

The old man remained silent, then said a few words in his own language to those around him. Someone quickly found a wrinkled shirt and put it on him. After buttoning it up carefully, all the way up to the neckline, he straightened himself ready to pose. Nodding at me with a smile in his eyes, he snorted softly, 'Yeah'. I felt sudden admiration and affection for this old man. His eyes were sending a new message: he could be a loving grandpa. The emotional exchange was quick and somewhat strange, but it was something only such an elderly man like this could initiate after judging me. I had the good fortune of being not only accepted by him, but also given the chance to draw him.

When I first saw him, I was attracted to something I had detected in him. I didn't know what it was, but now I was able to look at him more closely.

Two black flies were crawling at the corner of his eyes. His legs were thin, but his feet were very tough, and, just like his hands, were wrapped in thick calloused skin. His toes were all widely separated. This was a hunter who had lived his life in the desert, and this life had left its marks on him. I felt his inner power. It was this strength that I wanted to capture in my drawing.

As I began, others came around to watch. Although I didn't understand what they were saying, I saw smiles on their faces. The finished portrait, done in charcoal, looked strong and powerful. I showed it to Grandpa. He liked it. I felt this small group of Aboriginal people warm to me, and we began to talk. Justin told everybody how the kids had rescued me. He must have told the story well as everyone laughed. I asked Grandpa if he also painted.

'Yeah. I paint, and made this too', he said, producing a boomerang from under his pillow. 'Just finished. This is also art. What you think? Want?' I understood that he was telling me that if I liked it, I could have it, or buy it.

'Of course', I said, taking it from him and looking at it carefully. I knew already that the boomerang was a great Indigenous invention, a great treasure, and a symbol of wisdom.

I had seen many boomerangs in Alice Springs. It can function as a hunting tool to knock down all kinds of prey. The boomerang can also serve as a powerful weapon, like a sabre. And it can become a percussion instrument. During their ceremonies, they will often clap out a rhythm with the boomerang by making a sharp crisp sound to accompany their singing and dancing. The best kind of boomerang is made of she-oak or mulga, wood that is very tough and heavy. This sort of wood is usually chosen for making boomerangs that come back. Grandpa told me that most boomerangs don't do this.

I asked him about the one he was holding. He glanced at it but said nothing. Yet his expression told me that he was gathering his energy as Chinese do when practising *Qigong*. Then suddenly, I felt a strong gust of wind as the boomerang left the old man's hand, and returned with a soft 'chirp, chirp'.

Wow! Everyone applauded. The large woman sitting next to Grandpa spoke with admiration and pride, saying that she hadn't seen him do that for a long time. Throwing a boomerang so that it returns takes a lot of skill. My admiration for him had grown enormously.

'Can you sign your name on it?', I asked. 'I want to buy it.' This was the first Aboriginal artwork in my collection.

———————≈———————

Time passed quickly. A woman holding a bag of flour emerged from one of the sheds. She tore up a paper bag, put it on the ground, sprinkled it with flour, then shouted at a girl sitting behind her. The girl slowly stood up and walked over to reclaim an empty milk powder jar that was being carefully licked by a scrawny dog. The girl yelled and began kicking the dog that promptly scampered off with its head still stuck in the jar. The dog collided with a bare-bottomed child who gave a loud yelp. While the woman kept yelling at the girl, the dog finally got its head free and ran off in terror as everyone laughed.

Taking up the empty milk jar, the girl walked off, returning with half a jar of water which she handed to the woman. The woman sprinkled a little water on the flour, before beginning to knead the dough. As I watched her, I wondered if I would be eating Chinese flatbread tonight. The idea seemed crazy.

The woman dug a pit by the campfire with a wooden stick. She flattened some dough into a rough oval shape, and then threw it into the pit, burying it in hot sand. She then began kneading more dough. Walking over to her, I asked, 'Can I try?'

I expected her to look surprised, but she just replied, 'Yo!' She threw some dough towards me, as if she had been expecting me to ask. I broke the dough into pieces, sprinkled on a little salt, added a little oil, and kneaded it. If we had green spring onions, things would have been perfect, but I knew this was impossible. I looked around for a rolling stick and cutting board, before realising how silly this was. The woman began to dig another pit, oblivious to my embarrassment, and grabbing the dough from my hands, quickly threw it into the pit and covered the dough with hot sand. She was showing me that making damper need not be a very difficult task.

About half an hour later, the woman dug out the damper. She brushed off the sand, tore off a piece, and handed it to me together with a cup of water from the jar. The fresh damper smelled delicious, but I couldn't swallow it because it was covered in small grains of sand. What should I do? It was so embarrassing. Once again, Curly Boy came to my rescue, handing me something that looked like a black stick.

'What's this?', I asked.

'Goanna tail, want to try?', he replied.

This was the first time I had ever eaten goanna. It was an amazing experience, especially as I hadn't eaten anything the whole day. Curly Boy taught me how to peel off the skin to get to the meat inside, and with some effort, I managed to swallow the damper and the goanna tail together. I had to eat the food available. I kept wondering what would have happened if I had not been rescued. How would I have survived? Nothing was more important than survival. I told myself to get on with things as best I could.

It was night already and no one told me to go. It seemed that I could spend the night here. Approaching the campfire, I sat down with Grandpa and the others. Imitating what the young man had done earlier, I filled the pipe with the remaining tobacco, handed it to Grandpa, then took a hot coal from the fire and lit it for him. I watched as Grandpa took a few deep puffs, raised his head, and let out a big sigh of satisfaction. It was a wonderful picture that I saw before me: deep in the night, the elderly man sat by the campfire, facing the full moon hanging low in the sky and holding what looked like a Chinese pipe.

Pointing to the moon, Grandpa began telling a story in his own language to a child sitting across from him. Although I could not follow this mysterious story from a world beyond my imagination, I was content to watch Grandpa who was so focused and serene.

As Grandpa was roaming in his own world, Curly Boy used a handful of branches to sweep clean a space next to the campfire for me. In front of Grandpa, he wouldn't say much but just sat quietly, waiting for me to lie down. I wished I could tell him a Chinese bedtime story. It went like this: once upon a time, there was a temple on a mountain where two Buddhist monks lived, an old master and a boy… The old monk said to the younger monk that there used to be a mountain… where there lived two monks…

Taking out my sleeping bag and blanket from my backpack, I opened out the blanket as if it were a mat, like rice paper spread out for a painting.

The fire had died down, and the charred branches emitted a thick smoke that kept the mosquitoes away. People returned to their own hut, or lay huddled on the ground, like clusters of bushes in the dark night.

As I lay there, I thought about my family, relatives, friends, life and work in China. I missed my parents. My mother's words came back to me, 'Go, son, you need to see the outside world'. She was an enlightened woman, although she was reluctant to let me go. As her only son, I had never experienced an independent life away from home. She always treated me with special care.

'Take care of yourself, eat carefully, but don't save on food. Health always comes first', she said. 'Don't worry about us, we will be okay.' She believed it might be a long time before she saw me again.

To comfort her, I said, 'I won't be away long. I'll be back before three months at the most.'

'Write home, don't let us worry about you.'

Listening to what my mother was saying, I nodded and, holding back tears, hugged her. Later, I learned in a letter from my father that, while I was away, she would wait every day for the postman to show up. She knew that I wouldn't write to her every day, but she still hoped to receive something.

———— ≈ ————

I was born in China and grew up in a very difficult era. In the decade 1966–76, an unprecedented mass movement known as the Cultural Revolution brought about the rampant destruction of China's traditional culture that had developed over multiple epochs. This occurred soon after an earlier disaster during 1958–60, when the entire nation was engulfed by famine and countless people died of hunger.

I often heard my mother sigh, 'Hei, it's too hard to live, son. You must study hard and be a capable person.' Although just a teenager, I could sense how hard my family had to struggle to get by. Yet it wasn't until I grew up that I realised how much bitterness was locked in each of my mother's sighs. I was an obedient child, a good boy who showed respect to his teachers and friends. I was a polite and obedient youngster who did not fight, swear or smoke.

One day, a family friend visited and told Mum about how bad things were getting. Teenagers were fighting one another and were completely out of control. When our friend praised me for being a good child, Mum replied, 'It's not good to be too nice, because it makes it too easy for you to get bullied'. This was why Mum sent me to learn martial arts. For three years, I would wake up each morning before dawn and rush off to a forest near my home where there was a flat patch of clearing, to meet seven or eight other children aged between five and fifteen, including two girls the same age as me. During our first year, we learned different ways of stretching our arms and legs, a little footwork and some basic moves including a set of punches. Then we went on to learn some set routines. It was a very boring, tough process. Some could not cope and left, but others joined. Our master told us that if one of us was bullied, we had to all fight back together. This was the main reason for learning martial arts at that time. My own experience of being bullied during childhood has made me hate all forms of bullying and arrogance.

Mum was worried that I wasn't learning much at school. Activities like political studies, military training, exposure to factories and rural life took up most of our school time. 'How can school be like this?', Mum would ask. She knew the answer, but at that time no one dared to speak the truth. Apart from occasionally sighing or complaining in private, what else could she do? There was no way of resisting the status quo. While Mum couldn't fully explain the larger reasons, she understood that children who missed large parts of their education would later grow up to regret it. There was an old saying in Chinese: 'If you want to be a great person, you must study hard'. Such ancient philosophical sayings are deeply rooted in traditional Chinese culture and are passed on from generation to generation. Chinese families value education. Mum said that if I became skilled in something, I would survive. This was the simple thinking of a housewife.

It was our family friend who suggested that I learn painting. When Mum heard this, she quickly shook her head, saying, 'No. You wouldn't make enough money to buy food with that kind of skill.' What she meant was that it was not an essential occupation. But little other training was on offer. So, afterwards she said to me, 'Well, learn to paint for the time being. It's better than wasting your life.' She had no idea that later in life I would become a professional artist. So, our family friend introduced me to a teacher, Da-Liu, whom I addressed as Liu Laoshi or Teacher Liu. He awakened me to the potential of art as a career.

At first, I learned to draw basic sketches. Liu Laoshi told me to draw as many as I could, until I was able to sketch rapidly. Then he taught me technique, and the rest was up to me to practise.

Every day before and after school, I would go to a nearby vegetable market. Holding my clipboard in one hand, I would stand to one side trying to capture dynamic images of men and women, both young and old, either complete figures or just parts of the body. At that time, no one had a refrigerator at home, so everyone came to the market every day.

At first, I was very timid but, after a while, I found people looking approvingly at me. I was occupied and people were pleased to see this. In those days, it was common for people to worry about their children getting into trouble. As my confidence grew, my drawing improved, so I spent even more time at the market. It was not just the drawing that drew me there. The market was an interesting place. I liked watching people bargaining, especially the way that old women would take their time bargaining fiercely with the traders. No one was prepared to be taken advantage of by even a few *fen* or cents. Today, a few *fen* would buy nothing, but back then it could get you a bowl of vegetables. Chinese bargaining has a long history. While it may hide embarrassment of one's poor circumstances, many people also take pleasure in bargaining. Quite recently, at the Art Basel International Fair in Hong Kong, I saw sharp bargaining. Wealthy collectors warned me to expect this: 'Don't forget, this is Hong Kong'.

Every week, I selected a hundred drawings from my time at the market to show to Liu Laoshi. He would circle sketches he found to be accomplished, or would give me a brief explanation of what was wrong with others. When I got home, I carefully cut out all the circled sketches and stuck them on the wall for later reference.

In this way, I was taught by Liu Laoshi for three years. Every day, no matter what the weather, I went to the vegetable market, or sometimes to bus stations and anywhere else that people gathered, to draw different characters and movements, starting with body proportions, then adding shapes, movements and expressions. With moving characters, I learned to hold the motion in my mind before I tried to capture it with my pencil. I would try to outline the body as concisely as possible, to then complete later or draw entirely from memory. In this way, I trained myself to observe people and scenes, and to transcribe movement into my art. That experience became the starting point of my lifelong journey in art.

During any school excursions or activities, I always found excuses to escape, to have more time for my drawing, the thing that I really wanted to do. This soon landed me in big trouble, not only because I was absent from school activities but also because I was neglecting my leadership role. I was captain of the Red Guards, and I represented all the students at my junior high school. The fact that I held this position shows what a good boy I used to be.

After I started going off to the market, my teachers and many of the students were shocked at my change in behaviour. They warned that if I did not try to improve, I would be considered a bad boy. During that era, this logic sounded reasonable, but these comments upset me very much. From then on, I was looked down on and ridiculed as a 'bad boy'. I felt abandoned and ridiculed. The rebellious psychology of a teenager encountering the unreasonable political climate and social environment of the time had a huge impact on my development. It was a nightmare. Even today, thinking back to that time can give me heart palpitations and panic attacks.

It took more than one or two events to turn me into a 'bad boy'. But here I will tell just one of many stories, of situations that left a deep impression on me.

One day, coming home from school, I saw a crowd gathering. I knew what was happening: once again these people were watching somebody being paraded. It happened frequently. Although I was scared, I was curious to know who it was. Whose turn would it be this time? I wormed my way through the crowd. Hiding behind the adults standing in the front row, I saw three people standing together in the field.

They dropped their arms to their sides, bent over and bowed their heads. A group of students wearing Red Guard armbands surrounded the three accused. All were senior students from another school. On the ground lay piles of calligraphy, paintings and books, which would have been the personal collections of these three people. What would they do with them? Burn them?! I knew that something terrible might happen. Previously, I had seen people being criticised in the street, and even public insults and beatings. Red Guard students who up until then had been regarded as 'good boys' would join in these assaults. 'Rebellion' had become a very popular word. I found it crazy, hard to understand. Why did the rebels want to burn calligraphy, paintings and books? These old works of calligraphy and painting had survived for so many years and were cultural treasures.

The student leader continued shouting slogans. He threw an impressive painting into the pile of artworks and, fervently waving his hand in the air, shouted, 'Torch the lot!' A burst of malevolent fire sprung from his hand.

The whole crowd turned deathly quiet. One man who was whispering covered his mouth in shock. It seemed absurd that in China, in the middle of the twentieth century, such a tragedy could happen. Such sorrow lies at the heart of human history.

Recalling those childhood memories makes me very sad. I realise how much those experiences changed my thinking.

That night, looking into the campfire, I was thinking back, but eventually I fell asleep. Then, like a snapshot, I saw in my mind a portrait of the old man.

———— ≈ ————

The next day, when I woke up, the sun was already high in the sky. Before it could exert its full power on the desert, we set off again. The three boys were taking me on a shortcut to Uluru.

Before we left, Grandpa asked me to give him the drawing I had done. I did not understand why, just overnight, he had changed his mind. Under my repeated questioning, he lowered his voice and said, 'I had a dream last night, you know what I mean? I'm sick… headache… now.' I asked him what he had dreamed about. Then my own dream flashed into my mind. Surely, this was not just coincidence. In my dream, I had seen the old man walking in a circle with his hands behind his back. I didn't know what he was doing, but his walking was heavy and slow.

'Er, a not-so-good dream. I'm sick… spirit… out', he told me, pointing to his head. He didn't want to talk about his dream. But somehow it was connected to my drawing. Later I learned that often, Aboriginal people, especially older Aboriginal people, avoid being photographed, for fear of the flash. They believe that this strange sudden light will take a person's soul. Portrait drawing is different but there is some similarity.

'I'm getting old and weak. I want to get myself together', he said softly. If I gave him back his portrait, it would be like getting his spirit back. When I handed it to him, he took hold of my hands and said, 'I will be okay. See you next time.' Then he told me to hurry and catch up with the three boys. In that instant, I recalled how my mother looked when she sent me away.

Uluru is in the very centre of Australia, and it is the largest single rock in the world. An old man told me the legend about it. During the Ice Age, there were many small islands scattered about. As the climate warmed, the water level rose, flooding the smallest ones. People retreated to the largest island, but this was like a canoe floating on the sea, and in danger of being swallowed at any time. To save the people, heaven manifested its Spirit, and a huge rock dropped from the universe to anchor the canoe. Now it could float calmly, regardless of any changes in the waves. Australia is like that canoe on the sea and Uluru is the rock that keeps the boat steady forever. Its significance and sacredness are beyond human comprehension.

When we arrived, many tourists were already there. I stared up at Uluru, stretching out my arms in awe. In the morning sun, the rock gradually changed from bright red to reddish brown and hazy purple. These changing scenes only added to the mystery. I seemed to have wandered into a magical dreamland.

'Boy, what do you see?' I seemed to hear a deep voice floating towards me. I replied eagerly, 'It's a magnificent landscape, and the people living in this land are really great!'

I wanted to hold on to this moment forever. I turned to ask Justin to help me take a picture, but the boys were gone. I was deeply moved. The children had mysteriously appeared when I was lost, and now when I was safe, they had left. But they had also set my feet on a new journey.

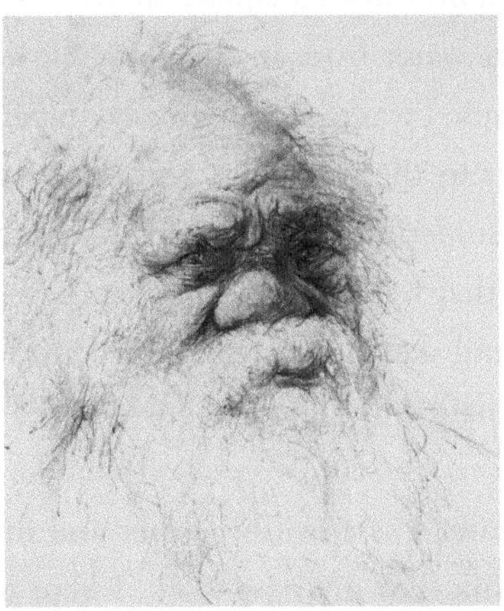

Rolley Mintuma, of the Mutitjulu community,
located at the base of Uluru, 2016.

4

Chinese Aboriginal

Returning to Melbourne after my first trip to Uluru, I locked myself in my studio to paint. The studio was behind a house in the southern suburbs of Melbourne, a small cabin only 25 square metres. In summer it was like a sauna, while in winter water froze in the glass. However, I didn't have the time to complain because I was totally engrossed in painting. It is well known that when the artist is in the throes of creation, a harsh environment and poor conditions can sometimes inspire and motivate that creation. It was in this humble cabin that I created my first batch of paintings in Australia. Hundreds of photos and sketches were scattered around my studio – on the floor, on the bed and nailed to the walls. Surrounded by these images, vivid memories returned.

In China, I had trained as a brush painter and my basic materials were rice paper and black ink. For my new work, I kept to these materials, and used strong brushstrokes to outline powerful figures in wash with black ink. My wild lines created powerful images of Aboriginal Australians. Such works later caused a lot of controversy. To gain a better understanding of Aboriginal people, I started going to the library, hoping to learn more about their history and culture. No one I met seemed to know much about them. When I visited local libraries in Melbourne's eastern suburbs, I found very few publications on Aboriginal topics, although later I found out that there were more published than I had realised, but it was still far from what one would expect. This was during the 1990s, and it seems that it was only in the early twenty-first century that other Australians really began to acknowledge

Aboriginal culture seriously. As an artist, I have my own unique antennae. My brief contact with Aboriginal people had made me realise that they were an ancient nation with a unique culture. From the limited information I had accessed, I learned that Aboriginal people had lived in Australia for 40,000 years, a timeframe later extended to 65,000 years. This figure is constantly being corrected by anthropologists. But I was puzzled and couldn't understand why such an ancient nation and its culture were largely ignored and unknown in mainstream society. I decided that this indifference had brought about the 'collective absence' of Aboriginal people in Australia. With my limited knowledge of Australian history at that time, I could only wonder why this was the case.

I realised there were so many more interesting things to learn and began thinking about the next phase of my return to the desert. Unlike my first spontaneous adventure, this trip would be planned. I was beginning to understand that the connection between Aboriginal people and their land could not be interpreted in a simple literal sense but was far more complex. This thought originated from looking at Aboriginal dot paintings, where the land was an ever-present theme.

In 1989, I went to Balgo Aboriginal community, located between Alice Springs and Broome, a very remote desert area, on the border of Western Australia. I had heard about this place in Alice Springs, while talking to a couple of men in a bar.

I chose a Greyhound bus again to travel from Melbourne to Broome, then on to the inner desert. As on my previous trips, there was almost no one in sight along the way except for a few occasional people at roadside petrol stations. This time, the sight of the desert didn't excite me and instead I had a feeling of calm and an expectation of the unknown.

Before leaving Melbourne, I had to extend my visa, so I was interviewed by an immigration officer. When he asked me what I had done in the past three months, I said, 'I was in the bush with the Aboriginal people'.

He was taken aback to hear this and asked, 'Oh, how come? Those are very mysterious people and places.'

'It all happened by accident', I replied. I really didn't know how to answer him because everything that had occurred was so totally unexpected. I took my time telling him about what I had experienced.

'Incredible stories. That's the first time I've heard of this from… a…' He broke off, unsure of how to articulate his thoughts. I suppose it surprised him to hear all this from a Chinese artist.

When I mentioned that I had been to Arnhem Land, the officer said that this was a place more difficult to enter than North Korea. I smiled, trying to look relaxed and feeling quite proud.

'You want to go back?', he asked. 'How much time do you want for that?'

'Three months', I replied, thinking this should be long enough to collect what I needed for an exhibition in China with an Australian theme. My friends in Melbourne laughed at me for being so naive. They thought I was unrealistic, with no long-term plan. To them, I was doing something inexplicable and unprofitable, quite unlike most urban Chinese – even though I had grown up in Hefei, which was a third-tier Chinese city. At times, behind my back, my Shanghai relatives called me a country bumpkin and I used to simply acquiesce to such ridicule. But now, for at least once in my life, I wanted to be myself.

'I'll give you an extra six months because I admire your courage', the immigration officer said. 'My only condition is that after six months, I get to hear more wonderful stories.'

There were no words to describe how I felt. I could only think to myself how lucky, how very lucky I was. It seemed that everywhere I went in this country, I met good people.

I had not expected to get this visa renewal. I was so excited. The Immigration Department was taking strong action against Chinese students who had breached their bridging visa conditions. If they were sent back, they faced the problem of repaying loans that they had taken to enable them to study abroad. Whenever these students gathered, they talked only about their visas, their jobs and how they had to skip study so that they could earn more money. They also grumbled about the discrimination they faced because of the language barrier. Their complaints of course were only vented behind closed doors.

I recall an incident at a language school in Melbourne, shortly after I had received my visa extension. One morning, the English teacher walked into the classroom with a newspaper in his hand and said, 'Look, everyone, who is the person in this photo?' All the students turned to look at me. 'Isn't this Lin?!', the teacher asked, and everyone in the class agreed that it was clearly a photo of Lin. 'But the name of the person in the paper is not Lin', the teacher declared. At this I was highly embarrassed, because I was standing in for Lin in the English class. The real Lin was at work. The teacher was holding a report in *The Australian* about my visit to Aboriginal communities. It featured a big headline: 'Chinese Artist Walking into Arnhem Land'.

Lin was my roommate. To save money, I had moved from my studio to a three-bedroom house that I shared with eight Shanghainese. The house was in very poor condition, featuring uneven floorboards, cracked walls and twisted door frames. It was a house that should not have been approved for letting. I was huddled in the living room with Lin and another Shanghainese. The two of them had been in Melbourne for over a year. One night when everyone was asleep, I heard a strange sound coming from the bathroom. Puzzled, I opened the door gently, only to see Lin, a rather arrogant Shanghainese, wiping away tears as he stood talking on the phone. He pleaded into the mouthpiece: 'Hang up! The phone bill will be too expensive. It will cost me a whole day's wages.' The person on the other end didn't want to hang up. Lin held the phone in his hand, his face grimacing in pain. Suppressing his emotions, he was speaking in Shanghainese dialect in a gentle voice: 'Listen to me, my dear…' I softly closed the door. Lin was very conscious of keeping up appearances and would not want me to see him in any kind of trouble. Returning to my bed, I heard my second companion in the room let out a heavy sigh. It seemed he was not asleep either and that he also was in great pain.

Others in the house told me more about Lin. In Greater Shanghai, a large city closest to modern Western society, he presented as a very stylish, well-off man. During the Cultural Revolution, following a change in government policy, two of the three children in his family were sent to a village in the countryside of Anhui province. Under the guise of supporting rural construction, the actual purpose was to reduce the burden on the urban population. Lin, the lucky third child, was permitted to remain in Shanghai, but because he could not get a stable job, he was supported by his parents. We call these people *xiao-kai*, a word originating from old Shanghai dialect, that refers to a rich boy without a business or profession who relies solely on his parents' wealth. Nevertheless, in front of his friends, Lin still pretended to live a glamorous life (although friends were rarely invited to his home). As he entered his forties, 'Xiao-Kai' (Young Kai) was becoming 'Lao-Kai' (Old Kai). When he had used up all the money left to him by his parents, he borrowed money to come to Australia. In the past, unlike most other Chinese students, he had never really suffered greatly. But now he was no longer wealthy and had to work in a factory, hoping to earn enough money to pay off his debts, and to get his wife and daughter out of China. I then heard that his wife's application for an Australian visa had again been rejected. This made Lin quite depressed. His wife gave him an ultimatum. If she couldn't come to Australia, then he had to return to China.

In the end, he decided to stay in Australia. One of the house mates explained that if you go back, you lose face, and must give up hope of achieving your life's ambition. Whatever happened, everyone struggled to hold on to the hope of one day living life like Australians. For this hope, they were prepared to give up the most precious years of their life. Lin once asked me, 'Have you ever had bread and jam for breakfast?' For him, it was a life of luxury that he had never lived. This was the life that many Chinese students wanted at that time.

I too had my hopes, but they were different. I wanted to stay in Australia because I had started to really enjoy life in the outback.

On the bus, all I could do was to dream, sleep, watch a DVD, and occasionally look out the window at the landscape rushing past. I could see that everything here bore the brunt of the scorching sun and the extremely hot climate. After a day and a night, I became drowsy and numb, the thoughts in my mind slowing. The next day, again watching DVDs, eating and sleeping, I started getting progressively more cranky.

About three days later, the bus arrived in Broome, where I stayed for a few days. Then I continued my journey, passing Fitzroy Crossing until finally getting off at Halls Creek, a small town with a mixed Aboriginal and non-Aboriginal population. I found many similar small towns scattered throughout Australia, some with only a few dozen people, mostly elderly. I wondered why these people didn't move to larger towns or cities. Since childhood, I had been taught that our lives should have 'meaning'. To be 'meaningful', we should go to bigger places to do 'meaningful' things. Later I came to realise that those so-called 'meaningful' things were in fact beautiful shackles that people had created for themselves.

From Halls Creek, I planned to go on to Balgo. But after several days of heavy rain, the two main roads to Balgo were blocked by flood water, so I had to wait for the roads to re-open for vehicles. Every day I would pass people in the town who, whether they knew me or not, greeted me enthusiastically with a 'G'day buddy!' or a 'Beautiful day, huh?'

One day, I met an old man who told me that he hadn't seen an Asian in Halls Creek for decades. No wonder so many people looked at me or said hello when I passed by. While chatting, the old man suggested that I call in at the town church, because Father Paul often travelled to Balgo. It seemed that God's envoys were everywhere, including in Aboriginal communities. Father Paul was a middle-aged British-Australian man who was short and fit. He had grey hair and a gold beard around his thin lips. He listened carefully as I introduced myself and then asked me why I wanted to go to Balgo. This community, he said, was not a tourist destination. It was not open to the public. As he spoke, he was busy packing his things, as though he was ready to take off at any moment.

I hurriedly showed him my permit that had been issued to me by the Balgo community. He read it carefully and an expression of surprise came to his face. I tried to dispel his distrust, saying that I didn't have much luggage, and I really wanted to go to Balgo – even that it was God's plan for me to have found him. At my persistence, he finally reluctantly said, 'Okay, enough. Get ready; we leave soon.'

I was secretly delighted.

His car was filled with food and cartons of mission brochures. Three young Aboriginal men were waiting by the car when I approached. The road to Balgo was terrible. We passed several small creeks and, because it was the wet season, there was water everywhere. Before long we saw an even bigger creek ahead. The water level was extremely high. Two cars were parked on the bank, one of them with both doors wide open. A white man sat with his legs propped up on the dashboard, the seat pushed well back and the radio blaring. He looked relaxed, as if he had already been there for a long time, waiting for the water level to drop before crossing. In the creek, the rear end of a car was sticking out of the water. A young man had tried to cross, but his vehicle was swept away by the flood waters. Even worse, a crocodile was quietly coming towards him. Two Aboriginal children saved him by screaming loudly and throwing rocks to chase away the crocodile.

Father Paul got out of the car to say hello and chat with each of the drivers of the two cars. After waiting two hours for the water to subside, they were almost ready to turn back. However, Father Paul began walking up and down the bank, mumbling to himself. I hoped his prayer would work, but looking at the situation, it seemed that the water level was not going to drop anytime soon. I started to gather some branches to boil some water for tea, but then I saw Father Paul take off his shoes and, despite the laughter of the other men, he walked until he stood waist-deep in the creek. As his body began to tremble, we yelled at him to come back, but when he did, he ordered us to get in the car. He was not joking: he was going to try to cross.

As the front of the car lurched forward, it set off waves of water crashing against the sides, but our weight helped to keep the car stable. Father Paul grasped the steering wheel with both hands, driving on an angle upstream to correct the downstream thrust of the rapidly running water. I felt the car shake, but at length it was held up by the water like a boat.

If the car stalled, or did not maintain its momentum, the water could easily have swept us away. Even if we had abandoned the car and swum for our lives, we would still have been in danger. The current was very strong, and it was likely that there were crocodiles. Perhaps one was already hiding somewhere, laughing at us fools. Father Paul was quite aware of this danger. 'Bad luck if a crocodile comes', he said. Thankfully, we got across unscathed.

In the next a few hours, we crossed several other small rivers where the water level was not so high, and we got across easily. Then, as it got dark, another big river blocked our path. Father Paul told us that this was the last big creek, after which conditions should be much better. We couldn't see the river very clearly in the dark, but from the sound of the water, we could tell that it was flowing deep and rapid. As before, Father Paul walked into the river. In the headlights, I watched him stretch out his arms, trying to keep his balance, testing to see whether his feet would remain on the riverbed. The water was above his waist. He struggled to return to the bank. Seeing that he was in trouble, with one hand I took a firm grip on a half-submerged rock and with the other, I reached out to grab him.

'Don't!', he yelled, but as the current swirled around him he had no choice. He grabbed on tight to my outstretched hand. I tried to pull him up, but his sturdy body seemed to have taken root in the riverbed. To allay his fear, I told him to relax, to believe in me, and to believe in God. My words 'Believe in God' must have calmed him. An invisible force seemed to propel him forward and I quickly pulled him ashore. As soon as he was safe, he drew the sign of the cross on his chest, then held and kissed my hand. Later he said that his rescue was the work of the 'hand of God'.

Our plan had been to spend the night at place on the other side of the river, but now it looked like we would have to set up camp where we were. But to my surprise, Father Paul once again ordered everyone into the car. He told us that, with thanks to the 'hand of God', he would be able to give us a big surprise. Between the rapidly flowing river, the crazy blood-sucking mosquitoes, and the dark night, what else could surprise me here? 'Get in the car. You will find out what it is when you get there', Father Paul announced. He drove along the riverside for about an hour, making only a few turns before we heard dogs barking in the dark night. We then saw people standing around a campfire and looking from the distance somewhat like Chinese shadow puppets.

An old man yelled out to quieten the dogs. Father Paul parked the car a dozen metres away from the fire, then walked a little closer while speaking to the people in their language.

I jumped out of the car and, like the three Aboriginal men with us, also leaned against the side of the car. We remained quiet while two dogs sniffed around us. 'You don't go there?', I asked the Aboriginal men. One smiled at me but said nothing. We were very tired and hungry, and no one wanted to talk. To the people here, we were intruders, not yet given approval to be here from the local host, so it was best not to move, to show our respect. We waited together silently, hoping to stay the night.

At last Father Paul beckoned us over to the campfire, where he was now sitting on the ground with a cup of tea. As we approached, Father Paul threw a few branches on to the fire, making it flare up and lighting up our surroundings. I was shocked! Four Chinese faces looked back at me. Father Paul smiled as I stared at them speechless, then said that it was God's work I should meet them. When he introduced them to me, I found that they all had Chinese names.

One of them slowly leaned across to shake my hand. 'What's your name?', he asked.

I told him.

'Oh, Chinaman?'

I nodded. 'Are you Chinese?', I asked, puzzled because his face looked Chinese but his skin was dark.

He turned to look at the others, as if he were looking for an answer, but no one responded. Disappointed, he turned and said to me, 'Lee. Everyone calls me Ah Lee.'

I greeted him in Chinese, 'Ni hao', but he only looked puzzled. Shaking his head, he tried to repeat my words, making everybody laugh. 'Aboriginal', he replied, then pointing around, 'We all Aboriginal'.

I was surprised to find Aboriginal Chinese in such a remote place. I was sure that their stories must be remarkable.

'Bro, yo from China, yeah?', Ah Lee asked. I thought that perhaps he called me brother because my Chinese name seemed strange, but he was too old to be a brother.

'Oh, no, I dare not be your bro. I'm a young man from China. You are my father's age', I replied, slightly panicked.

'Doesn't matter. I'm happy to see yo', he continued, looking back at me with excitement in his eyes.

He told me that they sometimes calculated each other's age when idle and bored, but the more they talked about their age, the more confused they became. 'I am sixty – oh no, seventy-eight years old', he said, counting the decades on his fingers, using a very traditional Chinese gesture.

He said that too many people were asking him his age, so now he just told them this age. Last year it was his age, and the same this year too. 'What about next year?', I asked. 'Same', he replied and laughed. For him, it wasn't important. 'But everyone tells me, I am Chinaman. Now when I see you… er, yeah… I am, we look the same, right?'

'Yes, we are the same: Chinese. Is your mother Aboriginal?'

'Yes.'

Then Ah Lee told me that his mother had died when he was a little boy. His Chinese father was a good cook, who would travel around cooking for people, black or white. Sometimes he returned and lived with his family for a while, but he did not get along well with them. In the end, he left and didn't return. People said that he had gone back to China, and he had a wife over there. So, Ah Lee had not known his Chinese father well. He knew very little of Chinese culture – all that he remembered was Chinese food. 'I like Chinese food, everyone like it', he said. Cooking food together had provided a way for him and his father to communicate. But it was because of his Chinese facial features that he could not forget his identity.

I asked the others what they remembered about their Chinese fathers or Chinese culture, but they were quiet and reserved, and not as talkative as Ah Lee. One of them, Ah Kee, said that he had been raised by his mother's family, but because there was not enough bush tucker in his country, he decided to move to this place, 'Chinaman Garden', together with Ah Lee and the others after his woman had died three years ago. As he mentioned the others, he stretched out his hands and raised six fingers, meaning that there were six Aborigines there who, like him, had Chinese blood.

I noticed that on one of Ah Kee's hands, the little finger was missing. He saw me staring and told me what had happened. When still a teenager, he had worked with Aboriginal people and some Chinamen on a cattle station owned by white people. One day, his boss was smoking opium in a pipe. When he looked around and couldn't find his pipe-stopper, he chopped off Ah Kee's little finger to use instead. Telling me this, Ah Kee stretched out his mutilated finger to show me again.

'The following year, the boss died.'

'Because of opium?', I asked.

'Probably yes', Ah Kee replied.

There was much opium trading in those earlier times, and many Aboriginal people were introduced to the habit by Chinese traders and by white people.

'What was it traded for?', I asked. Later, I found from historical records that it was for labour and sex.

Among the Chinese at the campfire was a middle-aged man who was also called Lee. Perhaps, the predecessors of these men had all come from the same village in China. I noticed that the face of this middle-aged man was not as Chinese-looking as Ah Lee's. Nonetheless, he still retained some Chinese features. The bridge of his nose was rather thin, like mine, and he had rather flat facial features. He told me that his grandfather was Chinese, so now he was here to look after the older men. 'My grandpa was a very good cook too, and he used to cook for the Hans family', he said proudly.

In the late nineteenth century, the Hans family was a very powerful local station owner who imported many young labourers from Southeast Asia – including Chinese, Malays and Filipinos – to work with local Aboriginals. At that time, the Chinese were engaged mostly in rough work, such as planting vegetables, building roads, transporting goods, and working in kitchens. The best job was to become a cook. These migrant men lived with Aboriginal people, and because both groups suffered discrimination from white Europeans, they gradually became closer. Because they were all living at the bottom of society, many Chinese workers and Aboriginal people married or lived together and had children.

Many Chinese people came to Australia looking for gold after 1850, when gold sites were discovered one after the other in Victoria and New South Wales. Later, mines in Western Australia and north Queensland also attracted Chinese workers. Most of these men did not speak English, and their way of living was different from that of white people, so they tended to live together, and gradually formed 'Chinese villages'. The Chinese not only kept to themselves but also worked very hard, and in this way aroused the jealousy of the local white people. Soon anti-Chinese sentiment was prevalent. The European workers claimed that the Chinese were dirty and not law-abiding. Because the Chinese did not speak English, communication was impossible. Also, the Chinese had arrived without their families, and were not committed settlers, wanting simply to make some money to feed their families in China. They were not investing in the new country and just taking away Australian gold. As discontent grew, colonial governments began to impose restrictions on these Chinese workers. In response, many began to migrate to less harshly regulated regions and to engage in different occupations apart from mining. For example, in the northern and western regions of Australia, the Chinese began working on road construction, as well as in mining, sugarcane planting, and various other business activities.

While chatting, Ah Lee lay on a blanket, one arm resting on his bent leg, looking lazily at a dog somewhere off in the dark. He made quiet pattering sounds as he sucked on a self-made pipe. To me, he looked just like some Chinese villager, even though we had met here in the bush and communicated more with body language than with English.

'Hey, I'm getting old', Ah Lee said as he sighed heavily. I wondered, who will take care of them now? It seemed that this task would fall on the younger Lee.

Father Paul told me how these men really wanted to understand their Chinese bloodlines. 'Didn't you see how excited they were when they first saw you?'

'Yes, I know, but what can I do for them?', I asked myself.

———≈———

That night, I couldn't sleep. Images of Ah Lee kept appearing in my mind. I also thought of Jimmy Chi. Before coming to Halls Creek on this trip, I had been in Broome where I met the Aboriginal-Chinese-Japanese songwriter, Jimmy Chi. Jimmy told me exciting family stories.

Jimmy Chi is since well-known for his musicals *Bran Nue Dae* and *Corrugation Road,* but we spoke less about his musicals and song-writing and more about his Chinese heritage. I remember when we first met on a pleasant morning in Broome. He told me that he could not talk for long, because he was just out of hospital. My first impression was of a happy man, who smiled while talking and he certainly looked Chinese. We sat in the front of his house. He said that if I didn't mind, he needed to lie on his bamboo reclining chair while we chatted. It was a lounge chair like those commonly used in Chengdu teahouses in China.

Jimmy asked me about China. 'Are you from China? Many people over there, yeah?'

'Yes, too many.'

He laughed, 'Migrate to Australia, we need more people here'.

Then he asked me to say something in Chinese. He wanted to hear me speak in Mandarin. So, I said, '*Jian-dao-ni-hen-gao-xing*', meaning 'Pleased to meet you'. He laughed as he tried to repeat my words, getting the pronunciation all wrong. But this turned out to be a good way to start on a relaxed chat. He said that all he really knew how to say was '*Ni-hao-ma?*' or 'How are you?'

Jimmy Chi's grandpa was a Chinese man called John Chi, who had travelled to Australia from China as a young man looking for gold around about 1860. He afterwards married Yamamoto, a Japanese woman escaping from a promised marriage in Japan. Their son, Jimmy's father, married an Aboriginal woman who often told her son about his Chinese ancestor and his mixed-race heritage.

Jimmy was first educated in Broome, then when he was twelve, he went off to boarding school in Adelaide. Afterwards he went to the University of Western Australia to study engineering, while also playing music as a hobby. However, after a car accident, he couldn't carry on with his studies.

I asked him how Chinese culture had influenced him. Jimmy said that he liked Chinese food. He also liked the way that Chinese men looked after their kids and families. He remembered that his Dad used to say, 'It's easy to make babies, but you got to look after them. You don't just make babies and run away.'

Jimmy was attracted to Buddhism as described by Lobsang Rampa. He readily believed in the paranormal and occult powers, and said, 'One day, I will show you. We Aboriginal people also know about it.' Jimmy thought of himself as a spiritual man, immersed in Aboriginal culture, but at the same time he didn't really want to talk about it.

'Your mixed heritages? Did they affect your childhood life?'

'Well, there was racism back then and still racists everywhere. It will never be any other way in this country', he said. Growing up, he had 'copped racism from everywhere'. He was rejected by his 'full-blood' Aboriginal relatives. Anyone who was not full-blood in a traditional Aboriginal community felt excluded, pushed out into a completely different culture. Perhaps that's why strong bonds often form between mixed-race people.

He later married a white woman and had two children. Speaking of his wife, he couldn't help showing such a sense of pride. That pride was later confirmed by his wife, who said that Jimmy would have liked her to be with him on all occasions.

I asked him what he thought about his identity. Taking my question very seriously, he replied that he thought of himself as Aboriginal. He considered himself an Aboriginal person from Broome, who had mixed Chinese and Japanese heritage. But then he added, 'We are raised to be human beings. Do you know what I mean? We shouldn't have racial discrimination, but unfortunately, it has always existed in our lives, in the past and today. Hasn't it?' At this point, he got up and walked into the house. Returning with a guitar, he handed me a sheet of lyrics. The song was 'Indiginee', which Jimmy had written with his friend Shane Howard. He stroked the strings and began to sing '… we are all a human family, whether it is white, red, yellow, or black…' His low, slightly hoarse voice expressed the full meaning of his words describing 'identity'. As he sang, his smile became brighter, and he no longer looked like a sick man.

Our meeting far exceeded the fifteen minutes originally scheduled. As we talked together, I had no impression of any mental problems. Instead, Jimmy indicated that he was really pleased to be talking with me, as I was the first Chinese from mainland China he had ever met. But on later occasions when we met and talked, I realised that his mental illness was gradually worsening. Sadly, the last time we met he could not remember me.

Jimmy Chi died in 2017. I heard from his wife that he wanted to be buried in the same cemetery as his cousin-brothers and not in the Chinese cemetery where his parents were buried.

As I lay at night in the bush, after my trip with Father Paul, I thought a lot about Jimmy Chi and Ah Lee. Their stories, told to me in completely different circumstances, had been the first to alert me to the relationship between Aboriginal and Chinese people in Australian history. Lying in the dark, I reached for answers to such questions: What should I do? … What can I do for them?

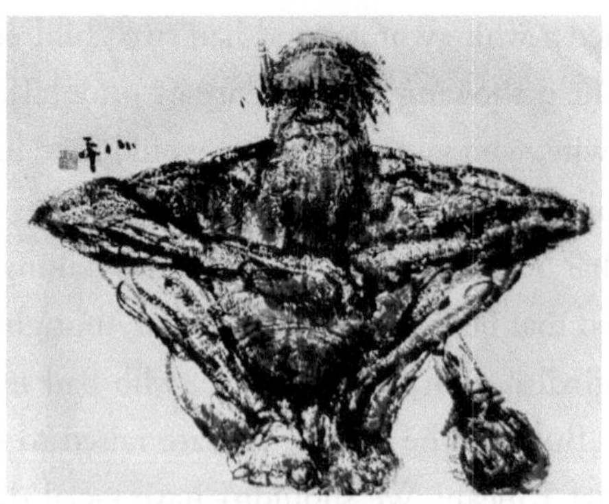

Aboriginal elder – an early exploration in
Chinese brush painting.

5

My Time at the Community
in the Desert

The next day, we borrowed a small boat and made several trips to transport the contents of our car across to the other side of the river, where we were picked up by people from the Balgo community. At one stage, Father Paul and I stood in the river holding the boat. Although we were cautious while wading out into the water, I was so nervous that I forgot to take the camera from my neck, and it got dunked. As a result, a roll of film with photos of Ah Lee and the others was ruined. I was very upset about this for days. While I thought I might be able to go back, it seemed that such opportunities did not come again, especially in the desert where very little can be planned beforehand. But, having crossed the river, what would await me in Balgo? I had no idea.

Balgo is a former Catholic mission in the dry and remote outback of Western Australia. It was established by German missionaries in 1939 and, at the time of my visit, it was home to around 300 Aboriginal people. The name 'Balgo' comes from the word *palkurr-palkurr* in the Kukatja language and means 'rice grass'. When I first arrived in this community, I found it very strange. The houses were arranged in a big circle, some small ones made from corrugated iron, and some older ones made from old iron tin. There were no streets. I wondered why they lived in a circle-shaped town and didn't put the houses closer to one another. Later, I learned that the famous Wolfe Creek Meteorite Crater – a pit 850 metres in diameter and 50 metres deep, filled with flourishing native trees – was located about 100 kilometres north of Balgo. Anthropologists believe that it formed over a million years ago when a large meteorite fell to earth. In Aboriginal mythology, this large crater is associated with *Ngarrinti* or 'Fly Dreaming'. The presence of the crater explains Balgo's circular design.

On my first two or three days, I wandered around to get used to the feel of the community and to take the chance to say hello to everyone, especially the elders. I explained that I was there to experience life in Balgo and to learn about their unique and ancient culture. I wanted to see if it would inspire my art. People are happy if you say you like it there, without needing you to give any reason. Best to just keep it simple. A young man dropped into a Kung Fu posture and asked if I knew Bruce Lee. As seen in the movies, he called out, 'Hey! Hey!' Everyone burst into laughter. In response to a call like this, his opponent had to square up: I went into a squat position and stared back at him fiercely while taking a few Kung Fu steps. I looked so scary and ready to fight that my opponent stepped back, retreating, and begging for mercy while the onlookers began booing.

I asked what his name was.

'Matthew, Matthew Jill.'

'Call me Master, and I will teach you Kung Fu.' I was joking, but he took me at my word and called me 'Master'. This was embarrassing, but everyone was watching so I had to abide by the rules of martial arts and had no choice but to teach him. After I had shown him the two main grasping movements used in Kung Fu, there was a round of applause. Hearing this, my initial sense of strangeness and difference quickly evaporated.

This routine surprisingly turned out to be a most effective strategy that allowed me to establish friendly relations in these communities. A little Kung Fu turned out to be better than any amount of talking.

After that, I was largely accepted in the community. People were willing to exchange a few words with me, acceded to my requests to draw or paint them or to photograph them, and to join their gambling circle and so on. My student Matthew Jill often came to me wanting to learn more Kung Fu. I did not dare teach him too much in case it created trouble, so I said that I would teach him to paint. He was very happy to hear this, so I prepared a sketchbook for him.

At first, Father Paul wanted me to stay in the church buildings. But I told him that, if it was possible, I wanted to live with an Aboriginal family. So, Father Paul introduced me to Rose, who would let me stay in her house. But I soon found out that this small and very simple house was only used if it rained. Most of the time, her family lived under shelters placed around a campfire that was the centre of daily life. After encountering this lifestyle on several occasions during my time in the bush, I came to like it. After living in the open, breathing fresh air twenty-four hours a day, living in a normal room felt like being locked in a box.

One cloudy and rainy day, I had taken shelter in a shed built with large branches and a tarpaulin and was preoccupied with sketching an old man called Matthew Jill, the father of Kung Fu Matthew Jill, who was one of the elders in the community. He didn't talk much but just squinted at people to show he was thinking. As I drew him, he toyed with a long pipe that I had made for him a few days earlier from a hollowed-out branch. A pipe like this reminded me of Ah Lee and the other Aboriginal Chinese men at 'Chinaman Garden', who had already found a place in my imagination. Jill filled his pipe with shredded tobacco. When he lit it and took a few puffs, it was incredible to watch two parallel columns of white smoke shoot from his nostrils, while his eyebrows furrowed anxiously. In a small shed nearby, three elderly men lay together. One of them was groaning and seemed to be sick.

Because Jill was sitting right under the edge of the roof, a sudden gust of wind showered him with rain. He wiped the rain off his long, slender face which was half-concealed by a grey beard. 'Boys…', he said nonchalantly. Having hardly heard him speak, I glanced around to see who it was that he was addressing. There did not seem to be any children about. I looked questioningly at Rose, who was sitting next to Jill, but she suppressed whatever it was she wanted to say. I sensed that something had happened, but no one was talking about it. Rose was also a painter, who often had a few specks of coloured paint on her face and arms. When she was painting, she would become immersed in her work, as she patiently added many small dots. It was time-consuming work, as I found out when I tried to help her.

The rain beat down rhythmically on the tarpaulin above us. Two women, who had also squeezed under our shelter, sat picking nits from each other's hair. The sick man in the nearby shed still lay there groaning. Out of nowhere, a few kids ran over and began playing in the rain. I carefully noted everything happening around me, with words and drawings in my sketchbook.

A naked little boy held out a piece of bread to bait an emu. It ran over to him, flapping its wings and boldly stretching its neck to peck at the bread, which made the kid quickly hide his hand behind his back.

'Hey, don't!', he shouted. The emu must have given his hand a good peck. Smiling shyly, the kid's friend grabbed the remaining bit of bread, and pushed the first kid aside. 'Look what I can do!', he said. The first kid, not happy with this, rushed to fight back. The emu stretched out his neck again, as if to stop them fighting. It was as if the bird were saying, 'Don't fight, it doesn't matter who feeds me'. The second kid, who now had the upper hand, smiled triumphantly, a row of bright teeth contrasting with his dark face. Placing the bread on top of his head, he arched his back, and stretched his neck forward towards the emu. The bread easily stayed on his head, because his hair was like a bird's nest. I quickly sketched the scene. The little boy was quite a performer. But the emu wasn't scared, as it tugged twice at the messy hair, pecking hard at the bread. The little kid screamed, and fell to the ground, holding his head, alarming others who were in the vicinity. A small group playing cards under another shelter shouted at the kid to shut up and stop crying.

Rose yelled back and swore at the card-players, as she angrily waved her arms about and caused paint to fly everywhere. Turning around, she grabbed the kid by the arm and lifted him up like a chick. His legs thrashed desperately, a metre off the ground. I was worried that his arm would be dislocated. Rose quickly examined his scalp through his messy hair, but evidently didn't find any serious wounds. As the child was still crying, she pulled out a breast from her dress and stuffed a nipple into his mouth. He stopped crying instantly.

'You brought it upon yourself!' She angrily spanked the child. When he began crying even more loudly, Rose reluctantly stuffed the nipple back into the child's mouth again.

With a child in her arms, it wasn't easy for her to bend over her canvas to paint, so I picked up a tool – a small stick wrapped with cotton – and helped her to make dots.

'Here, yellow', she instructed me.

I dipped the dotting tool into a pot of yellow acrylic paint and placed a few dots in succession on the canvas. I asked her why Aboriginal artists used dots instead of lines, as in typical Western art.

'Why? You have your way, and this is our way', she said. 'Tomorrow, you show me your way. Yeah?'

It sounded as if she hadn't answered my question, but I understood what she meant by 'our way'. Cultural practices are most precious in binding together a nation.

'You know, we used to draw on the sand', she said. 'Sometimes we still make sand paintings on the ground, with crushed plant and animal materials mixed with coloured ochres.'

Following her description, if the grains of sand were magnified countless times, wouldn't the natural landscape be presented in the form of 'dots'? Looking down from the sky, roads, rocks and rivers transform into lines or geometric patterns in the painting, and so the bush and large tracts of country are presented in dots of multiple colours. I imagined that these dots on the painting were like grains of sand scattered on the desert. The painter seems to condense the natural landscape into countless small dots with a sweeping view of the earth.

The kid in Rose's arms had fallen asleep. She showed me a red spot on his head, then pointed at the nearby emu and then returned to her painting. She began drawing an emu and explained that her original idea had been to depict a traditional story about a ceremony led by emus. It was one of the tales of ancestral creation that are often depicted in Aboriginal artworks. But now she wanted to add a group of little emus to tell a story about the events that had just happened. As she spoke, she drew and soon the outline of an emu appeared on the canvas.

'Okay, the neck is white, legs and claws… black. Here… yellow, you know what I mean?' I followed her instructions, carefully placing dots wherever she pointed. It took hundreds of dots to depict one emu. Helping Rose to paint later became a part of my daily routine. She began just pushing a small bottle of colour in front of me without saying a word, as if we were both too lazy to talk, but we understood each other. This made me realise an interesting thing. Our communication didn't depend only on language. There was communication through movements, sign language and facial expression. Some things not easily expressed in words could be conveyed by movements. Even when language was used, it was often only a few English words mixed with words in her native language.

The scrawny black dog lying alongside us heard something and stood up. Pricking its ears and looking vigilant, it listened intently for a few seconds then suddenly rushed off, knocking over a bottle of paint, and stepping on to part of the canvas. Some of the dots were still wet and blurred together. 'Yea!', yelled Rose. As we were painting outside on the ground, some disturbance by wind-blown sand was to be expected, and to find that the dog had walked on the wet canvas was also hardly surprising. But if the artist doesn't make a thing about it, no one will know.

About an hour later, I had a close look at the painting. There was a black child, followed by an emu leading two lines of smaller emus towards a large circle filled with black, representing a waterhole. I liked Rose's painting and her open mind. She was showing me how ancestral Dreamtime stories could extend into modern stories. It is how culture progresses and adapts.

'Emu is my totem', Rose said.

I looked at her. No wonder she hadn't said a word against the emu, but instead had scolded the card-players. A moment of understanding passed between us as she raised an eyebrow and a mischievous smile appeared on her face.

———————≈———————

The sick man was still moaning. One hand supported his head as his body curled in pain, and flies gathered at the corners of his mouth and eyes. His messy hair was like straw, and was dyed red.

'What's wrong with him?', I asked Rose.

'Headache', she answered.

'Having medicine?'

'Yes, Panadol, but doesn't help.'

I approached him and tried to wave away the flies hovering around his head. 'He should go to see a doctor', I said, but quickly realised that the red in his hair wasn't dye but blood.

'What happened?', I asked turning to Rose in surprise.

'He cut his own head with a rock.'

'What?!' I couldn't believe what I was hearing. Blood was still trickling from his scalp, attracting flies that couldn't be driven off. An infection was almost guaranteed. Anxiously, I proceeded to check his injuries, but immediately the elders lying under the shelter sat up to stretch their arms, pointing at me, signalling me to stop. I had no idea what to do, so I turned to Rose for help.

Rose was grinding clay from a red stone. One of the elders grabbed a handful of the stuff and slathered it on to the sick man's head, face and body. It seemed that the red clay was also used as medicine.

I was dumbfounded. Could this red clay really replace medicine? Rose who seemed to know my thoughts, explained that for many nights the sick man had dreamed about the devil, and now the devil would not leave him when he was awake. Because the devil was frightened of scarlet, all the man could do was to bang his head until it bled and put red clay on his body to scare the devil out. To stop the devil moving into another body, everyone smeared themselves with red clay for protection. As she spoke, Rose wiped red clay on my arms, face and head, smiling all the time. I think she enjoyed doing this to me – something she had never done to any non-Aboriginal person before. Moved by her smile, I grabbed a handful of red clay and rubbed it on her chubby arm. For a moment she froze, then chuckled. Hearing this, I dared to smear red clay on her cheeks and neck, leaving long red fingerprints. I was then overcome by my reckless behaviour. To hide my embarrassment, I pointed to a bulging scar on her shoulder and asked, 'How did it come about?' She hesitated for a moment, then looked back at the group of elders, and whispered, 'Tell you later'.

All this time Jill had remained completely indifferent to what was happening around him. Then I saw him slowly stand up, holding his hands behind his hunched back. Muttering to himself, he walked out from under the shed into the rain and was very quickly soaked. 'Hey…' I called out as I got up to try to stop him. However, Rose waved her hand in the air, gesticulating 'So what?' I thought that perhaps this was right, and Jill must have his reasons for doing what he was doing. Just as my Chinese compatriots failed to understand why I had chosen to spend my time living and working in outback Aboriginal communities. Without exception, they thought that I should stay in Melbourne enjoying the comfortable lifestyle that had never been available to us in China.

At that very moment, the pouring rain abruptly stopped and became a light sprinkle. Was this an illusion or did Jill possess some extraordinary kind of energy that could make this happen? It was incredible.

Jill disappeared into the rain. The men kept playing their card games, Rose kept painting her dots, the children kept running around playing, and no one noticed what Jill was doing. After a long while, I heard in the distance, chanting, singing and the sound of wood knocking against wood. From then on, every night, I heard this singing, quietly echoing around the campfire like a ghost, accompanied by the occasional sound of a bell ringing from the direction of the town's church.

———≈———

Since first meeting Father Paul, I had been wondering if Aboriginal people really believed in God. When I looked at the cross on the only 'sophisticated' building in the community, I tried to convince myself that perhaps this was true. As Father Paul had said to me, 'God belongs to all humankind'. Every Sunday night, some Aboriginal people, mostly women, would gather at the church to listen to Father Paul preach stories from the Bible.

One day, in the late afternoon, the sun was setting in the west. This was wonderful weather after I had been painting all day, so I started out on a walk. Approaching a group of gamblers, I went up to see the excitement. One of them tilted his head and looked at me. He shuffled the cards quickly and, with a cigarette in his lips, said, 'I haven't seen you for a long time. Where have you been?'

'Oh', I thought to myself, you're busy playing cards, so of course you haven't seen me.

Not waiting for my response, he asked, 'Are you rich?'

I patted my pockets and spread my hands out wide. He knew what this meant.

'Then, come and stand behind me', he said, as he threw $200 into the middle of the gambling ring. 'I'm going to win!', he shouted.

He made the crowd laugh. Bystanders never think that the bets are too big, because this makes it more exciting. They are interested mainly in seeing the fight between the players and to relish the frustration and anger of the loser at the end, and not so much to enjoy seeing any particular individual winning.

I watched the cards fly from the dealer's hands to land precisely in front of each gambler. They would all hold their breath and look carefully at their cards. This was the critical moment for the gamblers, and it was when their heart would beat rapidly.

By sheer coincidence, I really did bring the man good luck. He won a few hundred dollars. As the winner he was happy, but the losers were not, and they turned to me. Seeing the situation, I quickly fled.

Gambling is a favourite amusement for people in the bush. I am not sure when Aboriginal people first started gambling. Some say that they learned the practice from the Chinese, but others say that it was taught to them by the Macassans. Early on, when the Macassans traded with Aborigines, they introduced them to knives and other ironware, as well as to alcohol, tobacco, clothes and other daily necessities, some Macassan language, and various forms of entertainment, including songs and dances, and gambling when playing cards.

Next, I passed a campfire where Aunty Emily waved me over to sit beside her. She was squeezing mud on the ground, then wiping it over her head to dye her grey hair red. Her eyes were sunken and almost permanently closed, making me wonder if she could see anything at all. She asked me what I had been doing. I said that I had been chatting with people, drawing by myself, and helping Rose to paint, and that way learning a lot from her.

'Yeah, I see you walking around the community every day', she said, 'Have you got a skin name?' I had heard about people having a 'skin' name. She must have thought that I was beginning to fit into the community, because she briefly explained the concept to me, before adding, 'Never mind. One day, you will have one.'

This is a complicated but very important feature of Aboriginal culture. Everyone has a kinship or 'skin' name, which creates a systematic classification of relationships between Aboriginal people. There are eight different skin groups, and everyone will belong to one of them. I often heard people referring to others as their 'brother' or 'sister' because they came from the same skin group. People in the same skin group are not allowed to marry one another.

The water was boiling right next to Emily, so I asked if I could help to make tea. I threw a bunch of tea bags into the billy, used a stick to stir the tea, then used a stouter stick to take the billy off the fire. This was something that I had learned from Rose. Boiling water would only fill half the billy, so if I then filled it up with cold water the tea would be at the right temperature to drink immediately. Sometimes I put in a mound of sugar instead of cold water, and then poured this hot, sweet tea into cups containing powdered milk. I made two cups of tea like this, for myself and Emily. She motioned me to sit closer, then wiped a handful of mud on to my head, with a mischievous smile. I took this as thanks for the tea. Tears clung to the corners of her eyes. Her smile exposed a few stubborn, remaining teeth. When she saw that I didn't dodge away from the mud, she put a bit more on my arm as she said, 'God bless you'.

God? She had dabbed me with the red clay – the clay commonly used by Aboriginal people for ceremonies. Why would she then bless me in the name of God?

'Do you believe in God?', she asked.

I didn't know how to answer. Although I had no strict religious beliefs, many religious concepts have influenced me, including what Taoism says about this life, and what Buddhism says about the next life. Although this is quite different from Western Christianity, the lives of most Chinese people have been deeply influenced by these philosophies.

'Oh, you are white, but you don't believe in God?' She was somewhat sceptical, but then quickly added, 'Chinese, oh, maybe different'.

'Why do you believe in God? Does God exist in Aboriginal culture? Does believing in God conflict with your belief in Aboriginal culture?'

She looked at me while toying with a pile of the red clay, as if thinking about how to answer, then said, 'Paul is a good man'.

She hadn't answered me directly, but said enough to indicate her trust in the priest. She would believe what Father Paul said.

The day before, I had asked an Aboriginal man who always carried his copy of the Bible with him, 'Who is God?'

He didn't respond immediately, but stood shifting his tattered Bible from one hand to the other, as if judging how heavy it was, and replied, 'I don't know. But this little book says too much drink is not good for me. Father told me so.'

This exchange again showed the importance of Father Paul to the community. I had often heard Father Paul saying, 'When Indigenous people encounter difficulties and cannot solve them, the Lord God is willing to listen and help them'. Just a few days before, there was a girl in the community who asked for permission to dissolve an arranged marriage. The ancient Aboriginal practice of arranged marriage still occurs in remote communities, when stubborn elders believe that anyone living in a tribe must conform with the traditions and laws established by their ancestors. I found out that Father Paul had intervened, and the girl was only lightly punished and later left the community.

This reminded me of Darby Jampijinpa Ross, an Aboriginal painter and sculptor I met once in Yuendumu. He believed that he was eighty-five years old and told me he had three wives and seven children. As we spoke, he drew seven lines in the dirt with a branch, speaking the name of the child for each line he drew. Then he pointed to a girl sitting quietly on one side.

'She is my wife, too. She is pregnant, and we will have another baby', he said, smiling. The girl smiled back at him. She looked very young in her black jacket, as she focused on Darby's every word. I tried to speak with her, but she neither looked at me nor said a word in response. Her eyes were only on her husband.

I couldn't figure it out: did these old men still have sexual desires? I heard that they often asked others to find sea cucumbers for them to eat, as it was believed they contained some 'magic' that could act as an aphrodisiac.

That night I couldn't sleep and, as lay staring into the campfire, my conversation with Aunty Emily kept running through my mind. I was also thinking about how traditional Aboriginal culture and customs co-exist with modern Australian society.

In the past, many Catholic and other organisations used coercive means, starting with Aboriginal children, to change the traditional way of life, with disgraceful results. I often heard Aboriginal people say: 'Don't keep trying to destroy and change us. It won't work.' Past actions by bodies set up to 'help' Aboriginal people not only deprived them of their loved ones, but also separated children from the culture that they should have inherited. Rose once told me that she wanted to thank those foreigners who spent money collecting Indigenous art works: it was art that could attract people's attention and perhaps even change their minds.

The Aboriginal community at Balgo was strongly Catholic, but I still wondered about the role religion played here. Did the society in Balgo now reflect the Church's original motives? It seemed that knowledge of the Christian God had ultimately failed to change these Aboriginal people, but at the same time the Church organisation had not disappeared from their lives.

The social structure and traditions of Aboriginal societies have been affected by other cultures, but the people still consider traditional culture as the spiritual pillar of their being. This traditional culture includes laws and customs, public and secret ceremonies, and many very ancient traditions.

Today, Aboriginal people live within two conflicting cultures, at least in some respects, so how to manage the inevitable problems that arise remains a serious issue.

Dong, dong!

The church bell was ringing, and the sound pulled me away from my thoughts. Looking around, I couldn't tell which was a tree-shed and which was a bush, but the church stood out clearly. I quickly made a few drawings and added notes. Later, they would become the original drafts of paintings. There was a painting already in my mind: that of a woman sitting on the ground, intently and patiently putting different coloured dots on to a white canvas. On the chair alongside lay a tattered book, and on its spine, one could just make out the word: Bible.

As the church bell faded, the night became quiet. I continued staring at the campfire. Gradually, I closed my eyes and stopped thinking about anything. Usually, I would hear my breathing, gentle and smooth, then a deep singing voice would come through the air like a lullaby, sending me into a dream world.

But tonight, I heard a different sound, an irritable, bitter moan. I had the impression that the people were silently expecting something to happen. On the first day when I arrived here, Rose had told me not to take photos casually when I was out in the community. 'Don't ask about anything you shouldn't know. You will know when the time comes.'

I couldn't help but wonder what that time would be like. I opened my eyes, clasped my arms, and stared at the campfire, thinking of the boys that Jill was worried about. Did his disappearance have something to do with this? What was happening with the sick man? I hadn't seen him for a few days.

A dog beside me perked up on guard and barked loudly into the dark. Through the flames, I could make out three people quietly walking together. One of the tall, arched figures looked like Elder Jill. The last time I saw him, he was walking through the rain.

'Hi, J–', I couldn't help myself trying to greet him, but Rose shushed me quickly. She had also sat up, looking at the three figures approaching through the dark. She picked up a large branch and threw it on to the fire.

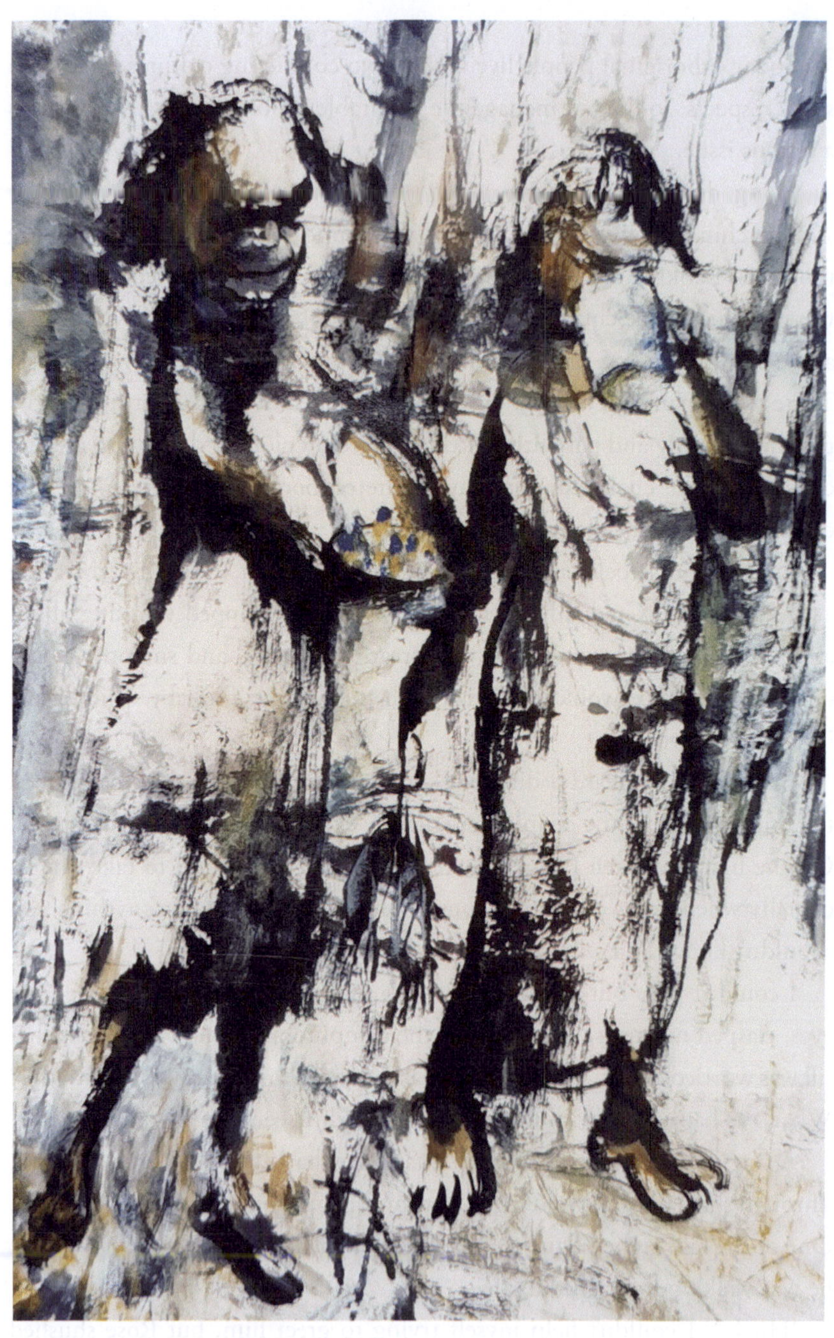

Two Girls Out in the Desert', ink on rice paper (1996), 84 x 60 cm.
This type of artwork is often created on site.

Flames leapt up and the fire made popping sounds. I could see her figure more clearly in the brighter light.

'Is that Jill?', I asked, pointing in his direction.

'Don't call him,' Rose whispered.

I stared back, my curiosity growing. Seeing my unwillingness to let the matter go, she raised an index finger and signalled me closer, 'Soon, you will know'. Although I was boiling over with curiosity, she refused to tell me anything more.

The next day, everything went on as usual, as if all were pretending that nothing had happened the night before. I remembered what Rose had told me: don't ask about what I shouldn't know, and even if I know, I shouldn't say what I shouldn't say.

At the time, the weather wasn't pleasant. Dark clouds kept coming and going, and it was uncomfortably humid. I helped Rose to paint, and I also walked from one campfire to another. In a seemingly random chat, a door to a mysterious world quietly opened.

———≈———

One morning, I got out of my sleeping bag, visited the bush loo, then collected a few branches on the way to bring back. I had something simple to eat, then made a cup of tea while looking through some recent drawings. I liked reviewing things that had happened and sorting out my memories. While doing this, sometimes ideas would surge up and later become a sketch or a painting. But I also wanted to paint my ideas more immediately with paintbrushes. Looking up, I saw Rose busy making breakfast. Her image kept coming to my mind: the yellow dress covering her plump body was streaked with paint of different colours. Just like her paintings, she liked to wear brightly coloured clothes. Another image came to me: now her dress was replaced by her painting. On her hip she carried a coolamon, a wooden scoop usually used for carrying food, fruits and even babies. She walked slowly towards to me, like a model on a stage, except her stage was the desert.

As I sat there lost in thought, Rose told me to get ready to go to the

Community Art Centre with her. This was a centre dedicated to helping Indigenous artists sell their work. The artists usually collect canvas and paint there, and later return with their finished artworks.

When we came to the Art Centre, a dozen or so people were already gathered there at the front, sitting quietly on the ground. Rose and I found a place behind them. It was the last day of the month, and for the artists, it was the day they looked forward to the most, because on this day, some of them received a cheque for the sale of their paintings.

We waited, but not for long. I was surprised at how many people had arrived. There were around 300 people in this community, and more than a third of the population liked to paint. Can so many paintings be sold? Rose shrugged and said that this was an easy way to make money. Admittedly, for some, it was the only way to make money other than the government allowance. Good or bad, there will always be someone who will want it, depending on the price. I wondered, as the French girl had, whether these paintings could be viewed as art, or whether they were simply products made for tourists. Since then, I have visited the centre several times, and indeed many good paintings were there as well as some excellent paintings. If there were repetitive works as well, this was to be expected. But what concerned me was how excessive commercialisation could be avoided in the production of Aboriginal art.

I like Rose's paintings, because they are always different, whether this finds expression in the colour matching or in patterns on the same theme – either way, such difference is difficult for the artist to achieve. It is inevitable for artists to repeat their paintings. Rose says that she sometimes dreams of images, which are always the most popular.

The door opened, and a young white man appeared: the manager of the centre. A commotion and a feeling of excitement ran through the crowd. The first person whose name was called rushed over to collect. The man waved his cheque in the air to make the others envious. This clearly made him happy but it made many others unhappy.

'Boo!', I heard jeers from the crowd. Rose explained that this was because someone had been called twice.

'Ro, Ro!', someone shouted. 'Oh, you are rich. Hey, don't you hear the cheque calling you?'

I heard someone talking behind me, 'How lucky she is. She got a cheque last month!' There was infinite envy in the words.

Although Rose was happy to have received her cheque, she confided that she would need to keep a low profile for a few days, to avoid some 'hungry buggers' she'd have to share the money with. It's the same in China. Traditionally, you are expected to share happiness and wealth with those close to you.

On the way back, I took the chance to ask her to be my model, to which she agreed happily. When I encountered new people, I often asked if I could draw them. About a week after I arrived in the community, a group of people, including some elders, indicated that I could have a 'drawing permit'. They did this simply by telling me, 'You're okay, man'. These were just a few simple words, but their trust meant a lot.

I spread a large sheet of rice paper on top of a blanket and selected only black ink to paint. The brush in my hand was like a three-section Kung Fu stick weapon that waved rhythmically above the rice paper. I attracted onlookers and some bursts of praise.

This type of painting requires a high level of skill. It is not like oil painting, where changes can be made repeatedly; instead, every stroke must be as accurate as possible. While I was painting like this, young Matthew came to see me. I gave him a sketchbook and taught him some basic drawing techniques and skills, and every few days he would come to show me his work. Then he said, 'I want to learn your way and then one day, I will be a real artist'. I was very pleased to hear him say this. For me, he was not just a Kung Fu disciple but my first Aboriginal art student.

While painting Rose, I took the opportunity to explain my painting technique to him. Because I was painting on the ground, Rose could easily watch the movements of the brush in my hand, and she also listened carefully as I explained things to Matthew.

'How long will it take for me to be like you?', Matthew asked.

'You don't need to be like me; your way is the best', I replied.

'Different, but also the best', Rose said firmly.

What she said was right. For artists, this is a simple truth and one that is most difficult to achieve.

While we were talking about painting, a dog quietly approached. Perhaps it was attracted by the nice smell of the ink. It nosed and sniffed the ink pad and tried to touch the ink plate with its foot. 'Hey, get out of here!', we all shouted. Frightened by our shouting, the dog ran right over the rice paper, leaving behind a few ink-stained footprints. It was normal when painting out in the open like this to expect some incursions from nature, but what I couldn't understand was why this dog had run across the painting instead of avoiding it. Matthew joked, 'The dog wanted to join us because it feels lonely'.

Matthew then said that he also wanted to try painting on rice paper. I put out a new piece. He picked up the brush, dipped it in ink, and looked at the nice clean sheet of paper, not knowing how to start. This was normal for any beginner. You must have the courage to pick up the paintbrush to try your hand at a brand-new technique, and this was a challenging task.

I suddenly discovered that there were two others by the campfire. They looked familiar, and I remembered that they were the two behind me who had spoken enviously about Rose at the Arts Centre. I hadn't noticed when they had arrived or how long they had been standing here. They stood aside in silence, without saying a word. After a while, when Rose came over and stuffed something into the hand of one of them, the two turned and left. Sharing happiness, wealth and pain is the consensus and culture of these people.

About two days later, young Matthew came to me with a small but quite long, rectangular canvas. He asked me to sit with him and, placing the canvas between us on the ground, he began painting. He told me to copy on my end of the canvas, everything that he did at his end. After about half an hour, he let out a long-drawn 'bum!' and I knew that he was going to tell me something. He explained that the two circles drawn on the canvas were the places where we sat, and the two U-shape forms represented us with our legs stretched out. Looked at from the top, the twisted, snake-like lines connecting the two circles symbolised our friendship. One side of each circle throws an arc to the other, indicating that just as I had once shown him my art and culture, now young Matthew was showing me his. The black background of the painting was filled with a mass of white dots.

'They are stars; we watch them when we fall asleep every night, Master. When you return home, you won't see them sleep with you', he said, 'but, if you still want to, come back'.

I was very touched by what he had said. I nodded but said nothing. We didn't need to say anything; we understood each other.

'Take it, it's yours now', Matthew indicated, then stood up and left. I still have this painting, which has twice been shown at the National Gallery of Victoria.

Looking at his back, I suddenly thought, why have I never heard any complaints from him about living in such a remote place? Rose and others were also not present. I asked some people, including Rose, and she said to me in a very peaceful tone, 'Because we belong to this land'. Although I couldn't fully understand the true meaning of 'belonging' at that time, it left me with much to think about. Only those who truly love their homeland will have such a complex.

I was not just thinking, but also turning those thoughts into a painting. Painting is the language in which I can truly express my thoughts. Sometimes, such expressions can take a long time to complete.

I started to compose the picture, then later I completed a large painting with the full figure of a man, with his hands hanging at his sides, his thick naked torso slightly bent, while facing a broad, flat stretch of land – a land of infinite imagining. I also painted a long strip of land in yellow and red that was deep, rich, vast and strong. The work is called *Our Land Is Our Life*, and I later designed it for the Mutitjulu Mural Group Project.

By now, I had spent much time in this community chatting and interacting, and I could feel an increased trust between us.

A few days later, I heard chanting and singing in the distance. The wind had now blown away the dark clouds, and the sun shone brightly overhead. In the late afternoon, I saw men, women and children walking out from the town in a southerly direction. Rose abandoned her brush and indicated for me to follow. I quickly picked up my camera bag and went with her into the crowd. Before me I saw people congregating in front of a huge white curtain like the back of a stage, and to my surprise, there, sitting in the front row was Jill, his face anxious and serious.

He waved me over and patted the space next to him. I hadn't seen him since that strange, rainy night. I had only heard his singing in the distance. When I took out my camera and asked if I could take pictures, he shook his head but then he nodded towards the video camera I had in my bag. Later, a white man who worked at the community store told me that although he had lived here for nearly two years, he had never been allowed to participate in ceremonies like this. He had only ever been to the occasional funeral. He was curious to know what I had done to have been accepted to this extent. I had no clear answer, but I knew that somehow it had happened.

Rose was sitting right behind me. Her manner towards me had always been quite open, but now she pulled me aside and whispered, 'Remember the kids that Jill was worried about?'

'Of course', I had always wanted to know what happened to those children.

'You will see them soon', Rose said.

Then I learned what had happened.

One night two months ago, when it was too dark to see the road, and the only sound was the odd dog barking, something happened very quietly. Seven children were awakened from their sleep and told to follow three elders. They walked behind the old man Jill, as he silently led them out of the village. Each child's parents stood watching in the dark, weeping softly. They knew that the children would be taken to a remote place in the desert, to go through the initiation tests that they themselves had gone through when they were young. The elders would pass on their traditions and customs and the stories of their ancestors to the children. This was Aboriginal law.

Now the children had returned, and the community was holding a grand ceremony for them.

Jill raised his hand and the noisy crowd fell silent. Among the crowd, women lowered their heads to suppress their tears; tension was building.

Suddenly, with a resounding 'Wow… yeah… la…', two boomerangs flew from Jill's hands to collide in the air: The ceremony had begun. To the sound of singing, I saw a little boy emerge from behind the curtain. Only perhaps five or six years old, his little legs were as thin as sticks and seemed barely able to support his body. A piece of cloth was tied around his head, and another wrapped around his lower body. He had red and black streaks painted on his cheeks, forehead and torso. He looked tired, and silently walked towards the crowd, his head lowered.

A few women had already formed a queue, each carrying a small bucket of water or food in one hand and holding a branch in the other. Slowly they walked towards the boy, keeping their heads down. They sobbed and as they wiped away their tears, then they flicked the branch at the little boy who barely reacted.

A second child emerged, and then a third. A heartbreaking cry came from the crowd, and another group of women stepped forward with food and water. One child was so small, he seemed almost skeletal. A woman stretched out her trembling hands and hugged him carefully, speechless and crying. The chanting, singing and crying blended together, with the singing desperately trying to overwhelm the crying.

The process of accepting this traditional knowledge was evidently very painful, far beyond my imagination. In addition to now becoming independent, the children had to be circumcised before they could begin their new lives.

At last, the biggest of the seven boys walked forwards, his torso wrapped in cloth. A man beside me told me that the boy had cut himself to prove that he had accepted Aboriginal law. I came to understand that even after these wounds heal, many scars remain. I had seen these scars on the chests of many Aboriginal men. This boy had clearly cut himself more deeply than the others.

Rose explained that this was their custom. This was a rite of passage that brothers and male relatives must experience when they grow up. Also, sisters or female relatives of the young males self-mutilate to share the pain of their brothers – that was how Rose had come to have scars on her chest and shoulders. Women, too, had their own laws and rituals to mark transition to adulthood, but these are secret things that men cannot know about.

That night, I sat at the campfire, dumbfounded. Just imagine a dark night, flickering flames, dust and singing in the air.

A child lay on the ground, painted patterns covered his body, only his face had been left untouched. An old man suddenly spat a spray of white liquid towards the child, so that white covered the child's entire face. More people approached, helping to pin down the child's arms and legs. Then, a few moments later, an ear-piercing roar cut through the night, announcing the birth of a new warrior. Majestic singing and screams of loss and grief continued. Everyone pulled at the scars on their arms, thighs, breasts, then began knocking my head with stones and wooden sticks. I was terrified and struggled desperately, but when I wrenched my eyes open, I saw nothing but the stars in the sky. I tried to calm down from my dream, but I could hear a woman's voice faintly. I sat up and listened carefully. Then I heard a man gasp. It was the sound of a man and a woman making love.

Due to my respect for traditional Aboriginal culture, I have never publicly shown the video I had made. Instead, it preserves my memories which I can then hide in my paintings. Just like many Aboriginal works of art, my paintings contain rich and secret meanings.

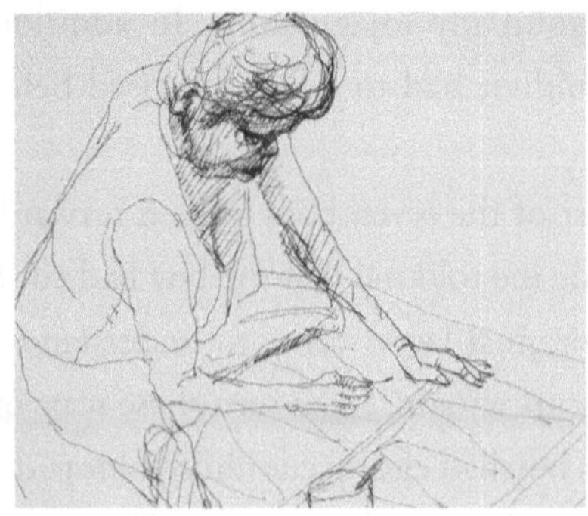

Watching and sketching an Aboriginal artist.

6

A Home Under the Tree

Broome is a very popular tourist town in the Kimberley, in Western Australia. When I first arrived there, people saw me as a Chinese artist who liked to mix with Aboriginal people. Some kept asking me if I knew Jimmy Pike, an Aboriginal artist. That caught my attention. From their tone, people seemed very proud to know Jimmy. So, I started to ask where I could find him. Finally, I was led to a black iron door set inside a long, solid high stone wall. If it were not for the tangle of barbed wire on the top, I would have thought it was the solid wall surrounding a family mansion.

I knocked on the prison door. When I faced the guards, I forgot everything I had prepared to explain why I wanted to see Jimmy Pike. I guessed the guard must have been thinking: who is this strange man? However, the prison guard was very polite. He waited for me to finish speaking, then told me that it was not the normal visiting time, but with the consent of the supervisor they would make an exception for me. He asked me to fill out a visitor's form, checked my passport, and left me to wait. It seemed that he had been expecting that I would come to see Jimmy. Later I learned that Jimmy's wife, Pat Lowe, had called them to allow this to happen. She had also guided me here.

After a while, the prison guard brought in a sturdy man with a beard that was braided with red thread and was quite eye-catching. Later I found out that Jimmy liked to play with his beard, and braided it into different styles. He was a man of medium build and he looked strong and tough, as I imagined a bushman would be. He looked directly at me, with a steady gaze. It is hard to believe that this well-known artist had committed a crime.

He in turn must have been wondering: who is this person? In his circle of friends, there would be no Chinese.

I needed to break the awkward silence, so I introduced myself, and then said, 'Hi. Everyone has told me that you are a great artist, and so I just want to meet you. I hope you don't mind.'

Not moving, he regarded me calmly but said nothing.

'I'd like to see your paintings, but it looks like I won't be able to see them this time', I said. 'How long are you here for?'

'A long time', he replied. Then, telling me to wait, he turned and walked towards an office and stood quietly at the doorway. After a while, an officer came out and Jimmy whispered something to him. The officer glanced at me and nodded. Jimmy beckoned to me to follow the officer, and we walked towards a room at the end of the corridor. 'Keep the door open and don't take too long', the officer instructed us as he left.

We entered a storage room, full of tools and office furniture. I saw a few small canvas boards on the floor or propped up in one corner. Jimmy walked over, turned them over, then, putting his hands in his pockets, looked from the paintings to me.

I carefully picked up a small canvas, about 50 centimetres wide and 70 centimetres long. In the dim light, I saw that it was filled with a pattern composed of many parallel lines, filled with some primary and some harmonic colours. The technique used was relatively clumsy. It was not like dot painting.

He pointed at a row of irregular squares. 'Here', he said frowning.

'Here?', I tried to understand what he meant.

'Yes, here.' This time, his finger pointed to the floor where we were standing.

A dot in the middle of each square. 'Cell and prisoner?', I exclaimed.

He snorted and nodded.

'What about these crossing curves?'

'Barbed wire.'

In the early 1990s, Jimmy Pike was one of the few Aboriginal artists who painted from immediate life experience. This was what attracted my attention when I first saw his work in the town gallery. Most Aboriginal artists chose to paint traditional Dreamtime stories using a dot method, but Jimmy's painting stood out, not only for its different subject matter but also for its different technique. Later I discovered that Jimmy's line drawing was unique among Aboriginal artists. No wonder so many people had spoken about him. It was a pity I couldn't take photographs in the prison at that time, and I don't know where those paintings ended up.

Tapping on the door, the officer appeared, so our time was up.

'See you tomorrow, hey, brother', Jimmy said to me.

By 'tomorrow' he meant that we would see each other again. Life is like this, full of accidents and inevitability. Sometimes tacit understanding and trust can develop with a short-term meeting and can lead to a strong friendship.

After my first meeting with Jimmy Pike in the Broome prison in 1989, I did not see him again until 1995. I got off the bus in Broome at eight o'clock in the evening and looked around, even though I wasn't expecting Jimmy to come and meet me at the bus stop. I was surprised when I saw a dark, strong man standing under the dim light. His beard was still eye-catching, now plaited in two braids. Apart from that, he hadn't changed much. He was still the tough bushman but looked more confident.

Seeing my surprised look, Jimmy said with a smile, 'You right?'

'Oh, yeah, and you?'

'Good', he replied. Despite this simple greeting, there was a tacit understanding between us.

The other passengers from the bus had already left, and only the two of us remained. Jimmy told me that he had been waiting to ask if I would like to go with him to a funeral in Fitzroy Crossing. I then noticed the blue travel bag set down beside him, with a pillow and jacket folded on top of it. I said, 'Of course' – I would go with him wherever he went. So, I jumped back on the bus again together with him. I tried to talk with Jimmy about what had happened since we first met, but I was too sleepy to talk after the long bus journey from Melbourne. I just wasn't up to it.

I don't know how long I slept, but when I woke, I found my head resting on Jimmy's shoulder.

We arrived in Fitzroy Crossing about one o'clock in the morning. How could we find somewhere to stay at this time of night? Jimmy, who seemed to know what I was thinking, just said, 'Let's go home'.

The night was dark and cold. I folded my arms across my chest and followed him. I knew from experience that the desert sun was scorching during the day, but the nights were freezing. While walking, I became badly scratched by bushes and almost tripped over a couple of times.

Jimmy told me to walk close to him, but not side by side. Soon I began hearing him hum a song in his language. He seemed to be walking home in a happy mood. I couldn't see Jimmy ahead clearly, but I staggered along following his voice.

It was an unbelievable night: no stars, no moon. I felt that I had melted into the blackness.

At this moment, Jimmy hummed a tune while we walked along. Relaxed and carefree, he seemed to blend into the night. This was a man I admired, a man I wanted to be.

'Here, we are home', Jimmy said. Walking along in a dream, I had arrived home without knowing it. I looked around and dimly saw a big tree, but other than that, I couldn't see anything.

'Help me get some branches', Jimmy said. 'So cold.' He rubbed his hands and breathed deeply. I quickly put down my backpack, collected some branches and piled them together. Jimmy lit some dried grass and carefully lay the branches on it.

I didn't expect that day and night temperatures would be so different in September in the outback. A few more branches went on the fire to make it bigger. We could hear dogs barking in the distance.

We couldn't lie down because it was too cold. So, we sat back-to-back and chatted. Then I thought of his wife Pat Lowe and asked him about her.

'She's well. She's been busy writing', he said.

She is a writer. 'How did you get to know Pat?' I was curious because I remembered scenes from my first trip to Alice Springs. The gap between

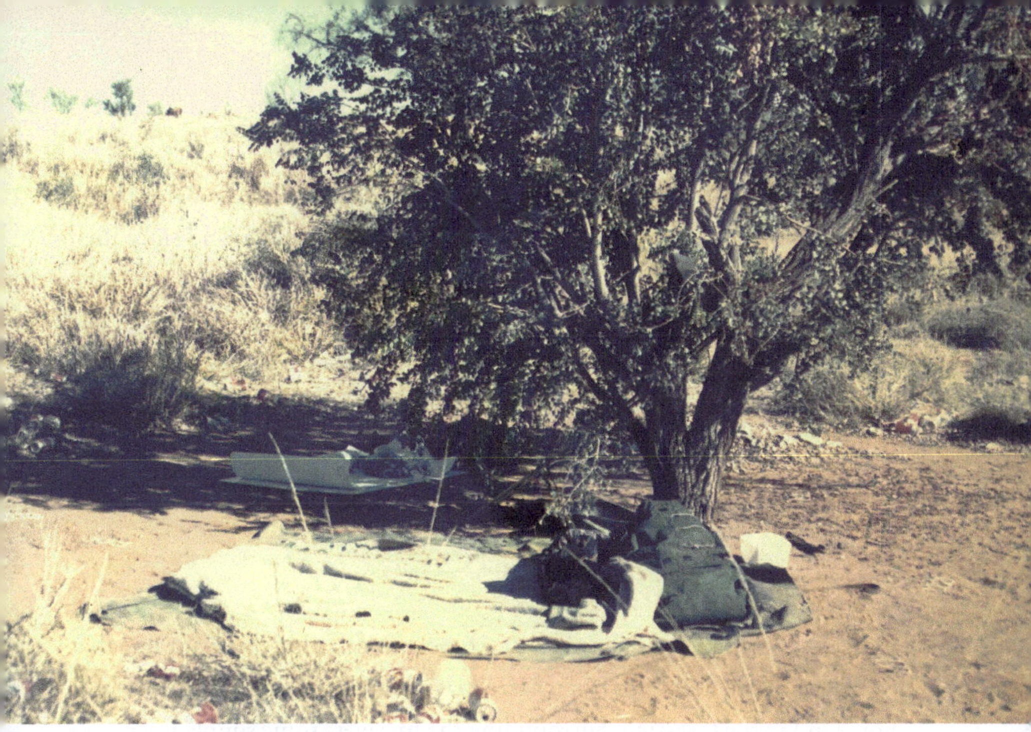

Jimmy Pike and I camped under this tree in Fitzroy Crossing.
We sat by the campfire, chatting and painting.

whites and blacks there had left a deep impression on me.

Jimmy said that he had met Pat in prison, while she was working as a psychologist. She was also a writer and was born in England. When Jimmy was released on parole, Pat quit her job and returned to the desert with him for three years. Last year, they had travelled to the UK for his exhibition and Pat was reunited with her family.

In 1972, she had migrated to Australia, where she found work as a psychologist. Seven years later, she met Jimmy, who introduced her to the space and isolation of his home in the Great Sandy Desert, and led her into a world that is regarded as being mysterious by outsiders.

Later, at a gathering of friends in Broome, I met an artist who had taught Jimmy in prison. He said that Jimmy was the quietest of the group. When you walked up to him and wanted to see how he was going with his drawing, or give him some guidance, he would look up and keep staring at you, as if to say: why don't you just go away? He would often lock himself in a room, and after an hour or two come out and surprise you with a painting. If he listened carefully to the instructor and observed what was being demonstrated, he could complete a work independently. Before long, Jimmy had signed up with a company called Desert Design, and since then he has become a great artist.

Jimmy asked if I had been back to China to see my family. I had not returned to China for many years. I missed my parents. If they knew that I was holding my arms tightly around my body, enduring the cold wind, they would be very upset and would want me to return home. I told myself that I must go back to visit them after this trip.

≈

The next morning, I discovered that we were under a big luxuriant tree that was like an open umbrella. It was a tree that vibrated with life and was Jimmy's home in Fitzroy Crossing. Surrounding the tree were some simple houses, in which Aboriginal families were living, and the whole area was fenced with wire. A rotting wooden sign nailed to a post read: 'MINGJERRIDY', and crooked words added beneath read: 'Keep Out'. This meant that we were in a restricted zone. Nearby was the wreckage of a car that had been painted all over with various swear words and pictures, and there was a large pile of empty beer cans and garbage everywhere. Jimmy clearly hadn't been back for a long time. A row of houses could vaguely be seen in the distance. I guessed that there must be a small supermarket and a petrol station, or maybe a bar over there, because these were indispensable in any small town.

It was a pleasant morning, and the clear air and warm sunshine were totally different from the cold of last night. Three children came up to say 'hello' to their guest. Jimmy was making spears and asked them to bring over some milk. After a while, a woman holding a child on her waist came over with a bag of bread and powdered milk. After a short conversation with Jimmy in their language, she promptly turned and left, without giving me a chance to say 'hello'. But she didn't hesitate in looking back at me. She might not have realised it, as she walked away, but I had an image of a slender, dark-skinned girl wearing an earth-red Aboriginal polka-dot dress, walking barefoot on the sunlit ground. The child sitting on her waist gave her graceful figure a natural curve. Her expression that was shy and calm, but curious, lent a wonderful dynamic and infinite beauty to the picture in my mind.

As I was busy thinking through these impressions, Jimmy asked me why I was in such a daze. He said that during the night, he dreamt that he went to China. 'Big mob people', he told me, as his eyes widened, and his mouth opened without knowing how to describe it. 'Everyone comes to see me and my paintings.'

'What did you tell them?'

'I didn't understand what they saying to me, but I told them: Xiaoping is my friend.'

That's right. I was very happy about what he had just said, thinking that one day, his dream should come true.

'But I'll take you to see our country first', he said cheerfully, humming a little tune as he had the night before, and creating a warm and pleasant feeling. I understood that Jimmy's intention was to show me not only his vast and far-reaching homeland, but also its spiritual meaning.

After breakfast, we rolled up the sleeping bags, putting them and some other things up in the tree to stop the dog getting at them. We went out early, before the sun was up. It was as though we were strolling through our own private estate, enjoying the beauty of the bush, and listening to the sounds of the birds. I slipped into a supremely wonderful state of mind. Jimmy told me to listen carefully: 'Bi-bi…. Bi-bi'. It sounded a bit like a shortened version of the English word 'people', and indeed the bird calls were warning that people were coming. 'When animals nearby hear this, they run or hide', Jimmy told me. Because of this call, the people here call it the Bi-bi bird. How interesting it all was. In the bush there was no shortage of all kinds of interesting things.

I plucked a purple fruit from a nearby tree. It looked ripe and was soft to the touch, so I threw it into my mouth just as Jimmy called out, 'No, poisonous!' It was too late. My tongue started tingling as if it had been pierced by a needle. Jimmy picked a few green-yellow fruits from another tree, which looked very much like the one I had picked, and he threw them into his mouth, telling me that these fruits were edible. 'Try these!', he said.

When I did, I found that this fruit had no bad effect on my tongue.

'How can you tell which fruits are poisonous?', I asked.

'Taste', Jimmy replied.

The incident reminded me of how, in ancient times, the Chinese doctor Shen-nong had personally tasted herbal medicines to ascertain their medicinal properties, and to see whether they were poisonous and, if so, the severity of their toxicity.

'Most Bi-bi birds will stop on safe fruit trees. They like to eat it, too', Jimmy added. This was the simplest and smartest way to identify safe fruit. It was the first survival skill that I learned in outback Australia.

Surrounding us, many different shaped anthills were scattered everywhere. Pointing to one of them, Jimmy said, 'Look that one, like a high-rise building in Melbourne. And this one, just like a couple: a man and a woman.' Looking in the direction his finger was pointing, I saw the couple kissing, while other small anthills looked like a group of people going to the market. We watched the ants, tapping them with our spears. We were two grown men playing like children. Jimmy made a spear for me. This was my first essential tool for living in the desert.

We came across a barbed wire fence with a wooden sign saying, 'Private Garden'. According to Jimmy, this was Aboriginal land. Since white people arrived here, they have used various ways and means to turn these places into private pasture. In some places, after years of negotiation, good conditions for co-existence have been established. When Aboriginal people did not want to relocate, there were two solutions: one was to reclassify land use to allow them to continue living on large areas of private land. This worked when the owner of a cattle station wanted to hire local Aboriginal people to work for him. The second solution was to avoid any long-term arguments and just return the land to its original Aboriginal owners. The one condition usually made in this case was that, although they could live here, the Aboriginal people couldn't sell the land. Many pieces of such freehold or leasehold land were administered by Aboriginal land trusts, or by church groups on Aboriginal missions, like Balgo.

Jimmy walked around with his head down as he showed me around.

Suddenly, he stopped and slowly squatted down to examine marks on the ground. 'It's turtle', he said. I was surprised and wondered whether there would be any turtles in such dry, sandy ground. Jimmy just said that there must be a puddle nearby. We followed the trail for a few metres and then stopped, as Jimmy announced that it was not worth chasing turtle in such hot weather. A good hunter did not readily waste his time and energy.

Jimmy's attention was then taken by other tracks. They looked like a dog's footprints. As we followed them, they became a little messed up. Jimmy explained that this was because the tracks were two or three days old, and they were mixed with human footprints. Not being sandy soil that provides deep footprints, the ground here was hard, so any footprints left on the ground were easily covered by floating dust. To show me this, Jimmy fell to the ground and breathed over it, sending a thin layer of dust into the air. I knelt beside him. Sure enough, I could faintly see a footprint – one that only desert people would find.

I used to hear people say that if a child gets lost in the desert, the child's mother will not look up and yell. Instead she will look down, searching for familiar little footprints. Everyone's footprints are different, just like human fingerprints, regardless of whether they have been made by bare feet or by shoe prints. Footprints hold details such as age, gender, weight and so on. When people want to avoid being tracked, they tie grass or feathers to their feet, and create the illusion of bird wings sweeping the ground.

The sun had risen quietly, and we looked for a somewhere to take a rest. Jimmy was attracted by a row of tiny traces on the ground. Carefully, he closed in on his target. I followed slowly. What would it be this time? We were getting closer and closer. Suddenly, the spear in Jimmy's hand plunged into the sand, and a small thing jumped out, sending sand up into my face. Taken aback by Jimmy's sudden move, I fell over. 'Ha, ha', Jimmy laughed. He had caught a locust. This little bug has six legs and is shaped like a spider. Although it hides in the sand without leaving a trace, a good hunter can still find it. At first, I was dumbfounded, then amused by Jimmy's prank.

Later, I found sand spiders that like to dig a small hole under the leaves where they make cobwebs. Out here, whether it was a small thing like a

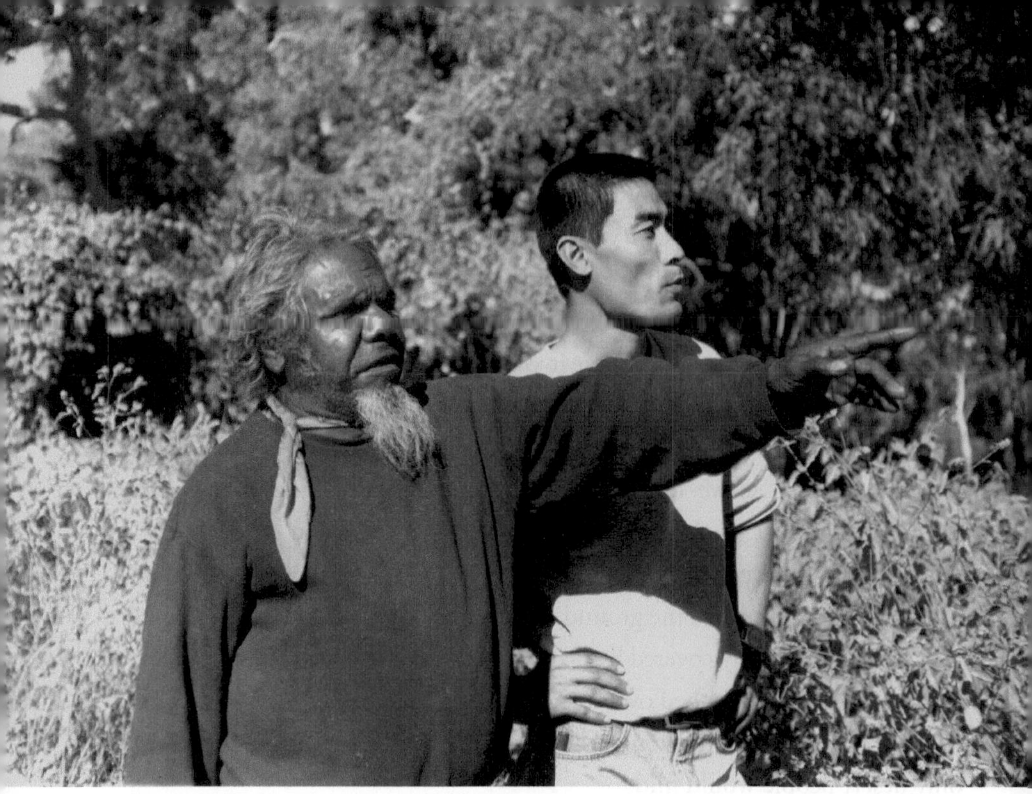

Jimmy Pike and Zhou Xiaoping, 1990.

locust or a large animal like a human being, all had to have a set of survival skills.

'Ha, ha', chuckled Jimmy as he walked ahead with his spear, still proud of his prank. I hurried to catch up with him. There were stones, mounds and shrubs everywhere. If I was not careful, I was cut by thorns or bushes. I tried to avoid them, but inevitably accumulated quite a lot of injuries. Jimmy asked me to follow where he walked, but also said that I must relax and not always stare at my feet. The bushes would naturally make a way for me.

Suddenly, Jimmy held up his hand to get me to stop. He looked all around, carefully placing his feet. I focused on his expressions and actions, and thought that he'd better stop playing pranks. This time I wouldn't be fooled. After a while, I gestured with sign language, What? He stretched out his hands with the palms facing forward and index fingers bent to indicate that he had spotted a lizard. Out hunting, we used a lot of sign language to avoid disturbing the prey. Sign language was also useful for long-distance communication. Jimmy said that to become a 'desert man', this was a basic skill that must be learned.

We looked around carefully and finally saw a hole. Jimmy analysed the shape and inspected the surrounds. Then he took out a small metal box, opened the lid, and used the shiny metal surface to reflect sunlight down into the hole. If you didn't have a piece of metal like this, you could use a knife or an axe. After checking the details of the entrance to the lizard's burrow, Jimmy didn't rush to alarm the animal, but instead went looking for the exit hole, which he knew would be nearby. Usually, a lizard burrow has two entrances or exits, often several metres apart. Sure enough, we found another hole 3 metres away. Jimmy asked me to guard one of these holes. Then he grabbed a handful of dry grass, lit it, and stuffed it into the second hole. He warned me to be careful, as these lizards knew how to escape from hunters. I dared not get careless as I stared at the hole. After a while, there was movement in the burrow, and a lizard's head slowly protruded, just for a moment, and quickly withdrew. Jimmy was impatient. He estimated where the tunnel led and threw his spear on the sand above it. This kind of tunnel is often deep and not easy to penetrate, but his action would scare the lizard, and perhaps make it run out by itself. But if the lizard protected itself by withdrawing deep in its burrow and by blocking the entrance from inside, it could take a long time for a hunter to get it out. A difficult and frustrating process. As it was, the lizard couldn't stand the heavy smoke and the knocking sound from Jimmy's spear and it charged violently out of the hole. It passed me so fast that it scared me, and I forgot to throw my spear. In an instant, the lizard was 2–3 metres away. 'Quick!', yelled Jimmy. As I heard his shout, I felt a spear whizz past my face and nail the lizard firmly to the ground. This was the action of a hunter: fast, clean and tidy. I was full of admiration.

Jimmy was born in the desert of Western Australia in the 1940s and had lived in a traditional Aboriginal environment from the time he was a child. Among the last group of real hunters in Australia and even the world, he was a very tough hunter who understood how to survive in the desert.

Jimmy was very happy. He had nailed his quarry just in time. He dug a hole and grabbed a few handfuls of dry grass. I helped to bring a few branches and we lit a fire. Then while he was preoccupied, I took out a sketchbook to record his movements. He was very interested in what I was doing and, after dealing with the lizard, he spread out a roll of paper, picked up a charcoal pencil and started drawing. Soon a slender figure appeared on the paper, with a camera on his chest and a backpack on his back. Meanwhile, I had drawn a black man with a goatee standing in front of the other figure, holding a spear, and looking for a lizard. In the picture, a nearby lizard stood looking at these two men. We finished our artwork by adding lots of ant hills in 'kissing' and 'hugging' poses or 'high-rise building' shapes. Our playful painting, and the delicious smell wafting from the fire, made us feel elated.

'Come on, let's do more!', Jimmy urged me.

I looked cheerfully at him then drew a big circle on a sheet of paper, followed by eyes, a nose, and a few missing teeth. When Jimmy saw I was drawing him, he also drew a circle on the same piece of paper. He drew very slowly, looking up at me repeatedly, constantly trying to correct his drawing. Then he added eyes, a nose, and a mouth. When his pen reached the top of the head, Jimmy said, 'Ermm, maybe a bald head....' On trips, I always cut my hair very short, so I retorted: 'Well, since you have given me a bald head, you must have a goatee!' We instantly burst into loud laughter. After that, our laughing and joking often pealed through the bush and followed our footsteps while our drawings recorded the unforgettable experience of two artists in the desert.

For the next few days, we wandered around, occasionally catching one or two lizards. As well as teaching me survival skills, Jimmy told me stories about what had happened in this land. One of the words he said most frequently was *jila*, a 'permanent waterhole'. One day, he pointed to a spot saying that he knew it would be easy to dig for water there. To prove his point, we spent about half an hour digging a hole that turned into a puddle about half a metre in diameter. Jimmy said that a long time ago, there were fish here and a dog-bird called Luuru who could call the wind and the rain. He travelled from west to east but found that everywhere across the land was very dry. No rain had fallen, and all the animals were suffering. They made miserable cries, hoping to be rescued. Hearing this, Luuru pecked the dry land fiercely with his sharp beak. He kept pecking and pecking, until finally he had pecked out a great many pits. Then he called for rain to fall from the sky to fill these pits. The rain fell and the pits formed permanent puddles that Jimmy called *jila*. Jimmy said that at the time, there was not much difference between humans and animals. To demonstrate, he drew a man on the ground with his finger: the man had a mouth like a bird's beak. The story continued that, every other day, a voice could be heard in the dark, and everyone was very happy to hear this voice. It was Luuru singing. He was calling for the wind and rain to come. From that time, Aboriginal people in this place have regarded Luuru as the spirit of rain.

I often hear people say that they cannot understand Aboriginal painting, because they do not understand Aboriginal culture. The stories behind the paintings are extremely rich and important and they constitute a history that every Australian should also know. Our understanding of Australian history should not be limited to the past 200 years.

———≈———

My lips were dry and cracked and my skin was like sun-dried orange peel. My stamina had been tested, but I was still full of energy. With Jimmy leading the way, we went to many places and, whenever we got tired of walking, we would sit back-to-back to rest, each taking out a sketchbook or opening out a large piece of paper, and then begin to draw.

One day, while we were busy drawing each other, I suddenly heard a loud voice behind me. It was Peter Skipps, and I could tell that something was wrong by his tone and expression. He was not his usual gentle self. I sensed that there might be trouble: Jimmy had kept drawing his picture when Skipps arrived, only greeting him with a short 'buzz'. Then there was silence, and no one spoke.

At last Skipps said something in their language, to which Jimmy responded by humming but not saying anything. Jimmy straightened up and tilted his head but kept his eyes on the picture he was drawing, looking as if he were still completely absorbed in it. In response to Jimmy's unresponsive attitude or perhaps for other reasons, Skipps raised his voice and, speaking gruffly, finally caught Jimmy's attention. Raising his head, Jimmy looked at Skipps and said something that I didn't understand. The voices of both men became louder and louder, and emotions were becoming high. They were quarrelling, and as their verbal exchange became even more fierce, I heard both mention the word 'Chinese'. Even so, I wasn't sure if the reason for their quarrel had anything to do with me. Jimmy stood up and rushed towards Skipps, who immediately puffed out his chest and roared like a lion. I quickly stood between them to stop the encounter, but the two angry men almost crushed me. I could feel them desperately trying to control themselves and neither wanted to act first in initiating the violence.

'What's your skin?', Skipps suddenly turned to ask me aggressively.

Stunned, I whispered, 'Gojok, from Arnhem Land'.

He paused a moment then announced, 'You wait, someone will come to see you, tonight'. With that, he drove away angrily. I understood that, in accordance with Aboriginal law, he had gone looking for the right person to talk to me.

That night, under the big tree, Jimmy and I sat by the fire, silently. Usually this was a time when I could ask him questions. He was never talkative, unless asked. This night we were not in the mood to talk, but I still had to ask, 'How did Skipps know where we were?' Was it because of our laughter? The smell of our cooking? We were far away from town. Had he tracked our footprints?

'Fire tells him where we are', Jimmy said. He explained that we had gone to some places where strangers should not be. 'But you are my friend, ours', he said angrily. He thought that Skipps was making a fuss because we hadn't let him know in advance. He was jealous. Jimmy asked in a concerned tone, 'Are you okay?'

'Yes, I'm okay.' Yet just thinking about the situation, I was still scared.

The water was boiling on the fire, and the hot steam made the billy lid splutter. I lifted the lid with a branch and made two cups of Chinese tea, hoping that a cup of tea on a cold night would ease our anxiety. Under my influence, Jimmy had got into the habit of drinking Chinese tea.

After this incident, whenever we caught a lizard, I knew that our cooking attracted attention. Jimmy told me that fire was an important way of transmitting information. If children went out hunting and could not get back the same day for any reason, they would pile up branches to make a large fire. This would show their location and show that they were safe.

Knowing how to master and use fire is very special for Aboriginal people. For example, a large fire is sometimes lit after a big hunting trip. In that case, the birds will sit in the trees and look at the charred earth, waiting for everything to cool down before landing to peck and feast on the charred insects and small animals. Jimmy warned me never to run in front of a fire, because it will smell you and chase you, and to be more careful if the grass is long and it is windy weather, because the fire can spread quickly. Also, he told me to keep an eye out for burned areas, where new trees and grass will grow again, because all things follow the natural laws of reincarnation.

That night, we waited for a long time before falling asleep. No one appeared. In the middle of the night, I was awakened by a bleak and scary cry emerging from the silent surroundings. Telling me not to move, Jimmy got up to check it out. Soon he came back and told me that a girl had died. I was shocked to hear this unfortunate news because I knew the girl. She often used to come to chat with us and sometimes brought us food. Once Jimmy had asked her in front of me if she liked me, and she nodded unabashedly. I had painted her many times. She was the girl who didn't talk much. A few days earlier, I heard that she had a headache after drinking too much, then afterwards there was a rumour that an enemy was trying to cast a spell on her, to kill her. This was unusual. Aboriginal people seldom use spells to hurt one another because to do so requires the exertion of much energy, and this loss of energy will hurt the person casting the spell. It was also not auspicious for anyone to be close to someone casting a spell. I heard that one way to curse is to cut some hair from a person's corpse, put the hair into a plastic bag, and then dig a hole to bury it. The clothes and belongings of the deceased should also be burned, while one chants curses non-stop, seated every day in the direction that the wind is blowing. By chanting, the spell condenses into a murderous aura that radiates outwards to find its target. A cursed person who is strong enough will resist the spell and cast a counter-spell, and a battle of casting spells begins.

When I thought of this in the dark, even with Jimmy by my side, my heart contracted.

The morning after the argument, Jimmy left without a word. I didn't ask where he was going but waited anxiously for him to come back. I guessed that he had gone to see Skipps. I hoped that Jimmy would be able to resolve things, otherwise I had no idea what would happen. I was also expecting that someone would show up to see me, which threw me into a restless mood all morning. Shortly before noon, I heard a car in the distance. I recognised it as Skipps's car. It stopped and Skipps and Jimmy got out. I gave a sigh of relief when I saw Jimmy's relaxed smile. Then Skipps told me, 'You are ours. Where do you want to go? I have a car.' To my surprise, the quarrel had made our relationship better. Jimmy, taking the initiative, reached out a hand to Skipps, and I hurried forward and grabbed both their hands. We smiled at one another.

As soon as I had the chance, I explained, 'I want to see the rock paintings around here'.

'No problem', Skipps replied. I was excited for several days. Without the consent of an influential elder like this, no one would be allowed to casually take me to see this rock art. His words constituted a permit.

'Go, let's find some meat first of all.' Jimmy always wanted to eat meat whenever he was happy.

'Are you addicted to meat just like you're addicted to drink?', I joked.

Jimmy first glared at me, and then ignored me. Many people feel that their life is lacking when they can't enjoy a few delicacies in their diet.

Skipps started the motor and stopped somewhere further off. Disappointingly, we spent all afternoon searching but failed to find any prey. Jimmy was gloomy and silent until after sunset. The surrounding ant hills had lost their appeal. He stabbed the 'high-rise buildings' and 'hugging and kissing couples' with his spear, before plonking himself down on the ground. I was also tired and just like him I, too, plunged my spear hard into the sand.

'Ouch!', Jimmy yelled as he jumped up instantly. What had happened? It was as if a spear had been shoved up his bum. Quick! I saw a lizard emerge from where Jimmy had been sitting. I grabbed my spear and instantly threw it, nailing one of the lizard's legs. Jimmy chased the creature, grabbed it by the tail, and held it off the ground. He had been sitting on a lizard hole overgrown with weeds, and when I plunged my spear into the ground, I had clearly disturbed the occupant. After our frustrating earlier hunting, we had never anticipated catching such a big lizard. It made us very happy.

I said to Jimmy, 'It's late. Even if we rush back, we won't get home before dark. But let's hurry back, Jimmy! Let me cook a great dish for us tonight. It's something you've never eaten before.'

'Okay, I'm hungry', he replied, as he grabbed the lizard and threw it over his shoulder.

On the way back, Jimmy was absorbed in thought. Then he asked me seriously, 'Can you cover up the smell of the cooking?'

Ha, ha … this was a compliment to my culinary skills.

That night, I didn't let Jimmy down. When a plume of oily smoke rose from the pan on the fire, the smell spread quickly, attracting children and dogs.

Jimmy reluctantly divided the bowl of food and rice among the children, but muttered: 'Can you think of somehow to cover the smell?'

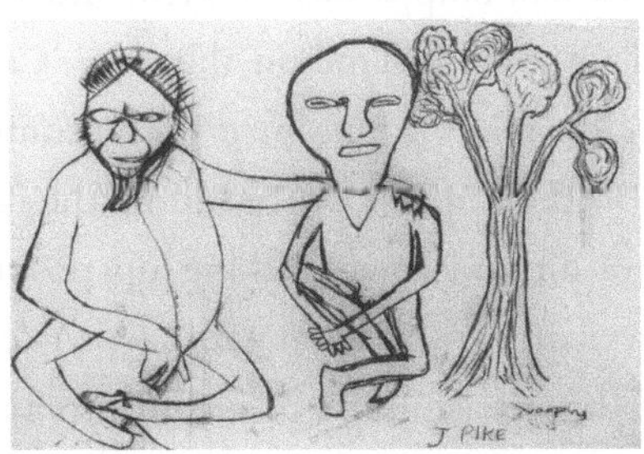

'Drew Each Other', by the late Jimmy Pike and
Zhou Xiaoping at Fitzroy Crossing, 1995.

7

What Do I Want to Be?

For days I had been thinking about petroglyphs, especially the very famous Wandjina petroglyphs of the Kimberley.

This day, I met Skipps at the petrol station, and I asked him when he would be able to take me to see some rock art, especially Wandjina art.

'Now', he replied.

Really? I was touched by his straightforward answer. I knew that I couldn't miss this opportunity, or I would regret it. The deal was that if I paid for a full tank of petrol, he would take me to see the rock paintings. I rushed to the shop and paid for the petrol. When I got back, I saw a young man sitting behind the steering wheel. Skipps introduced him, 'This is my son, Sam'. He would be taking me to see the paintings as Skipps had other things to do. I was a bit disappointed, because I thought that Skipps would know more about this art than his son. Skipps was an artist, and a knowledgeable man.

Sam was excited to be taking me on this trip, 'Come on, let's go!', he said. I thought that, like many young men in the community, he just liked driving. After I got in the car, this proved to be the case because for quite some time, we drove around town picking up people to come with us. About two hours later, our car was filled with six people, including a woman we called 'Mummy'. Jimmy wouldn't come but promised to wait for me to come back and to cook something for me that night. We would have rice, which we both liked. 'Yo, bring a lizard back', he called out.

Early on our trip we passed a cave, which Sam pointed out enthusiastically as having been his favourite playing place when he was a child. His father often took him and his brothers to stay there. They used to sleep on a big flat rock. Right next to it were big rocks with depressions that clearly had been made from the grinding of grain. Sam said that on the cave wall were faintly visible murals, featuring three dotted circles, the image of a lizard, and spears, but because his father and grandfather had painted these, they were considered recent works. Going further into the cave, the light was poor, and it was hard to see. Traces of rainwater flows were faintly visible on the wall, and water seeped in from the rocky mountain. On wet days, a pool would collect, and become a cold-water bath. No wonder Sam said that he used to like coming here to play.

We drove another half-hour and stopped at the site of the ruins of a house. Sam told me that this was where a grazier family used to live, along with their Aboriginal staff. I wanted to know more about them, but Sam told me to ask Skipps. The house had long been abandoned, and it was desolate and overgrown with weeds, but after careful searching, some of the brick foundations could still be seen. These bricks had been laid well, the work of a trained bricklayer, and I wondered who he had been. Walking quietly among the broken-down walls, I saw Mummy sitting in front of some collapsed brickwork. She slowly raised her hand to touch it, as if healing a traumatic memory. Just like the Hans family station, this station and others like it would have hired Aboriginal people to work for them. Their families were often left with stories or memories of that life, some of which are unbearable. This includes the history of the Stolen Generation, now familiar to all Australians. I wanted to ask Mummy to tell me her story, but I was too embarrassed. Not everyone is willing to revive those unpleasant tales of the past. Yet Mummy's silence conveyed the presence of powerful emotion, even though she kept her silence. When we got back into the car, a sorrowful mood enveloped us for some time.

I asked Sam if we were now going to see Wandjina paintings. 'Yo', he replied. Realising that no one wanted to talk, I started to think about Wandjina paintings which, until this time, I had seen only in books. The characteristic Wandjina is a white face, with no mouth, big black eyes, a vertical line between the eyes, and a halo on its head. Archaeologists believe that these rock paintings are at least 4,000 years old, and some can be traced back ten thousand years. The legend about them goes like this: a long time ago, Wandjina created the earth and everything on the earth, from the universe and the Milky Way, including Worora, Ngarinyin and Wunumbul people. These are the Aboriginal people who live across 200,000 square kilometres in the Kimberley region of northwest Australia. For them, Wandjina is the Spirit Creator. After finishing his work of making the earth and all its creatures and the first human beings, the Creator Spirit Wandjina sank into the water, where many new aquatic lives began. So, Wandjina is also revered as a powerful rain spirit. I knew that in this area, traditional Aboriginal law and culture were still very strong.

I broke out of my thinking about Wandjina when Sam turned off sharply on to a small side road. Soon I couldn't see any track ahead, only weeds, rocks and a few sparse trees on either side. A big rock appeared on the horizon. As we approached, it became bigger and bigger until it became a mountain. Shrubs grew everywhere around it, some nearly as tall as a person. The bush here was in its original, untouched state.

I looked at Sam suspiciously… 'Is this our destination?'

'Yes. Behind the mountain', he said.

The mountain was steep. Would we have to climb it? Sandy reassured me that no climbing was needed. There was a path leading to the other side. I was puzzled, but I copied the others and pushed away the scrub around me with a stout stick, looking for the path. After a long time, someone shouted, 'Here, I found it!' There was a broken bridge hidden in the grass. It had been constructed by putting two big tree trunks parallel alongside one another, then laying thick branches crosswise over them. The bridge was about a metre wide and 7–8 metres long. It squeaked as we walked on it, and for me it seemed to be the painful groans of something long abandoned and almost completely forgotten.

After crossing the bridge, we continued to approach the mountain. I was told that we needed to find a large crack or fissure that would lead us through to the other side. I have been to many different mountains, but I had never seen anything like the large crack that we at last found in the rock. It was the secret way that Sam had told me about. The gap looked very narrow, and I couldn't see where it went. Cautiously, I followed Sam's lead, squeezing through the narrow space and in the process cutting my chest and back on the sharp stone. I worried about Sam; he had a big belly. A couple of times I wanted to go back, but this was impossible as all the others followed behind me. Eventually, we emerged and what awaited us was indeed a big surprise.

'Wow, what's this?' I was stunned, and it was impossible to describe what I saw. Sam smiled at me. Not knowing me well, he didn't say much, but his smile told me that he was pleased.

It looked as if the big mountain had been sliced into two halves, with an open stretch of water between that was about 10 metres wide. Emerging at the point where the two half-mountains met, the source of the river could not be seen from the outside, keeping this place secret from the rest of the world.

Sam and the others stretched out their arms, ran around and yelled. They were talking to the trees, the half-mountains, the water, and everything there, to all these things and to the spirits, telling them that we were here. This was a special secret place, and it held its own mystery that impressed itself on me. All the Aborigines who had come on the trip, except for Mummy, plunged into the water. Looking at them, I felt a strong urge to join in. I shouted, 'I'm coming!' and threw myself into the water. The cool river water drew the heat from my body and washed away all my exhaustion. I lay quietly, letting my mind and body fully enjoy the tranquillity of that moment. I experienced a kind of exquisite pleasure at reuniting with nature in this place. Had I come to Peach Blossom Spring? This was the name that Chinese people use to describe a beautiful and peaceful realm.

In China, there was once a great poet called Tao Yuan-ming, who lived around 365–427 CE. He wrote a very famous poem called 'Peach Blossom Spring', describing how a fisherman accidentally discovered a beautiful peach blossom forest and then a mountain with a gate. He got out of his boat and made his way through a narrow passage in the mountain, then he came to a big village with neat rows of farmhouses standing in a wide, flat land. Around the village were fertile fields, separated by intersecting roads, beautiful ponds, mulberry trees and forests of bamboo. The sounds of chickens and dogs were heard everywhere. Men and women in the village wore the same clothes as people outside the village. All these show a message: peaceful. The elderly folk and the children all appeared to be very happy. The villagers told the fisherman that they had been living there for many generations and knew nothing about the outside world. Long ago, their ancestors had led them to this isolated place to escape a war. A few days later, when the fisherman was about to leave, the villagers warned him, 'Don't talk about this place to outsiders'. Scholars later discussed how the poet had imagined an ideal society with beautiful scenery, abundant resources, simple customs and a tranquil life. They called it the Utopia of the East.

Lying in the water, I thought that nature had provided just such a place for the Aboriginal people. Then, looking up at the mountainside, I saw a big rock wall covered with paintings. They were not the Wandjina paintings I had been expecting. Even so, they still made an amazing petroglyph about 2 metres high and 10 metres long, containing images of goannas, kangaroos and human figures carrying spears. It was not hard to imagine the figures of different sizes all jumping and running about and their quick responses and actions whenever they saw animals, and their excitement when catching prey. This rock art clearly portrayed the life of Aboriginal people at some long-ago time. It's a pity that they didn't have a written language and couldn't leave an explanation about why they had created this mural. Nonetheless the mural itself provides a complete documentary record. Aboriginal stories, and their rock and cave paintings, can often be interpreted as allegorical myths.

What most interested me in the rock art was a small design looking like an airplane. Its fresh colour indicated that it had been newly painted. This was evidence that the tradition of rock art here has continued, and that contemporary life and art were emerging in traditional Aboriginal art forms.

I closed my eyes and pictured myself standing in front of the rock painting holding a Chinese brush. I knew that the circles in this petroglyph could symbolise a waterhole, a place, a certain rock, or a specific person or thing. The circle was an iconic symbol of Aboriginal culture. I imagined drawing my own circle, representing myself standing in a dreamland or wonderland. In my picture, there would be three Aboriginal elders sitting, watching me paint, while children played and laughed in the water. We would be living in a happy and peaceful world, just like the village described in 'Peach Blossom Spring'. To my great surprise, I had found the 'pure land' described in this poem, not in China, but far out in the desert of a foreign country. The poem written by a Chinese poet 1,600 years ago linked these places together. For me, this was a miracle.

Sam found a billy and started making tea. A place like this never lacked billies or saucepans, because early visitors usually made sure to leave such items for later arrivals. As we gathered round the fire, someone, with a weird smile on his face, remarked that this was the perfect place for escapees. It was clear that he thought this was the place to hide if he was ever in trouble. We all laughed.

After years spent travelling between Melbourne and the outback, I now know that it is not easy to break away from secular society to lead a simple life without quarrels and complicated interpersonal relationships. But at least there is the knowledge that I have a place like this to sometimes escape to. It is a perfect place, especially for Chinese *Qigong* practice.

As I drew myself out of the water on that first visit to the 'secret place', I asked Sam, 'Where does the river go to?' He didn't know, because he had never followed it. I thought of Skipps and wondered if he could be persuaded to show me where it led.

While we were chatting, I noticed a dark cloud quietly drifting across the sky. It was time to leave. We hurriedly doused the fire then pissed on it on our way back to the car.

Dark clouds were gathering fast. After driving for about twenty minutes, the clouds were directly overhead, followed by thunder and lightning and heavy rain. It was difficult driving the car on the muddy road, and the wheels kept sliding in the soft ground, but we somehow managed to continue for about an hour while there was still some light. We all knew that we had to keep going. The car struggled in the quagmire until finally the engine stopped. This was really worrying, because it was not a good place for the car to break down. Sam pressed his foot hard on the accelerator, to try to get the car moving, but his patience was running out. There was a sudden loud explosion, and a dazzling green light flashed in front of the car. We quickly jumped out into the rain, staring at the car, waiting to see if there would be another explosion. I stood there hugging my arms around my chest. No one knew what to do.

The rain was getting bigger and bigger. I couldn't stop myself from rushing back into the car. The others reluctantly followed. For some unknown reason, I had taken the front seat. Two of the men in the back began arguing louder and louder, until Mummy shouted, 'Hey, shut up!' We all fell into an uncomfortable silence.

'Can we try again?', I said to Sam. I thought we might fluke it, but Sam said nothing, and wouldn't even look at me. I think he knew what had happened.

'What will we do tomorrow?', I asked.

'Don't know', he replied, shifting himself into a more comfortable position.

I knew I asked silly questions, but I was surprised by how quickly the others let go of the problem and drifted into sleep. I wondered how they could be so unconcerned. But that was the way of the people of the desert. First, I heard Sam's snoring, and then other snores came from behind me, as if snoring were contagious. Before long, different snoring sounds, from light to heavy, came from all around the car. I closed my eyes and tried to rest, but the sultry heat and the stink of bodies became unbearable. I rolled down the window. The rain had stopped and there was no wind. Putting my head out, I breathed in the fresh air, but all too quickly a few mosquitoes landed on my face. I quickly rolled up the window and tried to blot out my exhaustion and hunger, and the torture of the mosquitoes.

A few stars came out but, in the blink of an eye, they were gone. I tried to make myself more comfortable and relax my mind. I knew that I wouldn't be able to sleep, so all I could do was to sit and wait for the dawn. My mind was racing. I asked myself: it seems that every time I travel, I encounter some trouble or danger, but each time, I come through it, and I get used to it. Perhaps I am adaptable because I'm still young? Young people always do reckless things, sometimes repeatedly. And then after a while, the so-called 'dangers' start to be regarded as commonplace.

I sat there thinking about Jimmy. He would be waiting for me back home. I wondered what he had cooked for us. He liked a barbecue. Whenever we caught lizards or something like that, he always cooked it on a hot plate. I thought that if I had the seasonings, I could try to cook lizard tail in the same way as the Chinese roast duck. It would taste great. My mind wandered again as I remembered how Jimmy and I would sometimes ate big fat witchetty grubs, throwing them into the fire to cook. They taste like silkworms. I thought: I should coat them with flour and fry them like chips; they would be delicious.

As the night wore on and I still couldn't sleep in the cramped car, I started worrying: what if the car cannot be repaired tomorrow? And then: why am I here? Was it to experience life, or for the sake of my art? Or to deepen my understanding of nature? While I liked the free and open life of the outback, I didn't think that I had the courage to leave beautiful Melbourne and live out here permanently. And then what about China? Everything that had happened to me was changing my plans about returning there.

I sat in the car, thinking about what had happened to me in the past six months. Before my extended visa was due to expire, I had a second interview with an immigration officer. Not the same officer as the first, but he asked the same question: 'What have you done in the past few months?'

I explained that the main thing I had done was to visit remote Aboriginal communities in Arnhem Land in the Northern Territory. I didn't tell him the name of the specific place, as it wasn't well known. I told this officer lots of interesting stories about my life among Aboriginal people. He asked how I communicated with them, and I explained that it was mainly through body language. The officer liked my stories about how I had made friends through Kung Fu and by cooking Chinese food for everyone.

I told the officer that another thing I had done was to touch up the Chinese characters on tombstones in the Bendigo Chinese Cemetery. I had a strong reaction to these tombstones of Chinese gold miners who had come to Australia from the mid-nineteenth century. Many of the tombs were now more than one hundred years old and were beginning to tilt and fall over. I thought that the names of the dead should be clearly seen and remembered. These ancestors had no relatives or descendants here, and being a person of Chinese blood, I felt an obligation to do something for them. So, for two months, I brought sandwiches every day and took them to the cemetery, where I rewrote the characters on each tombstone with red paint. Some tombstones were so worn that I could only recognise the characters by feeling the impressions.

I calmly told the immigration officer: 'This was the most careful and practical thing I have done'.

He looked at me silently, as if he had forgotten that we were in an office in the immigration building. I said that I had met some Aboriginal people with Chinese forebears, like Ah Lee in the Chinese Gardens. I wasn't sure what the officer felt about all these stories, but from his occasional nods and his expression, he seemed interested.

He told me that I could apply for permanent residency and continue what I was doing. I was very excited to hear this. I remember the sincere way he treated me, even to this day. Ever since, I have believed that I can make a special contribution to this country and society. I was granted a permanent residency visa as a person of special talent. Every time I think about it, I feel lucky. It meant that my new life could begin.

However, as an artist, I soon found that it was very difficult to support myself through art. I realised that, for an artist like me, living in a beautiful city like Melbourne was no easier than living in the desert. At least I didn't have to pay for rent, food or transport while I was living in the desert.

Soon I had a girlfriend called Ke Pufan. We got married, and I spent more time in Melbourne. I began by working in a factory making sofas and as a kitchenhand in different restaurants. One day, the second chef was sharply reprimanded by the main chef. They quarrelled and the second chef threw down his iron cooking ladle and walked out. The boss became very angry and paced up and down the kitchen, cursing. She made many phone calls but couldn't find anyone to replace the second chef, even on a temporary basis. Eventually, she turned to me. Thankfully, I didn't let her or the main chef down that night. Fried meat balls, grilled satay skewers, fried rice – I was taught only once how to cook them. All fried food, including things like fried bananas and fried ice-cream, were done by the second chef. It wasn't difficult for me to learn how to do all this. After that night, I surprised even myself. I learned that if I did not want to be an artist, I could be a cook. My Aboriginal friends all liked my cooking. Seeing me get off to such a quick start, the boss asked the main chef to train me as a second chef but made it clear that I would not get the full second chef salary until I was trained. However, the boss had picked the wrong person. No one can expect an artist to become a second chef. Shortly after I had earned enough money for the Greyhound bus ticket, I quit my job and started on the road again.

Another time when I was in Melbourne, I worked in a factory making moulds. The boss would give me a drawing and ask me to make a simple mould. He knew that I could read the drawing, even though I hadn't ever studied how to do it – this kind of thing was never difficult for me. Miscellaneous odd jobs were never hard, but at the end of the day I was always tired, because I could never stop thinking about my future life in Australia. How could I continue to be an artist? When I got home after work, all I wanted to do was painting. As soon as I spread rice paper on to the floor, all my worries disappeared. I couldn't afford an easel and a big painting table, so I spread out a blanket and lay on the floor to paint. This became a habit that I continue to this day.

When I wasn't happy with my current life in the city, it was easy to recall good memories and experiences that I had had in the bush. The thought of returning to the bush kept coming back to me. I missed the desert and the people there.

As I was thinking about all these things that had happened in my life, I looked out the side window at the sky, where some stars appeared then later disappeared. Although I tried to relax, I couldn't stop thinking. Then I saw a flash of bright light in the broken side mirror. What was it? I tried to wake up Sam, but he just hummed twice and ignored me. I didn't dare get out of the car to find out. The light persisted like a will-o'-the-wisp, but I refused to look at it, and tried not to think about it. Many inexplicable things can happen in the desert. Elves are good and bad by human standards, and they know that when people think of them, they will follow you. Thinking of them, my heart began to tremble. I stayed up all night like this, restless. The next morning, when I told Sam about it, he said that it might have been a firefly. But I knew that the light from a firefly could not have been as big or as bright. Then Sam quickly motioned me to forget it. I seem to understand what he meant. We had something else to worry about.

Sam checked out the car and discovered that the water tank had exploded, and the fan belt was broken.

'Can we fix it?', I asked hopefully.

Sam grabbed the two ends of the broken belt and shook his head with a helpless expression – not a good sign.

We started to talk about what to do next. I would have liked to return to 'Peach Blossom Spring', giving little thought as to how we would get out of there afterwards. Somebody suggested that we should walk back home, but this would take a few days. Then at last, Mummy suggested that we could walk to nearby FiFi station. If we went there, the grazier would give us something to eat. Thinking this was the best option, we headed off, but secretly I was rather grumpy. Everyone else was walking slowly, talking and laughing, even fighting together in a friendly way, as if they had just had a meal and were taking a walk in their backyard. They took all problems in their stride, with such a relaxed attitude. But even these desert people could not withstand the sun. After about two hours in the heat, they started to become listless. The crows above us cawed their complaints about the hot weather. But we kept on walking, so slowly.

Along the way, we came across a small creek, so we stopped to cool down and drink. The water was very clear down to the creek bed. Like everyone else, I put my lips on the soft water, took a deep breath, and a stream of cool water ran down my hot throat. It was better than my favourite ice-cream. While Sandy squatted in the water, I sat on the creek bed, having a cool bath. My body seemed to be absorbing water like a sponge. But this pleasurable feeling did not last very long. We faced another situation soon after we started walking again. I had started to feel weak and uncomfortable. I thought: maybe it was because of my hunger? So I picked up some fruit from trees growing by the roadside. Most were unripe, sour but not poisonous and I thought that swallowing them would be better than swallowing saliva and nothing else. I dropped two berries into my mouth. The astringency caused the inside of my mouth to crack. Then the discomfort got worse. I sat down weakly against a tree, closing my eyes, and holding my head with one hand.

'You alright?', Mummy asked.

I shook my head, feeling weak and drowsy, then I saw her take a piece of damper from her bag to share with me. It was probably a week or two old. I chewed each bite with some water. In a daze, I felt someone touching my arm, then my forehead and my hair. Mummy was muttering as if she were praying. It reminded me of the old man with his head covered in red clay in Balgo. Although I had lost the ability to think clearly, I knew that I was suffering from heatstroke. Mummy's muttering in a monotonous voice made me feel comfortable and peaceful. I was slipping out of consciousness and wondered: am I going to die? Thinking about it later, I realise that when people die in this kind of situation, there is no pain or fear; it is more like a feeling of peace on entering a dream. In retrospect, according to common sense, people with heatstroke would not think that they are about to die, but the environment here is different, and the heat is a most ruthless killer.

I don't know how long I was like that, but I gradually got better. I opened my eyes and saw everybody sitting around me. It was like a scene from a Kung Fu movie where practitioners gather around to concentrate the healing power of nature, to deliver it to the injured person in the form of *Qi* energy.

'Feel better?', Mummy asked.

I took a few deep breaths. It was as if I had just woken from a deep sleep. I really felt different. Although my body was still weak, I thought that we needed to move, to get to FiFi station before dark. Fortunately, everyone still walked fairly slowly, so I could keep up. It was a long and difficult road. If I hadn't experienced it personally, I would never have believed that it could happen in real life. Usually, we see it only in movies: a group of survivors fleeing, supporting one another, walking in the wilderness under a scorching sun.

———————≋———————

Finally, we arrived at FiFi station where a white guy lived by himself.

'Oh, bloody hell, where you come from?', he yelled at us. Seeing his hideous, angry face, my heart trembled. Sam stepped forward and said gently, 'Sorry to disturb you, but could we have some water or tea?'

'Bloody hell, tea? Why should I give you tea?'

Sam was appalled by him. We stepped back, looked at one another, but no one said anything, although their eyes showed helplessness and resentment. After some time, Sam asked me to intercede. We needed this man to contact the people at Fitzroy Crossing. I had to try again. But he didn't want to talk to me at all, and kept complaining.

'Bloody hell, what're you doing here?' Obviously, our arrival had put him in a very bad mood. He went back into his house and sat down in front of the television. Through the open door and window, I saw him walk into the room, sit down, then stand up and repeat this all over again. Finally, he walked into the messy kitchen and took a pot down from the top of the dusty cupboard. It looked like it hadn't been used for ages, but he wasn't washing it. He dropped a bunch of tea bags in it, poured in some water, and put it on the stove.

I stepped aside quietly and sat on the ground with the others, tired and hungry, unable to think about anything. We were all depressed.

Constant swearing came from the room as the man tried to make a phone call. 'Hello? Bloody hell!' He was very annoyed when he got no answer on his radio intercom phone. He slammed the receiver down on the table. The last time I had seen such old communication equipment was in war films from the 1970s.

About an hour later, I was lying on the ground, almost asleep. 'Hey, what are you waiting for?' I vaguely heard someone shouting. Opening my eyes, I saw the man standing there with a piece of black beef in one hand, a tea pot in the other, and a large piece of black bread under his arm. I thought

I was dreaming. When the man said, 'Bloody hell!', I reluctantly woke up.

'Oh, Sam, this is not a dream', I said. Sam and the rest of us looked so silly sitting there. I didn't know where I got the energy, but I rushed over to take the food. 'Thank you, thank you', I said.

Although everyone was very hungry, we ate in a restrained way, No one talked. Sam poured tea, and we shared the single cup. The beef was cooked meat taken from the freezer and heated in the microwave. After our meal, one piece of beef remained on the plate. Sam cut it into several small pieces, and we hid it quietly in our pockets. We all knew that this guy would never give us any more beef.

That night, we slept in a storeroom with one quilt but no beds or blankets. Each of us found our own spot to lie down in, but many ferocious mosquitoes kept driving me crazy. I covered my head with a cloth and was kept busy killing mosquitoes, as they still bit through my T-shirt. I tried my best to calm myself down, like Sam and the others, and just go with the flow.

It didn't work. Once again, I stayed up all night. I began to miss the feeling of sleeping in a soft bed – what a luxury for people walking in the desert.

The next morning, I was awakened by a voice. I realised that I must have had a little sleep, probably in the early morning. When I walked out, I saw the guy again in a bad mood.

'Good morning', I said carefully, but he didn't respond. He just walked in and out of his house, still trying to reach the people at Fitzroy Crossing. The longer he failed to get in touch with them, the angrier he became. He was so anxious to send us away. I still didn't dare ask for his name.

Eventually I heard, 'You have to fucken hurry up. Get these bloody guys out of here. I don't have enough food to feed them', he yelled at the phone.

The other person said, 'Don't feed them, then. What the fuck are you yelling at me for?' They quarrelled on and on. Listening, I learned that it was raining heavily in Fitzroy Crossing. Not long after, the guy made another loud phone call, arguing with a mechanic.

We sat together with our heads down, but I saw a smile on Sam's face. I knew why, because I had the same feeling. The guy inside was more anxious than we were. We were here because we didn't have a choice.

At lunch time, he made a big pot of soup with potatoes, radishes and cabbage. I took the opportunity to ask the man for his name. 'Rod', he snapped, putting down the pot, turning his back, and leaving the room. Bloody hell! It was my first bit of conversation since yesterday. However, Rod's bad mood had lessened slightly because he had finally made it through to the mechanic at Fitzroy Crossing.

We were sitting around the table having our soup. No one spoke. We ate less desperately than the day before, but we still didn't make a sound. I couldn't stand having to be so careful and anxious.

By the afternoon, we were still waiting anxiously.

We wandered around, hoping to catch a goanna, leaving Rod to argue with the person on the phone. Rod wanted us to leave as soon as possible. Unfortunately, it wasn't going to happen. It was still raining heavily at Fitzroy Crossing. We just had to wait. It really tested our patience. My legs began to wobble, and since there was not enough food, I desperately drank more water.

The third day was just the same. To distract myself from my hunger, I started to draw on paper, and gradually became absorbed in my work as I tried to use my skills to summarise what had happened yesterday into a sketch.

By the fourth day, Rod had become quite mad, and was cursing from morning till night. Sam and the others constantly walked to the crossroad to see if there was any car coming. I pulled my hat over my head to block the light and lay drowsily on the grass. There were too many mosquitoes at night and too many flies during the day to get enough sleep. While I lay there, yesterday's conversation with Rod kept coming to my mind.

He had asked me if it was difficult to become an artist. I said that my current situation proved this to be the case. Then he asked why I was with these Aborigines.

'Bloody hell, how do you mix with them?', he said.

I really didn't like him talking like that. Still, seeing that our group of six had eaten his food over the past few days, I gave him a brief explanation to satisfy his curiosity.

He looked at me for a while and asked again, 'Why?' It seemed that he really couldn't figure it out.

'You don't like us?', I asked.

He hit a plate that was on the ground with his stick, signalling that we weren't too bad.

What could I say? To be fair, he was not such a bad 'bloody hell' man. Although he didn't like us, he still fed us every day, even if it was only one meal. He started complaining and talking a lot, frequently interrupting his story with 'bloody hell…' He usually lived here alone, so he talked about himself. It was an interesting tale, but I couldn't keep my mind on what he was saying. I just pretended to be listening, while all I heard was in fact his nagging tone.

Looking at his rough, wrinkled face, I thought: will I ever become like him?

'Why do you like to be with them?' He was back with the same question.

I shrugged, 'Why not?' But after he had asked me the same question repeatedly, it came to be insulting.

Did I need an impressive reason to prove that my life was meaningful? I could ask why someone like him had chosen to live in such a remote place. His insistence that I should provide some deep and meaningful reason was absurd.

He became impatient with my constant hedging, 'Don't fucking talk nonsense to me'.

'What the fuck do you want to know?', I replied angrily, surprising myself.

'Your story. You're a story man.'

He didn't seem to mind that some foul language had crept into our conversation. Everyone living in the desert had stories to tell. Later I regretted that I hadn't listened to his story. If I ever meet him again, I will record it.

In fact, the question Rod asked me was exactly what I had been thinking about in the car a few days previously.

The well-known Aboriginal artist Rover Thomas was once painting a small picture. He said to me that he was doing it in exchange for a dinner ticket. 'You have to go back to where you really belong.' Rover's painting used only two colours, yellow ochre and black. He asked me to put white dots between these colours. Then he pointed to the black space and said, 'This is Darwin, surrounded by a lot of garbage'. I thought, it's just the same in Melbourne, or anywhere that people are happy to live together in a great concrete pile. It's their choice, or perhaps they don't have a choice. Rover told me that the yellow ochre space represented his country. He asked me what my choice was. I couldn't answer him. But it made me ask myself other questions: who am I? Where do I belong? I kept trying to find answers.

I was awakened from my dreamlike state by a burst of shouts, 'Toyota! Toyota!' Looking up, I saw Sam waving desperately as a repair truck approached from a distance. I quickly ran over and told Rod, 'Here comes help!'

'Oh, the exciting news has finally arrived, even if it's a bit late', he grumbled. He slammed the wooden spoon in his hand down hard on the big wok, because he was already preparing another meal for us. 'Thank you, Rod, thank you very much', I said with sincerity, folding my hands together in front of my chest as I bowed to him.

'All right, get out of here. I hope it doesn't rain again on the road', he replied more warmly, without the swearing that had characterised his conversation over the past few days.

So, he finally got rid of us and could return to his solitude. What would it be like for him without us disturbing him? For whatever reason, I still thought of him as we travelled back to Fitzroy Crossing. If a person like him was alone for a long time, loneliness would be like an ever-present fly that one couldn't drive away… annoying, but something one could get used to. After meeting Rod, I vaguely saw what I could become – not like him, but not quite like a normal person either. To be honest, I didn't like to face this contradiction in my life.

I straightened up and, folding my arms, wondered what I would be eating that night. Would Jimmy be at home waiting for me?

It was already dark when we returned to Fitzroy Crossing, but there was

Jimmy sitting on the side of the road beside the petrol station. He told me he had been waiting there for me every day. Now, 'Let's go home', he said.

———≈———

Back home under the big tree, I slept for two days to recover from my exhaustion. After that, people would come around to watch me and Jimmy painting and to hear what had happened to us on our trip. I told them most of it but didn't mention the secret place. They especially liked my stories about Rod. After that, 'bloody hell' became a sort of joke between us.

Jimmy told me that while I was away, he had gone to the funerals of his relative and the girl. He didn't go into details, and I didn't ask for any. But I felt sorry for the girl. Then when we talked about Rod, Jimmy really opened up. 'I was in the garage, next to gas station and heard him arguing on the phone with people. Wow! Unbelievable, he was so angry.' Jimmy told me that he had gone there every day, and that was where he found out about our situation at FiFi station. He knew that if he went to China, I would take good care of him, just as here, in his country, he was responsible for me.

I paused, as a thought came to my mind. 'Jimmy, let's make an exhibition together.'

'Yeah', he agreed immediately. There was a tacit understanding between us.

While we were painting and talking, some Aboriginal people gathered around us. They liked to spend time under the big tree, making noise, joking or even arguing. Today, for some unknown reason, two people, one young and one old, were arguing. Gradually they went from quiet to loud disagreement, shouting and jumping around. Finally, their expressions became quite serious, and with the veins bulging on their necks, they looked like two protagonists in a play. Their looks and fierce expressions made us laugh, while some people slapped at the ground. The young man, who held a stick in his hand, reached out with it towards the crotch of the old man. He gestured with both hands to separate something, then turned around still singing. His opponent was a shrivelled old man who showed no sign of weakness. With his legs hunched, he held up two fingers like a stick ready to strike and made a gesture. Seeing everyone laughing, I asked the people around about what the young man and the old man were arguing about. The one I asked was laughing so hard that he could hardly breathe, but after a while he explained that the two men had started arguing and then quarrelling. The young man had said that he would chop off the old man's cock and hang his testicles on his belt for decoration. The old man replied that he would slowly cut the young man's little 'chicken' down the middle, give it to a wild dog, and make the dog ecstatic. This was the first time that I had heard such talk from Aboriginal people, but it is the sort of humorous folk culture that every culture has.

Such fun-filled atmosphere attracted people but didn't affect our painting. Jimmy and I still painted, and then chatted under the tree, back-to-back, every day. When we felt tired, we just lay down, and let others do whatever they wanted. Jimmy looked at a picture that I was painting.

'Well, there should be people', he said, and drew a little man under a tree. 'This is me.' Responding to what he said, I also drew a little figure under the tree. The two people were back-to-back. Then Jimmy drew grass around the tree. The understanding between us had reached the point where we knew how to draw together without discussion. Over the next few days, we painted like this, depicting our lives and what was happening around us, defining our understanding of this land.

Jimmy was one of the few Aboriginal artists I had seen who could draw. His painting skills had come from his early training in Western art. But he used the traditional content of Aboriginal culture, expressing it via Western painting techniques in his own artistic style. He was the first Aboriginal artist I had collaborated with, and our collaboration was carried out impulsively. Our paintings that consisted of random ideas were impulsive and temperamental, and sometimes betrayed a certain madness. They record our friendship, the most important facet of our collaboration.

The night before leaving the tree that was our home, I made some delicious fried rice. We invited Skipps to join us. He said that he could smell the alluring aroma of this Chinese cooking from a long way off, and he would miss it very much.

Skipps asked me, 'Do you like it here?'

'I think so', I replied.

'Then you should come back. We like you, like your cooking', said Skipps laughing.

That night, as we chatted around the fire, Skipps was particularly talkative. I am a lot quieter, but I really appreciated his warm, cheerful personality. I watched Skipps through the flames. Then I turned my gaze to Jimmy and started to think of a new painting. Everything I had experienced over the past days flashed quickly through my mind, but with a single recurring image: under a big tree in the wilderness, two artists sit back-to-back, as they chat and talk about painting. In that state we forgot about everything.

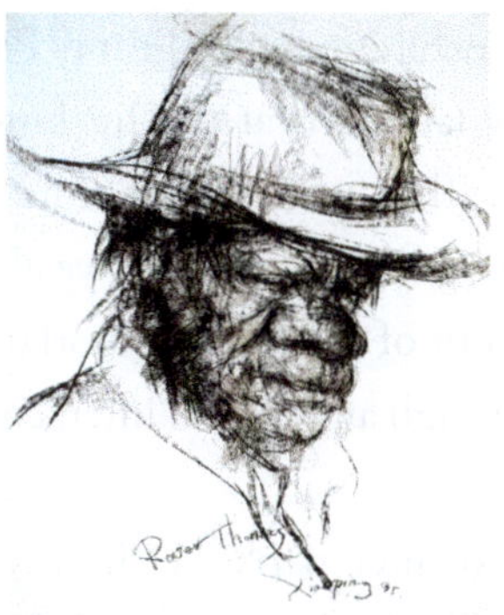

Rover Thomas, Darwin, 1995.

8

First Aboriginal Artist in China

For some years, I had been planning to bring to reality my idea of doing a joint exhibition with Jimmy Pike.

The day of 7 November 1996 was one I had been looking forward to. It was the day that my joint exhibition with Jimmy Pike, 'Follow an Australian Aboriginal', was officially launched at the Jiu-Liu-Mi Art Museum in my hometown city of Hefei. This was the first time that my work had been exhibited in China since my departure eight years ago, and it was also the first time that an exhibition of Australian Aboriginal art had been held in China. This happened through an unusual interaction between Chinese and Aboriginal artists.

The exhibition fell into three parts: (1) Jimmy's paintings that told his dream stories linking his people, their land and the spirits; (2) my paintings expressing my own view of Aboriginal people and my understanding of their culture; and then (3) our collaborative paintings that revealed how inspiration had sprung from the experiences and interactions of two artists from two very different cultures meeting in the remote desert.

Jimmy, his wife Pat and I attended the opening ceremony.

Our Chinese audience had no previous exposure to Australian Aboriginal art. They didn't understand it very well but left messages in the guestbook to indicate their reactions, such as: 'the paintings are very strong', 'the dots have a sense of rhythm and tension' and 'there is both a strong national language and a modern sensibility'. Some people saw features reminiscent of Chinese folk art, including Shanghai Jinshan Peasant Painting and Shaanxi Folk Art. I was aware that by this time, the simplicity and many other features of Chinese folk art were becoming lost due to excessive interference from local governments. Why would anyone want to reform folk art? It's incredible and just the same as someone trying to straighten out the eyes and nose in a Picasso painting. My fellow artists knew that Jimmy's art was far from simple, even if they didn't understand the full meaning of his paintings. His use of colour, itself, was much finer than that employed by many artists trained in the Chinese Academy of Fine Arts.

My old master, Zhou Bin, who had taught me traditional painting, said:

The first time I walked into the Exhibition Hall, my eyes lit up. I haven't had such a feeling for many years. I think everyone who comes here will feel the same. Usually, I never praise my students in public, because they still have a long way to go in the development of their art. But today I must break this convention. I am proud of this student, because he has extended the artistic concept of 'learning from nature' from the Chinese environment to the land of Australia. These cross-cultural works are unique and refreshing. I would like to suggest that we take this as a model for our future teaching.

In China until the 1990s, artists spoke only briefly about art but without sensationalism or flamboyance. Traditional art concepts and forms continued to dominate the entire field. Then following China's reforms and opening to the outside world, Western contemporary art flooded in. Some Western art collectors started to promote the earliest Chinese contemporary artists in the international market and received widespread attention. The former Swiss ambassador to China, Uli Sigg (1995–98), collected nearly 2,000 contemporary Chinese works. The Belgian collector Guy Ullens also appreciated contemporary Chinese art, which made up 80 per cent of his collection of over 1,700 items. Contemporary art suddenly became very fashionable in China.

Chinese artists realised that strictly adhering to the conventions of their traditional art and to concepts passed down for hundreds of years would not allow them to survive in this new market. Everyone was working at a loss, except for rebels who had been exploring new forms and who had been surviving somehow outside the system. The commercialisation of Chinese art had begun.

Three years later, in 1999, Jimmy and I held our second joint exhibition in China, this time at the National Art Museum of China. It was the first time that the museum had exhibited works by Australian Aboriginal artists. Later, Australian Aboriginal art, music, dance, painting and photography were gradually seen more often in China, where these art forms now receive widespread attention. Even so, China's understanding of Aboriginal art lags far behind that found in Europe, the USA or Canada. In 1989, an important exhibition, 'Magiciens de la Terre', was held at the Centre Pompidou in Paris. It included works by Aboriginal artists, expressing their complex spiritual relationship to their land. The Quai Branly Museum in Paris now has a permanent display of Australian Aboriginal art. Rover Thomas was one of two Aboriginal artists to exhibit works in the Venice Biennale in 1990.

My focused observations, academic research and long-term study of Australian culture have led me to conclude that Australia is an immigrant country based primarily on Great Britain's culture, that only later absorbed compatible elements from multi-ethnic cultures of both the East and the West. Nonetheless, in the world of art, it is the Indigenous culture that for me most truthfully represents the characteristics of this country. During our two exhibitions in China, Jimmy and I presented lectures on Australian Indigenous art and culture.

So, how does one appreciate these Aboriginal artworks? This was the question asked by most Chinese audiences. In one exhibition, there was a painting titled *Snake* or *Kalpurtu-makari*. The painting shows a human face rather like a Chinese paper-cut but with the body of a snake. Jimmy told me that it represented Kalpurtu, the rain spirit, who can call the wind and rain. Whenever people in the desert are threatened by drought or lack of water, they pray for the rain spirit to come. In the painting, the rain spirit has long hair and a beard. Chinese audiences became more interested in this painting when provided with an explanation of the story behind it.

On one occasion, someone in the audience pointed to a painting titled

Waterhole and asked, 'What are these lines that go around like intestines?' After I had translated Jimmy's explanation, they all laughed. Jimmy was very happy when audiences wanted to know the meaning of his paintings. He replied in English but mixed in quite a bit of his native language, making it sometimes hard to understand. Luckily, I was there to help. He said that '*Japingka*' or '*Jila*' means a permanent waterhole. Whenever the weather is very hot, everyone will gather there. When he was young, he often went there with his family. For him, this is a sacred place, where ceremonies are often held. Whenever I translated for Jimmy, people would invariably comment that his language was unfamiliar, but they really liked listening to him speaking. In an interesting way, it was somewhat like singing.

Jimmy said that the paintings showed 'water, roads, traces and people'.

The audience began looking for these symbols in the paintings.

If the vague curving lines are roads, and the circles are waterholes, where are the people?

'There', Jimmy said.

'Where?' Everyone was trying hard but still couldn't find them. This was because they had such a strong mental concept of how a person should be drawn that they were unable to discover symbols representing people within an abstract pattern.

'You can't, but I can.'

This remark reveals the thinking and intuition of an artist from the desert. Everything that happened there was engraved in his mind. 'Sometimes. No need to paint the people, but they are there.'

Much Western abstract art and other types of art are not well understood in China. But even so, the vocabulary, imagination and way of thinking of artists generally resonate with Chinese audiences. Artists whose works are best appreciated are those where there is some understanding of their cultural background. Aboriginal art is not only abstract, but it is also rich in spiritual meaning and symbolic realism. Both simple and complex abstract symbols are used to tell a story. Once the culture and story behind it are explained, the art becomes much richer and more meaningful.

The same process can also be found in Chinese art. The flowers, birds and insects that appear in Chinese paintings are also often symbolic: a floating fish tail or a few water plants on rice paper will evoke memories of water, so there is no need to paint the water itself. Just as Westerners who want to understand Chinese painting must find the symbolism captured within it, to understand the art of Aboriginal people, we need to understand their culture, their spiritual world and their way of thinking. It is only when we locate the paintings in context that we will grasp their meaning. The geometric symbols found in Aboriginal paintings are a special language, a set of hard-to-crack codes. Only those who have mastered these codes can truly understand the artworks' rich connotations.

Apart from 'Dreamtime stories', Aboriginal artists also paint many interesting ideas from the present. To illustrate this, I will tell two stories that happened many years after the first Aboriginal exhibitions held in China. Reggie Uluru is an Aboriginal elder from Mutitjulu in Uluru. Born and raised in the desert, he speaks the Yankunytjatjara language. For most of his life he worked on cattle stations, then after that as a park ranger and tour guide in Uluru–Kata Tjuta National Park. More recently, he has been living in a nursing home in the Aboriginal community of Mutitjulu. Sometimes he paints a few small paintings, often humming a simple tune while he works. It is a pleasure to watch him. He liked to ask me how he should paint and what was needed to make the picture more beautiful and complete. If I didn't come up with any useful ideas, he would roll his eyes to show that what I was saying was of no help. Nonetheless, he would always finish his work and enjoy the process. At the end, he would say, 'Finished', then push the painting to me – meaning that I needed to pay for it.

These small paintings by Reggie are quite different from those of Aboriginal artist Malya Teamay, who bases his work on only a handful of main stories and an equally small number of images: a small lizard, emu tracks, or a U-shape indicating a group of people sitting together. His reliance on these few symbols resembles the practice of Chinese artists of using just a few simple images: goldfish, shrimp or grass. In ancient times, Chinese artists often drank liquor and tea, wrote poetry, while taking sheer delight in the process of painting. I love traditional Chinese paintings. They can appear serene and natural, but at the same time they can also have profound meanings depending on how viewers choose to interpret them.

For me, Malya Teamay's paintings possess more levels of meaning than Reggie Uluru's, and he explained one of his works to me: 'A long time ago our Aboriginal laws were very powerful, but after the white people came to our land everything changed. The traditional culture gradually changed.' The disappearance of traditional culture seemed inevitable. The laws and customs became weaker and weaker under the impact and challenge of foreign cultures – a situation that greatly worried the elders. In response to their concern, Malya drew an interrupted straight line on the painting to indicate, 'The law, broke'. He explained how people had come together to discuss what should be done. So, below his interrupted lines he had drawn several U-shaped symbols forming a circle, representing a group of elders holding a meeting to discuss how to revive their laws and customs. Further down the painting is a strong, complete line, to indicate that the law had returned to its proper strength through the joint efforts of everyone. All were now confident about the continuity of their culture: 'It's like this straight line'.

In the 1970s, the Japanese collected a significant number of bark paintings in Arnhem Land, northern Australia, and established a private museum in Japan. Later they discovered that the story behind each work was missing, and to understand these stories more accurately, they sent people to learn local Aboriginal languages and to find the individual artists who had created the paintings. They asked each artist to tell the story behind their painting, in their own language. This was very important, because many artists have limited English, and the wonderful and important stories behind the paintings could easily be missed. These records not only help audiences to understand these artworks but importantly also prevent anyone from fabricating stories to satisfy public curiosity. Such made-up stories can seriously mislead the public and limit their understanding of Indigenous culture.

From the beginning, Aboriginal people have created their own spiritual world. They express the stories of what happened in the past and in the present through music, dance, painting and stories. Although contemporary

Aboriginal art has absorbed some aspects of other cultures, and has become more diverse, it still retains the unity of Indigenous culture. Through traditional and modern artistic concepts, an ancient world and a modern world become vividly connected. Indigenous art demonstrates to the world their unique contribution to the development of human culture. This is the meaning and value of Aboriginal art.

————≈————

When I was in the desert, Jimmy showed me his country. Now, I had the great opportunity of introducing Jimmy and Pat to ancient Chinese culture. While in Beijing, we made an excursion to the Great Wall, and in Shaanxi province, we saw the Terracotta Warriors in Xi'an. In my native Anhui province, we visited the famous ancient Huangshan Mountains and Jiuhua Mountain. Beijing was once the city where I wanted to live so much. Walking along the streets through bustling crowds and seeing so many huge neon billboards made us feel dizzy. New buildings had sprung up everywhere, the shops were crowded, and entertainment venues were lively. The city was full of life. But Jimmy had mixed feelings. He told me that he couldn't breathe with the pressure of the surrounding skyscrapers and the huge crowds. I can appreciate the sensitivities of desert people because I, too, have had similar experiences. In the desert, living in a vast open space, one's vision is stretched to the limit. Over time, the sense of space becomes all pervasive. Whenever I return to the city from the bush and find myself back among urbanised people who had been honed by modern civilisation, I feel panic and unease. Where this has happened to me, it has come after only months in the bush. For Jimmy, who has lived in this sort of environment for his whole life, it is not difficult to imagine the huge impact the city would have on him. In the city, many bush people say they feel lonely. It feels like entering a 'box' full of debris when they are living in a place like Melbourne. They have no mental connection to this kind of environment.

Therefore, every time I came back from the communities in the desert or the bush, I would stay in a nearby town for a few days, have a drink, and

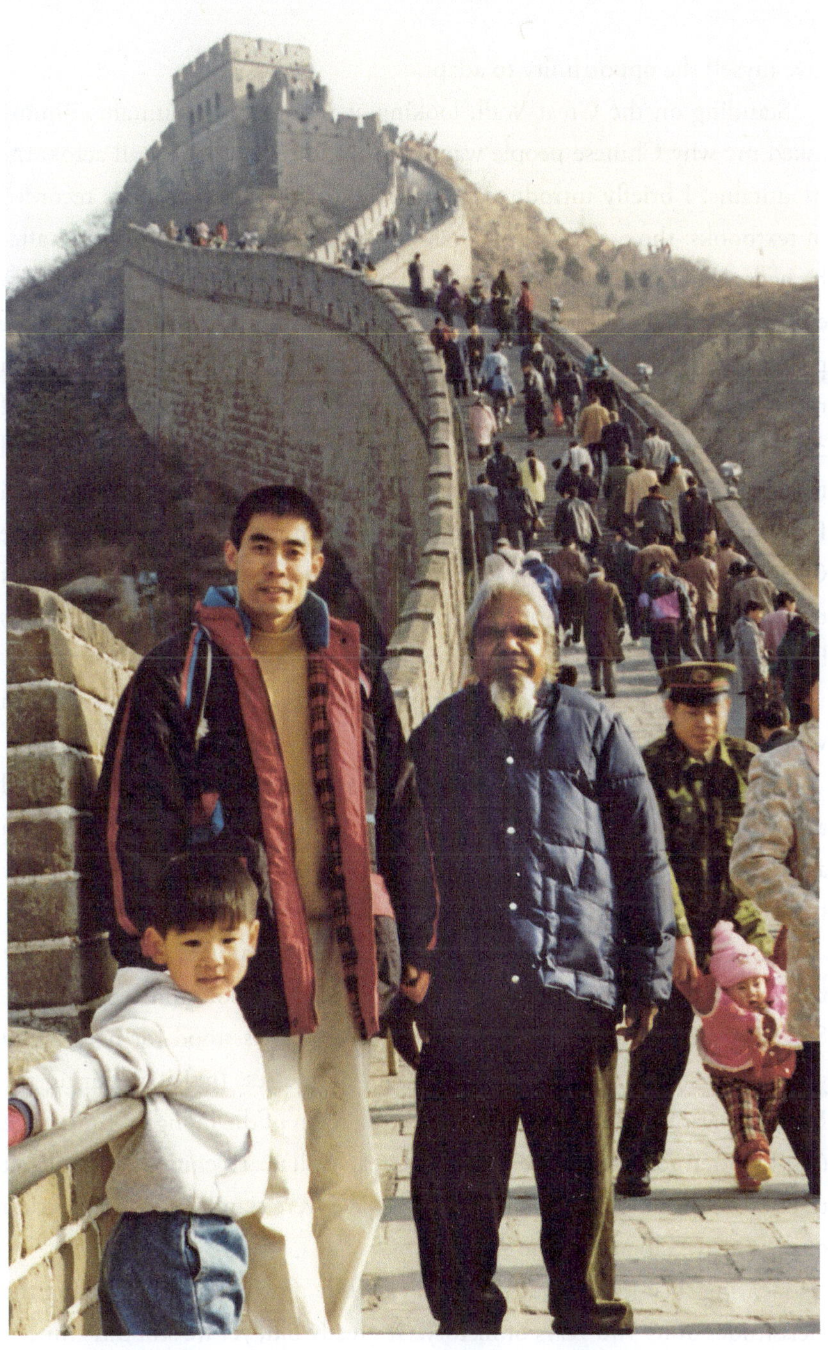

Jimmy Pike in China, 1996. That year, we held a joint exhibition in my hometown, Hefei. Jimmy was the first Aboriginal artist to exhibit in China.

give myself the opportunity to adapt.

Standing on the Great Wall, looking at the rugged mountains, Jimmy asked me why Chinese people wanted to build such a great wall across the mountains. I briefly introduced the history of the Great Wall as recorded in textbooks: the earliest Great Wall had been built by Qin Shihuang after he had vanquished six separate kingdoms in 221 BCE, to become the first emperor of a united China. The one thing that still disturbed him was the persistent invasion of his new country by nomadic tribes of the Xiongnu riding down from the north. He sent General Meng Tian with an army of 300,000 men to attack the invaders, and over time the Qin armies forced the Xiongnu to retreat all the way back to a place called Mobei in the Gebi Desert. They did not pursue the Xiongnu any further, because most of the Qin army were infantrymen who had difficulties fighting the horsemen of the Xiongnu in the desert of Mobei. However, to stop any further incursions by these nomads, the Great Wall was built.

After listening to my story, Jimmy murmured, 'We should have such a wall too'.

Hearing him say that, I was shocked but tried not to react. As I looked at him thoughtfully, I noticed that on the other side, Pat was giving him a fierce look. I had never seen her glare at Jimmy like that before. Jimmy turned around nonchalantly and walked away, to avoid Pat's gaze.

I told them that the Great Wall was an ancient military defence project that was an engineering feat with the longest construction time in the world. Since the time of the Western Zhou dynasty, it has stood for over 2,000 years and extends for more than 21,000 kilometres. In 1505, during the Ming Dynasty, in the eighteenth year of the reign of the Hongzhi Emperor a 650-kilometre section of the Badaling Great Wall near Beijing was rebuilt. It took more than eighty years to complete. We were standing on that section of the Great Wall at that moment.

Hearing this, Jimmy put his hand carefully on the wall, as if feeling the vicissitudes of its 500 years of history. 'It's really old, yet we still can climb it and touch it', he said. 'In my country, we have the same.' He always seemed to be thinking about Aboriginal culture and history, and his attachment and affection for his own land was evident. Everything in his country was always close to his heart.

At length Jimmy murmured, 'Great people, great country', to express his respect and awe for an ancient history and culture from a desert man with his own ancient culture and history.

The Terracotta Warriors in Xi'an are one of many cultural highlights in China. When Jimmy first saw thousands of these carefully crafted soldiers looking so realistic and full of life, it seemed to shock him.

Qin Shihuang was the First Emperor in Chinese history. When he was alive, he gave orders for people to dig a large pit about 5 metres deep that extended over an area of 13,260 square metres around his future tomb. He had underground buildings constructed in this pit, where they put pottery figurines of men and horses. These figures included more than 8,000 life-size soldiers holding bows, spears or broadswords, and there were also tens of thousands of wooden chariots, pottery horses and bronze weapons. After the First Emperor died, his mausoleum was hastily completed over the next two years by his son Qin Li. The mausoleum took a total of thirty-nine years to construct.

'These all built for the funeral of one person. He must be a big boss', Jimmy said. He couldn't believe it.

'Yes, he was once the biggest boss.'

During China's 2,000-year imperial history, the emperor was the symbol and supreme representative of autocratic rule. According to the records, from the time of the first Qin emperor in 221 BCE, to the forced abdication of the last emperor in February 1912, there were 422 emperors in China over a period of 2,132 years. The last emperor was called Puyi. In his memoir, *The First Half of My Life*, he wrote:

I have been emperor four times. The first time was when I was three years old and inherited the throne of my ancestors. The second was in 1917, when Zhang Xun was restored to power as interim president in Beijing and supported my restoration as emperor for ten days. The third was in 1932, when the Japanese helped me to the throne of their puppet state of Manchukuo in the northeast. This role ended with the end of the war in 1945. Fourth was when I became a citizen of the People's Republic of China and obtained the right to vote and to be elected.

During his lifetime over two thousand years ago, in his project to unify China, Emperor Qin Shihuang led troops to fight in many places across the country. From ancient times, the Chinese believed that there was a life after death. So, Emperor Qin wanted that, after his death, his army should remain with him. He believed that if his warriors were put underground with him, then his life in the underworld would continue as it had on earth.

The warriors in the pits are figurines that have different and very life-like faces and bodies. By this time, artisan capability of creating realistic sculptures had reached a very high level. The original terracotta warriors and horses were painted in bright and harmonious colours, but after being unearthed the paint rapidly oxidised and the colour disappeared, turning into a white ash. Archaeological studies indicate that the figurines had been manufactured from the time the Qin first unified the country in 221 BCE up until 209 BCE. So, they were made over a period of about twelve years, by tens of thousands of artisans.

Faced with these magnificent figures and the cumulative impact of the entire mausoleum, Jimmy declared several times, 'It's amazing!' He said that while it was a pity that his culture had no written language, Aboriginal stories, painting, music and ceremonies kept a record of the past. He never forgot to associate things he saw with things from his own culture.

After listening to this story, Jimmy said, 'Whether it is Chinese or Australian Aboriginal, this is a treasure belonging to the big family of mankind'.

———≈———

From the Terracotta Warriors, now known as one of the Eight Wonders of the World, I led Jimmy back to the wonders of nature by taking him to see

China's most wonderful mountain, Huangshan.

But first, I had to tell Jimmy about the origin of the name.

One year, Emperor Huang Di (2717–2599 BCE) sent his servant Fuqiu to find a suitable place for making an alchemical elixir of immortality. Fuqiu searched for three years, and finally returned to tell the emperor about a group of high mountains he had found to the south of the Yangtze River. Because these mountains consisted of black rock, they were called 'Yishan' and would be suitable sites for undertaking alchemical experimentation. So, the emperor led Fuqiu and some other servants to Yishan. After many years of arduous searching, they collected the herbs they needed for their alchemy, and finally made an elixir. After drinking this elixir, the emperor was reborn and became an immortal. From this time, Yishan was renamed Huangshan, after Emperor Huang Di.

Huangshan has undergone millions of years of geological change, and growing among its complex criss-crossing rock crevices can be found towering trees and an extremely rich diversity of plants.

Jimmy had bad knees, so he had to take the cable car up the mountain. As the car passed big trees hanging on to the rocks and emerged through a sea of cloud, Jimmy grasped my arm firmly. I could feel his hands shaking. He said that he was a hunter, and his feet did not leave solid ground very easily. He believed that he needed the earth to support his body and spirit.

I thought that the best way to calm his fear was to divert his attention. Standing in the slow-moving cable car, I pointed to a mountain in the distance and asked Jimmy what it looked like.

After looking at it for a few seconds, he said, 'Well, it's a bit like a monkey, isn't it?'

That was it. The Chinese think of this mountain as a monkey shading his eyes with his hand, while looking out at the sea of clouds.

'Haha!', Jimmy nodded and laughed, then started looking for other peculiar rocks on the mountain. Over 120 odd-shaped rocks in Huangshan have been given names.

Soon, our cable car was buried in fog. Among the four wonders of Huangshan – its peculiar pine trees, its rocks, its cloud seas and its hot springs

– my favourite is its cloud sea. Due to rapid changes in temperature and humidity on the mountain, a magnificent cloud sea often forms throughout the year, but especially in winter. As we entered the cloud, I closed my eyes, emptied my mind, and tried to relax, even although I could feel the strong clutch of Jimmy's hand. It seemed as if I were carrying him, like a spirit, and entering the clouds. A single word describes the experience: beautiful. It is a beauty that blends body and mind with nature.

When we alighted from the cable car, we were standing at the top of Huangshan, 1,650 metres above sea level. Jimmy was totally overcome by the majestic scenery. He didn't try using words to describe it, but took out a sketchbook to draw his impressions, just as I had in the Australian desert. Jimmy naturally aroused the curiosity of onlookers. This was probably the first time that Chinese had seen a foreigner paint their mountain landscape. Jimmy was embarrassed to see them looking at him. As I stood aside watching, I recalled my meeting on the mountain with Miss Helen. Everything had started here, and now, eight years later, I was back at this starting point.

Next, we went to Jiuhuashan. But first we decided to visit a small town in Qimen county to look at ancient houses. There we found a small restaurant with only two square tables. When the restaurant owner saw us, he was somewhat stunned. 'Big brother, what would you like to eat?', he asked, addressing me but looking curiously at Jimmy and Pat.

'Is there any meat?', I asked.

'Of course. No meat, no business.'

We ordered two vegetable dishes, two meat dishes and two bottles of beer. Jimmy likes to eat meat. A few days earlier, I forgot to order meat dishes and he became quiet and talked less and less. Following Pat's reminder, I got him stuck into a great plate of meat, and after that he looked like a different person. He also loved eating the baked sweet potatoes that were sold at street stalls in Beijing.

By the time the food and beer appeared, the small restaurant was full of people. They made loud comments about the three strangers. It was the first time in my life that I had experienced so many people watching us eat. It was as if we were monkeys in a zoo. I was worried that Jimmy and Pat would feel uncomfortable, but they didn't seem to mind, so I quietly let it go.

Someone in the crowd began to hum a local song. The local people were just managing to get by, but they looked happy. The restaurant owner said that when they saw that we were happy, they were happy too.

After the song was over, someone began singing another one, and then the owner joined in with his song. Jimmy listened happily, picked up his chopsticks and began clicking them on the table in time to the rhythm. The owner suggested that Jimmy should come and sing.

By this stage, we had eaten our four dishes and were drinking beer. Jimmy became elated and sang a song while tapping on the table with his chopsticks. Everyone applauded, and there was cheering and tapping on the other table. It turned into a special party, an unprecedented gathering of Chinese and Westerners in this small county town. After a round of applause, the owner made up a new song:

A foreigner came to town
He is eating and drinking and singing
Everyone is listening and watching happily.

Jimmy quickly stood up, putting his hands together in response to the enthusiasm of the onlookers. Afterwards, Jimmy often recalled the occasion, 'These are very, very good people'. He liked their enthusiasm and boldness, just as I liked the simplicity and magnanimity of the people in the desert.

When we came to Jiuhuashan, Jimmy became particularly excited, in fact elated. As he entered each pavilion in the temple compound, he would burn incense, so I teased him, 'If this goes on, you will become a Buddhist'.

Jimmy replied, 'Buddha is not part of our religion, but Buddha, like our Creator, should be respected. I am in China now, and I worship this big happy man, but what I think of in my heart is our own people.'

The stone steps leading down from the mountain were very steep. Because of his bad legs, Jimmy went down in a sedan chair carried by two men, a service usually provided only for elderly Chinese people. Jimmy said,

'The feeling of sitting on a sedan chair is no better than walking. When I see the sweat on the faces of the carriers and hear the tired squeaking of the sedan chair, it grieves my heart.' To relieve his guilt, Jimmy paid the carriers twice the normal rate.

Interestingly, all these seemingly small events cropped up later in his paintings. This is how an artist observes life and accepts and respects different cultures. When Jimmy painted the mountains, he made their outlines fall by continually switching the direction of his paper or canvas. These paintings could then be hung horizontally, vertically, or even upside down. The natural landscape of China emerged in a unique way from Jimmy's paintbrush.

When people come to China, it seems essential that they visit places like the Forbidden City. Jimmy expressed great amazement when we went to this place, but it never appeared in his paintings. He had a stronger interest in nature, in places like Huangshan and Jiuhuashan. Nature was always closer to his life.

After Jimmy's trip to China, he sent me some unfinished paintings saying that I would know how to complete them. They show not only our life under the big tree, but also impressions of our travelling together in China. This was how we collaborated.

Jimmy Pike died in 2002.

I made a special trip to attend his funeral. After the funeral, I went back to the 'home'. The tree was growing more luxuriantly than ever, but the surrounding weeds were growing wildly as well. Beer cans were strewn everywhere. The home needed a new host.

I leaned against the tree, as if I were back-to-back with Jimmy. I could feel his warm body. Everything that happened here slowly reappeared in front of me, scene by scene. What had impressed me most was his braided beard, so playful. Together, two desert men had walked around, hunting in outback Australia, and they had also climbed Huangshan and Jiuhuashan in China. No matter where we went, when we were tired, we just sat down to draw. Without speaking, we could understand each other's thoughts. His harmony with nature, his devotion to painting, and his respect for traditional customs enlightened and helped me to understand life and art.

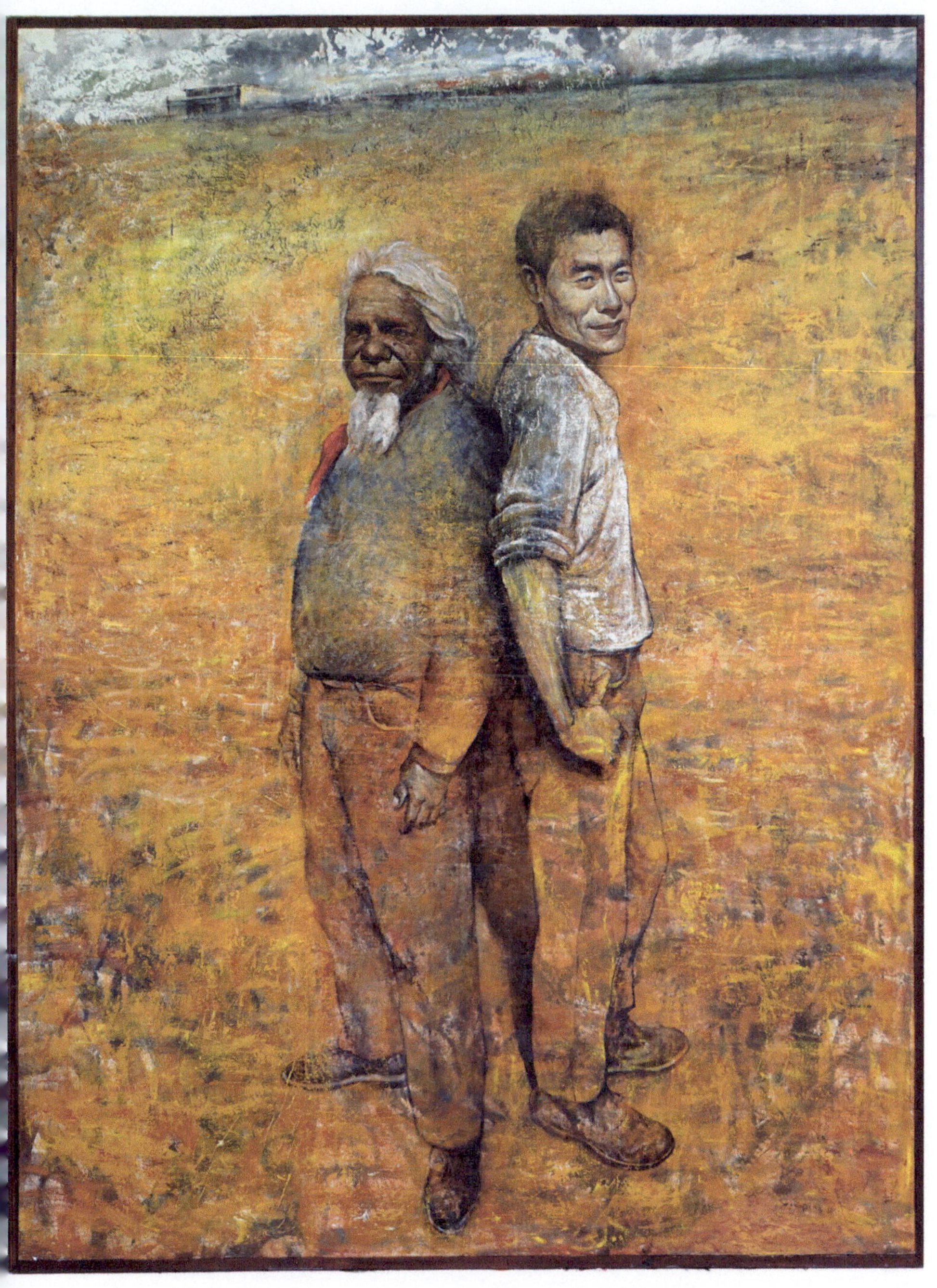

Back-to-Back Bushmen (1995), acrylic, 207 x 154 cm.

Life in the desert made me realise that Aboriginal survival skills determined their culture. There are many Australian Aboriginal stories and myths relating to water and animals. This is not accidental. It is the result of a long period of interaction between people and nature, sufficient time to establish the feeling of mutual affection between them.

In memory of this strong friendship between Jimmy and me, I painted a work called *Back-to-Back Bushmen*. It shows two men standing back-to-back in the desert: Jimmy Pike, a tough hunter with a confident expression, and me with an immature smile. It is close to life-size, and the two portraits occupy the whole canvas. At the top of the painting is a thin sky, below it a tree, later changed to a house hanging between the sky and the earth. That was our home.

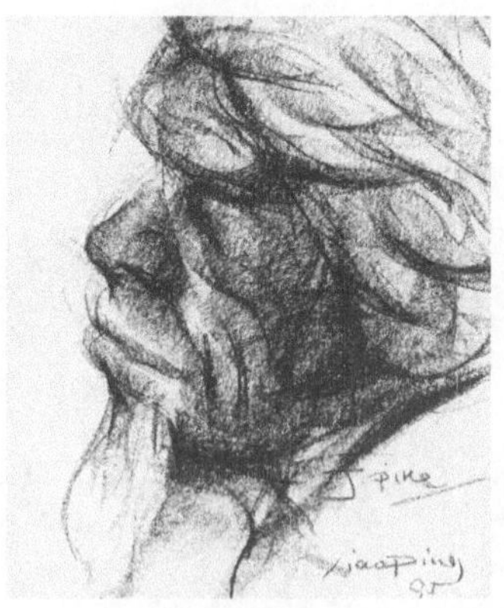

Jimmy Pike, Fitzroy Crossing, 1995.

Part Two

In Arnhem Land

I'm going to tell you now about what happened in Arnhem Land. Arnhem Land remains an unknown and mysterious place for many people, but I have developed a very deep connection with the place. My Gojok skin name among Aboriginal people came from there. What impact did this place have on me as an artist? My artistic creation has also matured amid various controversies.

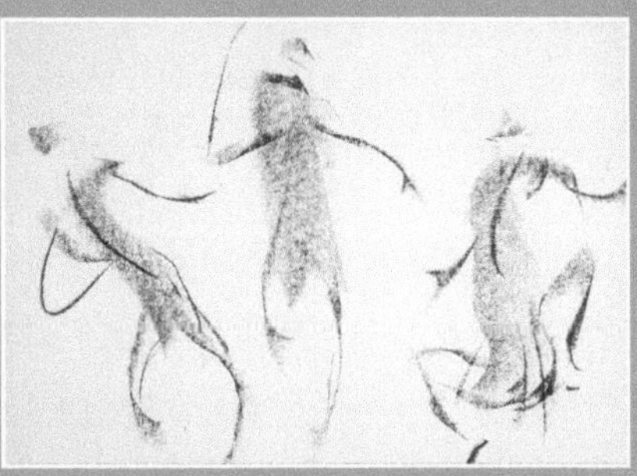

Drawing of dancers, from my dream.

9

Life in Arnhem Land

It was very early morning. Mist awakened me. I stretched out a hand from my sleeping bag to wipe my face that was as wet as if a bucket of water had been thrown over me.

The surrounding bush at dawn was very still, even the birds were not awake. The sound of dew falling from leaves was clear and sweet, like drops of water hitting the surface of a calm lake. Occasionally, somewhere in the bush, I heard the sigh of a kangaroo although the sound of snoring people was much louder. I wrapped myself tightly in my sleeping bag and just enjoyed the 'concert' surrounding me, the refreshing cool and humid air, and the peculiar breath of the trees. This wonderful moment almost made me forget the cold. After a while, I began thinking about getting up and making a fire to warm myself, but I decided that it was still too cold. So, I just drew my head deeper into the sleeping bag and let my thoughts wander.

The first time I heard the name 'Arnhem Land' was in a bar in Alice Springs, in 1988. Later I met Bob, a man from the Northern Territory Land Management Committee, who suggested that I should go there, because he could see that my interest in Aboriginal people was not just a tourist's passing curiosity. On his recommendation, I went directly from the desert in Western Australia to Arnhem Land in the Northern Territory, where traditional Aboriginal culture remains well preserved and relatively intact.

That first time, I took a bus from Alice Springs all the way north to Darwin. With the help of two of Bob's friends, I got a permit to visit the Maningrida Aboriginal community in Arnhem Land. At the time, I didn't know how lucky I was. A few years later, when Bob's friends talked to me about that trip, they remembered this young Chinese man with little social experience, who seemed almost child-like. But this man's fascination with Aboriginal people and his persistence had really moved them.

Arnhem Land is on the northern edge of Australia, extending over an area of approximately 92,000 square kilometres. The nearest city is Darwin. There are no well-established ports, although some cargo ships visit with heavy items. The main transport is by road or car. However, during the wet season, many roads are closed, and then people can only fly in or out.

On my first trip, I took Airnorth from Darwin, flying in a small nine-seater plane. I was so excited. Looking out the window, I saw a few mountains, but many stretches of water connected by small and medium-size rivers. Due to the rainy season, the ground was covered in water. Frightened by the sound of the aircraft, different animals – including buffaloes, kangaroos and wild pigs – ran for cover. Occasionally, I could see a column of white smoke rising, indicating the presence of people. I heard that many Aboriginal people have lived here all their lives and never been anywhere else. I couldn't imagine what kind of environment and what sort of people would be waiting for me there.

I flew directly from Darwin to Maningrida airport, a small place with only one runway, but a very important facility, especially in the wet season when the community relies on small planes for supplies. Bob's friends in Darwin had arranged for a schoolteacher to meet me at the airport. He looked at me and, although he might have been wondering where this Chinese person had come from, all he said was: 'Are you ready?'

'Ready', I replied, scarcely believing that I had finally arrived.

The teacher told me that we would be going straight to Yikarrakkal outstation. As he drove, he told me a little about himself and the family I would meet. The Northern Territory government had set up schools in remote communities where there was a high concentration of Aboriginal people. An 'outstation' was a place where one or two Aboriginal families lived together. There were many such family-based outstations around Maningrida and scattered all over Arnhem Land, where several hundred people lived in some of the bigger communities. If there are enough children in an outstation, the school in the community will send a teacher there.

The teacher was particularly interested in my background and why I had come. As with so many other people, I don't think my answers really satisfied his curiosity. But we nonetheless had a good chat.

Looking at the landscape, I compared it with the desert. I thought that although I rarely saw people in the desert, there was a vast view. Here in the bush, I couldn't see anyone either, but surrounded by trees, it was like walking in a maze. I was in a very different environment.

Yikarrakkal outstation was only about 60 kilometres from the community airport, but because the road was in very poor condition, we often had to detour through the trees. It took us a long time to get there.

Looking around, I glimpsed a small white spot looking quite conspicuous in the bush. The teacher said that we were almost there. I started to feel excited. Gradually, the spot became bigger and bigger until I recognised that it was the flat roof of a house. Then I heard dogs barking, letting people know that we were coming. The people who had made the smoke I had seen from the plane were finally going to appear in front of me.

I saw a dilapidated tin house and two wooden sheds standing on the open ground. There was also a large, open shed with several tables and long stools, and a small blackboard hanging on one wall. The two wooden sheds seemed abandoned. Although I knew that I was deep in the bush, I was having difficulty understanding this simplicity.

Mick Kubarkku lived here with his family. When I met him, the first thing I noticed was the scars on his chest, like those I had seen on Aboriginal people in the desert. Then I noticed his beautiful long curly hair. The teacher told me that Mick was a painter and a typical bushman, reluctant to leave his home. Once, he held an exhibition at Darwin Museum. After persistent coaxing from the organiser, Mick had attended the opening ceremony to let the audience meet the artist. The next day, he went shopping, and on the third day, he returned to the bush. He knows who he is, and he knows where he belongs.

My appearance at the outstation aroused great interest, especially among the children, who surrounded me whispering to one another. One bold child quietly approached, stretching out his hand to try and touch me. Later I learned that people called him 'Luo-Luo'.

'Bruce Lee, do you know him?', Luo-Luo asked suddenly.

I was taken aback that the name of this famous Hong Kong star of Kung Fu was known out here. Bruce Lee was just that famous!

'You look like him.'

'Oh, really?' At that time, I had long hair, and was tall and thin, 'Of course I know him. He's my cousin', I joked.

'Where is he?', another child asked.

'Is he still alive?'

'Hey, how do you talk?'

Someone hit the back of his head. The scolded boy looked aggrieved and quietly hid behind the other children. He didn't say anything more. I had not expected that Bruce Lee would be so important to these Aboriginal children.

Seeing everyone was so interested, I quickly added, 'Bruce Lee has already passed away'.

The children were saddened by this news and became silent. The serious looks on their faces were moving. The child who had been scolded, and was hiding behind Luo-Luo, raised his head to show his small face that was smarting with tears. To relieve the atmosphere, I quickly offered to teach them some Kung Fu movements. A few bright sparks immediately adopted a Kung Fu posture, making everyone, including the older men and women, laugh. 'Hey, hey!', I improvised a posture for them. Supposing this to be authentic Kung Fu, everyone laughed even harder. Luo-Luo copied me, sliding with one foot, and moving forward sideways, guarding his chest with his left hand, and punching out with his right, 'Hey!' The process starts slowly, then erupts with explosive force, 'Hey, hey!'

Luo-Luo was taking it all very seriously. 'Come on, more, more…', he said. The children were extremely excited to meet a real Chinese Kung Fu 'master'.

'Okay, one more', I said, demonstrating a few more fighting movements.

Amazingly, this was the best introduction that I could have made. It was much better than talking.

'Okay, let them clean up', Mick ordered, pointing to the campsite.

The children were keen to continue enjoying themselves, but it was getting dark and we needed to unload the car. The boy who had been scolded was particularly helpful. He brought things from the car, swept out a clean space for me with a handful of branches, then helped me to open my bag and organise my belongings. The other children collected branches to make a fire, and some went to the river to fetch water. It was dark by the time we had finished. The teacher took out a bag of bread and gave it to Luo-Luo and, with the children following behind, they disappeared into the night.

Looking at their backs receding into the night, I suddenly thought of Justin, Sandy and the curly-haired boy who had saved my life when I was lost in the desert. Although I never saw them again, their smiles, behaviour and figures have always remained in my mind, and they appear in many of my artworks.

A few years after my first visit, I returned to Yikarrakkal outstation. Not much had changed there, and the children still clamoured to learn Kung Fu. I had been employed as an Artist-in-Residence at the Aboriginal School in Maningrida. At that time, the population was around 800 people. It was hard to know how many precisely, as so many people lived away on outstations. In the community there was a store to supply daily necessities, a Chinese food takeaway which people liked, and a video store holding many popular Hollywood action and Chinese martial arts movies. This was why everyone knew about Kung Fu stars like Bruce Lee, Jackie Chan and Jet Li. Many of the children wanted to exchange a few actions or learn martial arts from me. They thought that all Chinese knew Kung Fu. The Maningrida community also had a school and a clinic. Back then the clinic had only one nurse to provide medical care, although every fortnight the flying doctor came in from Darwin.

As I lay in my sleeping bag, thinking about past visits, my thoughts were interrupted by a sudden burst of noise. I poked my head out of my sleeping bag and saw that it was already light. Three dogs were raising dust and biting at one another while fighting over a bone. A woman shouted at them and made her two babies start crying. I watched her pull out her breast and shove the nipple into the mouth of the baby with the fiercest cry. She straddled the child on to her hip and, helped by another elderly woman, she tried to take care of other children. Although they didn't have the busy role of city housewives preparing the family for school and work, there were inevitable noisy mornings in the bush. The women of this family took good care of their children. I often saw them setting off with a short digging stick in one hand, and a dilly bag hanging from their head or shoulders to gather some bush tucker for their kids.

I got out of my sleeping bag and rushed into the bush to have a long pee.

A girl fetched a billy of water from a pond, set half of it aside in another pot, then set the billy on the campfire. These people made tea in the same way as the Aboriginal people did in the desert. When the water was boiling, the girl threw in a handful of teabags, added half a bag of sugar, stirred it, and then poured in the cold water she had set aside. She handed me a cup of strong tea. After a few sips, I felt a lot more awake.

I asked Luo-Luo to come to help me roll up my swag. During the first few days after my arrival, I often noticed that my sleeping bag was wet and smelt unpleasant. Then one day when I came back from fishing, I found a dog lying on my unfolded swag. I yelled at it, knowing that this wasn't a good sign. And sure enough, I saw a puddle of yellow staining my sleeping bag. I was left very angry and screaming, but totally helpless. The children yelled too but also laughed and made fun of the fuss I was making.

'Leave some of its scent on you to show welcome', Mick said.

'They already have. A dog pissed on my lap the day I arrived.'

'Ha-ha, they like you.'

I thought: oh please, don't like me like that! Those scrawny dogs drove me crazy. They not only pissed on me, but put their snouts into my sleeping bag in search of food, or pissed on my paints and art materials, as if in revenge for not being fed. I could accept these small things, but not the big thing that happened next.

I woke up one morning, feeling very itchy all over my body. I thought that it was because I hadn't showered for a few days. I scratched but this only made things worse, especially on my legs. I sat up and saw two skinny dogs lying comfortably on my quilt, cuddled up together to keep warm. Trembling slightly, I stretched out my hand to drive them away, then lifted the quilt and gave my leg a little scratch. Then I felt something like little sparks fall on the back of my hand. I hurriedly looked down. What I saw made me so scared that I jumped up and ran to the river, stripping off my clothes as I ran, then throwing myself into the water. What had frightened me so much was the sight of hundreds of fleas hiding in the hairs on my legs. It was cold in the early morning, and I was shivering all over. I picked up a handful of silt from the bottom of the river and frantically wiped it all over my head and body, but it didn't stop the itching.

After these lessons, the first thing I did as soon as I got up in the morning was to roll up my bedding. Sometimes I would put it up in a tree to protect it from being damaged or taken away by dingos. My bed roll, which in Australia is called a 'swag', was so important. The early white settlers all had one. It was convenient to carry and allowed them to sleep wherever they liked. More than a hundred years have passed, and today, people like me couldn't live without it in the bush.

I took out a bag of shredded tobacco and began to slowly roll a cigarette. Beside me was a cup of newly made tea sitting on an inverted iron bucket, because I didn't intend to share it with those dogs. I got up, reached to light my cigarette with a piece of charcoal from the fire, then took a few puffs. It felt great, and, totally relaxed, I opened my sketchbook and concentrated on making notes and sketching or drawing some of my ideas. I was not left in peace for long. A boy soon ran over to ask me to teach him Kung Fu, but Mick stopped him, saying, 'Go away, don't disturb him'. This made me realise that putting down these notes and sketches was like homework, something I did every morning to review what had happened the previous day. It turned out that Mick's observation of me was as incisive as mine of him.

I looked down at my last diary entry: 'For the first time, I feel different… like at home'. Then I tried to think about the way in which I felt different. First, I was relaxed. After my previous experience I now knew how to live with Aboriginal people in the bush. They were all very friendly, so I felt at ease, and I was less obsessed with getting on with work or life than before. I was less fussed about things, and I did not feel upset about not having a bath every day, let alone complain about not being able to eat well. In fact, we did have access to a lot of seafood that was regarded as expensive back in the city, including fish, prawns, sea cucumbers, shellfish and turtles. If we wanted to, we could have them every day. The difference was that we had no condiments, and there was no fine kitchen here. So what?, I told myself. By grilling on the campfire, I could turn out food that was much more delicious than what was produced in any BBQ restaurant. But I needed to understand what I had lost and gained to truly accept my new circumstances. Most importantly, I realised that I now felt a sense of security, just like I had at home in China. In fact, from the moment I had walked on to this land, unknowingly I began to be influenced and changed by an array of things.

In the four years since my first trip in 1988, I had visited many Aboriginal communities, including Yuendumu, Balgo, Kununurra and Fitzroy Crossing in Western Australia, and Yirrkala, Elcho Island and Ramingining in Arnhem Land. Some places, like Maningrida, I revisited or stayed at for a longer time. These experiences allowed me to develop a deeper understanding of Aboriginal people and the natural environment, especially after I had settled down for a few months in one place. I lost the tourist mentality and developed a sense of belonging. Like a seed, this sense began to sprout quietly in my heart.

I stared at the fire blankly, immersed in my own world. I had a habit of falling into this kind of daze, especially after dark when there was nothing to do. Mick and the children would never bother me when they saw me like this, although sometimes Mick would say, 'Hey, city kid thinks too much, worries too much'. But I know that a lot of the time I wasn't thinking about anything, it was as though I had forgotten where I was. Here, I was away from it all, with no complicated interpersonal relationships to deal with. I could just take lessons from nature and life itself.

In the afternoon, Mick asked me and the children to help him collect bark. A few days earlier, he had agreed to show me the process of bark painting. There were not many stringybark trees suitable for use in bark painting near the outstation, so we decided to go looking a bit further away. Mick drove the car through the bush, carefully bypassing muddy quagmires, stretches of stagnant water, fallen trees and the peculiar 'high-rise buildings' made by ants. Although the steering wheel seemed toy-like, in these difficult conditions, Mick drove like a veteran. At one point I noticed a 'No Entry' sign nailed to a tree. On it something was written in very poorly formed letters. Curious, I asked Mick why it was there. Surely, only locals came here?

'Sh…' Mick whispered immediately, making a gesture for me to be quiet, 'They are here'.

I looked at him. The mysterious expression on his face made it clear that he was not joking. 'It's secret, ceremonies, here for spirits', Mick said quietly. I understood from him that because secret ceremonies were often held here, the place, over time, had become a gathering place for spirits. The sign warned anyone who might come here, to keep away.

I looked out of the window. It was as if countless pairs of big, wide-open eyes were watching us. My heart shrank, imagining transparent and elegant ghosts as seen in movies. Then I remembered an earlier experience. Once in Western Australia near the Aboriginal community of Kununurra, I came upon a big tree lying across the junction of two normally clear roads. Every time I wanted to approach and try to remove it, someone always warned me to stay away. After this had happened a few times, a kind young man, who saw how bewildered this made me, explained quietly that a secret ceremony was being held nearby. The tree was a sign to tell people to stay away. Putting his face near my ear, he murmured, 'Understand? Be careful when you see obstacles like this in the future. It may be a warning. If you run into an evil spirit, you will be in big trouble.'

Right now, I experienced this strange feeling once again.

We didn't dare stay but drove off quickly through the bush. At length, we came to a rocky mountain that was criss-crossed with many cracks. Hundred-year-old trees were growing tenaciously in the rocky gaps. Mick told me that there were many rock paintings here. I had seen some like them before, painted under protruding rocks like pictures hidden by a hat brim. When I looked up, most of them were faint and fuzzy, and some could barely be seen. Time had cast its shadow on them.

In one place, it was very hard to reach the cliff. 'How could they paint them in such impossible to reach places?', I asked Mick.

Mick explained, 'Mimi, the fairy Mimi who live among the rocks. They can fly over the walls.'

Judging from the images, Mimi are extremely thin and slender. It is said that the Mimi were the first to teach Aboriginal people how to catch and grill kangaroos and other animals. They selected the most intelligent people among the earliest Aborigines and taught them various skills, including how to paint stories on rocks and bark and how to sing and dance in ceremonies. These wise elders then taught the skills to the rest of their people. According to archaeologists, the rock paintings here could be traced back 60,000 years, or even earlier. The local Aborigines believe that the rock paintings found in places beyond their reach were painted by Mimi. Because the Mimi live in crevices in the rock and they usually rest during the day and travel at night, Aboriginals take care to respect their privacy and will not disturb them. They believe that the Mimi will not harm people or impinge on their lives unless they are seriously disturbed. While tales of the Mimi may seem hard to believe, to date there is no good alternative explanation for how these rock paintings were painted in such inaccessible places.

There were also some recent, newly painted works that were notable for their fresh colours, and their different images and content. My friend Wamud once made a rock painting. One year, shortly before Christmas he had taken his family on a short trip in Arnhem Land. When they passed the rock country, they decided to stay there for a few days. During that time, he had a dream, which led him to draw a big kangaroo on the rock. He said that he had done this with the help of a few Mimi spirits who had appeared to him in his dream. He said that he had done the painting exactly as the spirits had told him to do. In terms of form, it revealed a distinctive personal style, with some regularity and many details. Although these new paintings lack the concise form of the old ones and cannot have their ancient meaning, as the centuries pass, they too will come to be seen as great art. During the creation of Wamud's rock painting, he and his family danced and sang in front of it every night, and he told the children the stories that lay behind it. The details are very personal and secret, only revealed to him and his family.

Rock painting has continued uninterrupted in Aboriginal culture. The paintings record human behaviour, interactions with the natural world, and emotional symbols. Their form and purpose have gradually developed from the simple recording of daily life and stories of spirits into more consciously artistic creations. The themes have also gradually changed. This continuous and rich content is a very rare thing to find among the different cultural heritages of the world. For me, Arnhem Land is the biggest museum in the world – one that perfectly combines art, the humanities and nature.

The origin of art coincides with the origin of human life, and it exists both objectively and with strong subjectivity.

Mick stopped the car and, pointing out the window, explained that very few people had been here so we should be able to find what we wanted. With him as guide, we started to look for 'Stringybark' trees – a type of eucalyptus with a particular bark, a thick bark made up of delicate fibres. Aboriginal people often used it as a material for building the roof and walls of their huts. Artists used it for painting. We found many of these trees. At first Mick tried to cut off the bark, but after blunting several knives, he gave up. He knew that this kind of bark did not come off easily. Finally, he joined Luo-Luo to continue cutting. I watched Luo-Luo cut around the root of the tree expertly, and then make another cut right around the tree at a level just above his head. He then made a small crack between the upper and lower circles, peeled off a corner, inserted his knife, and pried a few times. In this way, a complete piece of bark peeled off easily. Seeing him working so calmly, I wanted to have a try. It took me a lot of effort to make the bottom cut and I was breathing hard before I finished. I was trying hard but lacked sufficient strength. Suddenly, I saw this thin child appear beside me. He grabbed my knife and called a bigger boy to come and crouch down near him. He jumped up on this boy's shoulder and, flourishing the knife, he began the top cut. Even so, the little guy was too small for this hard work and had to stop to catch his breath from time to time. The other children laughed and urged him to come down. Instead, he tried even harder, persisting until the last few cuts were finished, even as his little face turned black and purple. After jumping down, he sat on the ground with one leg bent, and his arms covering his knees, his little tummy rising and falling fast. He was panting. Mick said that in the past, this job had been even more difficult, because the bark had to be peeled off with a stone axe. In those days they would use human ladders or use branches as ladders. Once, Mick said, he and his companions had peeled off a very long piece of bark. From his gestures, I gathered that it was about 3 metres long. He had used it to complete a stunning painting.

We can imagine just how high the cost of bark painting is.

As we stood there, collecting bark, I saw a dog run over to Mick. He hummed, and the dog took off into the bush, but after about 10 metres, it stopped and looked back towards us. 'Sh…', said Mick, and we immediately fell silent. Mick casually took hold of a rifle held by one of the older children, bent down, and moved carefully towards the dog. Mick usually looked a little lazy, doing everything in a very unhurried fashion, but now he changed into an action man covering the distance rapidly. Several of the older children followed Mick closely, keeping a proper distance behind. The dog hid carefully in the grass as he went, looking back at Mick from time to time. I did not dare to follow. With the smaller children, we made too much noise.

'Ping.' The crisp sound of gunfire echoed through the bush. The first to rush back was the dog. He had quickly rushed to bite his prey before leaving it to his owner. After a while, Luo-Luo appeared dragging a kangaroo behind him, while holding another small kangaroo in his arms. He threw the kangaroo carcass on to a freshly made campfire. Tongues of fire quickly removed the fur from the body. The little boy looked thin, but he was a very capable little helper. Seeing him hurry over and take charge of things, it was not difficult to understand why Luo-Luo was one of Mick's favourites.

My eyes rested on the cute baby kangaroo. It wasn't clear what they intended to do with it. Mick guessed what I was thinking. 'The animals here have always been our food', he explained. To survive in the bush, you had first to feed your stomach. The little kangaroo would survive or not, according to the laws of nature. When the Ancestor created this world, he had taken into consideration the needs of humans.

After a while, Luo-Luo dragged the kangaroo carcass out of the fire. With the help of another child, he didn't hesitate in plunging a knife into its bulging belly and making a deep downward cut. The internal organs fell out and a spurt of blood suddenly splattered all over his face and body. He soundly cursed, making the other children burst out laughing. Someone pulled the intestines backwards and forwards, then grabbed a piece of the viscera and cut it off. They pushed a branch through it, passed it through the fire a few times, dipped it in kangaroo blood, then handed it over to Mick. Sitting beside him, I could see that it was a piece of liver. Mick took a bite then handed the stick to me. I hesitated, gathered up courage, then took a bite. The remainder was stuffed into the mouths of the littlest children. When I looked back at Luo-Luo, he was roasting the kangaroo heart on the coals. After some time, he reached out to grab it, but it was too hot, and he instantly withdrew his hand and cursed. More laughter from the children. Luo-Luo blew on a small piece of the heart that he had staked with a branch, and carefully took a bite. Then, as before, he passed the stick to the other children. One child took a bite and tried to grab the rest of it, but before he could get it in his mouth, I heard someone say, 'Don't eat it all, share it'.

Looking at the cooked kangaroo, I thought: why not make a Chinese dish with kangaroo meat? I couldn't remember how many days it was since I had enjoyed the smell of rice. I really wanted to have a Chinese meal.

Mick told Luo-Luo to throw the piece of bark he had cut on to the fire. The new bark was still wet and had rolled itself up like a tube. After some time on the fire, much of the water was removed, and the outer skin had burned off, leaving a solid piece of inner fibrous tissue. The bark slowly opened out again. This instant was the first step in the creation of a bark painting.

———≋———

That night I told everyone to relax, because I would cook something for us all. First, I got two children to help me to build a 'stove' from a piece of wire mesh stretched between two big rocks. It took a bit of practice to get the fire to burn just right. A stack of dry twigs will burn quickly and fiercely and make a fire good for boiling water, whereas a branch as thick as an arm will burn much more slowly with a relatively stable heat. Stir-frying requires very high heat. A tree trunk as thick as your waist is good for putting on the fire at night, as it can keep going for a few days and be used to prepare a pot of rice. The residual heat from burned charcoal also has its uses.

Some of the bark we had cut during the day provided a cutting board. Luo-Luo found two abandoned tins. The shallower one served as a frying pan, while the larger one was good for cooking rice.

It had become dark. Everyone silently gathered around the fire and watched me take a few unusual green leafy vegetables from my bag.

The first thing to go on the chopping board was the kangaroo meat. 'Cha-cha!' I sharpened the knife by drawing it back and forth on a stone a few times, and then cut up the meat. Removing kangaroo skin was much easier for me than peeling bark. My quick actions surprised the children. When I was trying to peel bark, they had laughed and thought that I was bad at using a knife.

The pot on the fire had become hot. I poured in some vegetable oil. There was a sudden swishing sound, a flash of black, and everyone looked around to see what had happened. I reached for the kangaroo meat but felt nothing. 'Hey, where's the meat?' I couldn't believe the meat was gone. At the outstation there was never any theft. A few children helped me look. Then the crowd yelled, 'Taken by the dogs!' It seemed there were no rules in a kitchen without a table. Dogs would casually come to share the meat. Everyone laughed. The sound of their laughter hovering around us in the dark, gave me a feeling of warmth and family.

I quickly cut another piece of kangaroo meat into small pieces and threw them into the pot, then brought out a small bottle of soy sauce.

'How did you think of bringing these things?', Mick asked.

He was surprised too, as I was myself. When I went shopping for food before coming here, I had casually thrown a few Chinese seasonings into my shopping basket. Unexpectedly, I was given the opportunity to use them.

In addition to giving people an interesting taste, Chinese cooking is also quite a performance. I had few ingredients and couldn't cook lots of dishes, but I could beat pots and bowls with knives and a spoon. The food was kept moving as I shook the pot with my hand as a Chinese chef would do. While I cooked, I muttered something in Chinese that no one understood. They all sat on the ground intently watching the 'chef' perform his magic. It was too dark for me to play with the knife in my hand, otherwise they would have seen me as Bruce Lee: tall and skinny, and with long hair. I picked up a branch and made up a pair of extra-long chopsticks, using them to toss the food around in the pot. Soon I had a large pot of diced kangaroo meat fried up with sliced potato and carrot. I picked up a piece of meat with the long chopsticks and tasted it, then sprinkled on a pinch of salt. I knew everyone would like it when it smelt so delicious. I was just as proud as Mick had been when he made that shot.

Someone sitting in the dark praised the fragrant smell of my cooking, and someone else agreed. Then I heard Mick say to his woman, 'Why don't you learn?' They all began talking and laughing. Chinese people have been making fried dishes like this for hundreds of years, but just as I learned when I tried to make a good boomerang, it is not that simple.

I asked all the children to queue up, saying, 'Don't worry, enough for everyone'. The children couldn't wait to squeeze up in front of me. I used an empty can to spoon rice on to each plate, then added a half-spoon of vegetables. When Luo-Luo's plate appeared in front of me, I did just the same but holding out his plate he looked up at me, and said, 'More, please'. He was the smartest of these children. I liked him, so I gave him a bit more rice and some more vegetables. As soon as I'd done this, everyone lined up behind him began asking for two spoonfuls. I had wanted to have a good Chinese meal, but in the end all the meat was gone, and I had nothing but a few vegetables that were left over in the pot.

Everyone thought it was a wonderful meal. Mick and his woman praised the food a lot. Seeing them eating happily, I felt very happy and

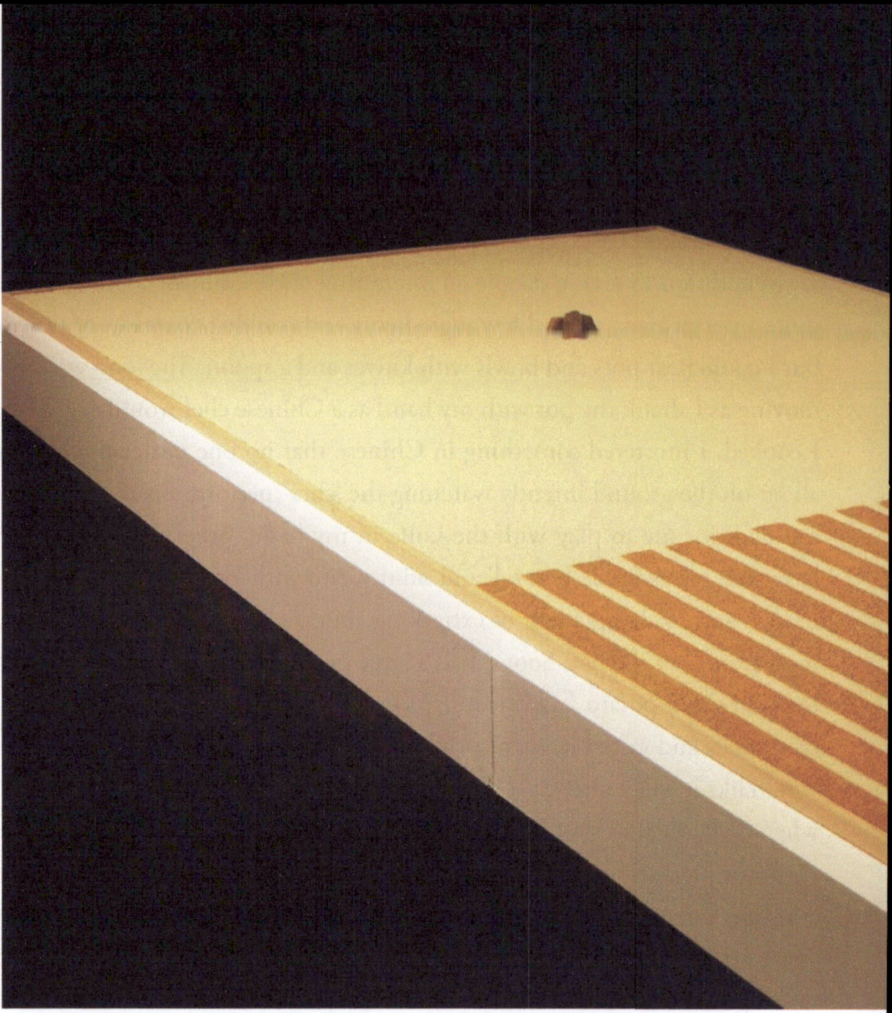

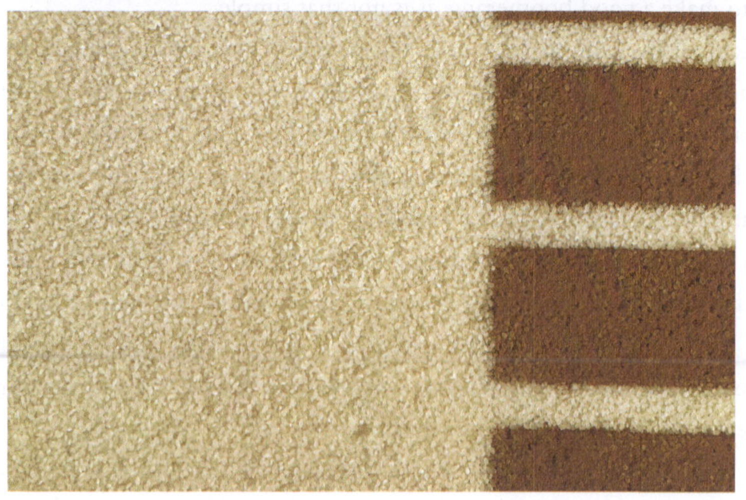

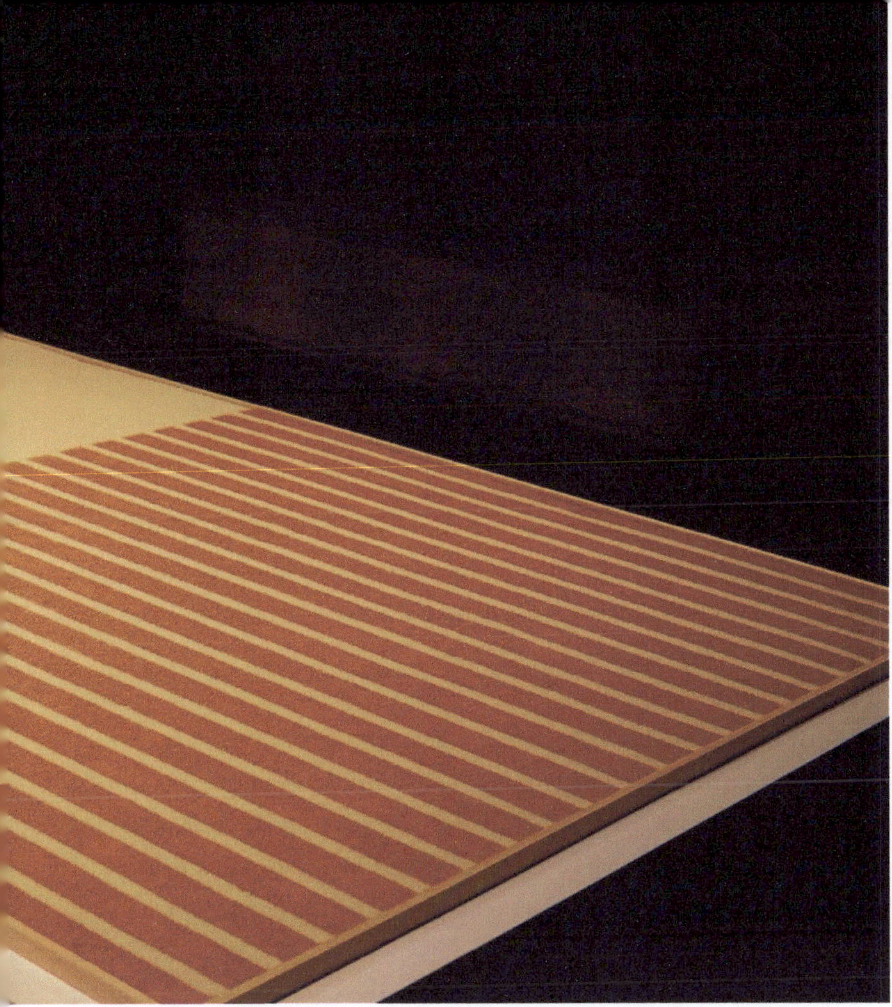

Above: Zhou Xiaoping, *Life, Land*
(2024), installation, materials: rice, ochre
and stones, 400 x 800 cm.

Left: detail

In this installation artwork, I use rice
as a medium to portray the significance
of land, nature, life and love for family.
Rice is a favourite Chinese staple and it
has also become a popular food source
for Aboriginal peoples, so it conveys a
cross-cultural message about the shared
meanings found in everyday life. Ochre
in the artwork symbolises land, and
the relationship found in both ancient
cultures between life and the earth.

proud. But then I felt someone pulling on the corner of my coat. Looking down, I saw two shiny eyes in a small black face. He held out his empty plate and stared at me.

'Want more?', I asked.

He nodded. Among the children, he was always timid and introverted, never saying much. The other children always made fun of him.

I told him there would still be some rice in the pot.

'All gone', someone announced in the dark.

Looking back at the child, I pushed all the rice from my plate on to his. He still looked at me without a word, then turned around, and walked away. Watching his back disappear in the dark, I wished that I could cook a fine meal for these children every day.

In the first few days of our trip, everyone had shared the convenience foods that I had brought in: tinned food, instant noodles, rice and potatoes. Later, I shared their food: kangaroo, wild pig, fish and damper. Occasionally we caught a sea turtle. The eggs in its belly were as big as chicken eggs. I made 'tea eggs' for everyone by boiling the turtle eggs in water, to which I had added tea bags and salt. If we caught a buffalo, then we had enough food for several days.

Although life in the bush is hard and tough, there are also bitter pleasures, taken with no sense of entitlement. In the bush, no one complains about how terrible life is. In contrast, city people have too many desires, which bring trouble and make them complain.

After a few days, the piece of bark had flattened out after heating, drying and pressing. We cut off the rough edges and trimmed the bark slightly, so that we could paint on it. Mick brought out some red and yellow ochre, some black charcoal, and a white powder (gypsum) – the four traditional pigments used for painting.

I was already sitting there enthusiastically watching every movement that Mick made. He poured a little bit of water on a flat stone about the size of a hand, then ground a piece of rock rich in red ochre on it for a while. Last, he added a little bit of PVA glue, explaining that in the past they had used gum rather than this glue to stop the colour falling off. Next, he picked up a very stubbly old paintbrush used for oil painting, dipped it in his freshly ground red ochre and start to apply a base coat on the bark. He painted very awkwardly, like a child just learning. The stubbly brush held very little colour, so Mick had to dip it again with nearly every stroke. He started complaining that the brush was bad, became increasingly angry and then at last threw it away. He now picked up a piece of bark off the ground, tore off a strip and smashed the end of it with a rock, and then put the strip in his mouth and chewed it until he produced a new brush. Trying it out, he was finally happy, 'Oh, much better'.

Mick now ground down a stick of charcoal to form a pool of black colour. This reminded me of the inkstones and ink blocks used for Chinese painting. With his black colour, Mick drew the outline of a crocodile. Then, mixing powdered white clay with water, he added white lines to his picture. He painted very carefully and seriously, stopping to look and think after he added anything. When he took out the yellow ochre, I said, 'Let me grind it'. Copying his earlier actions, I ground the ochre much in the way I grind my ink stick that I have been using for years. It made me feel good to observe this similarity.

After this, it seemed that Mick had nothing else to do. He picked up a big cup he had beside him, drank a few mouthfuls of tea, then slowly got up to go to the toilet. When he returned, he was holding a bunch of bright grass stalks bearing flowers with yellow petals. He rubbed these colourful green stalks and yellow flowers back and forth through his big black hands. What was he doing? Was he making a wreath to place on his woman's head? I couldn't see Mick being so romantic. But then I noticed that all that remained in his hand was one strong stalk with a soft tuft at the top. He had made a long slender brush. Grass stalks, tufts of hair and pieces of bark are all used by Aboriginal artists to make their brushes.

While artists in Arnhem Land continue to use traditional methods, Aboriginal artists in other places have begun to use all sorts of brushes, painting tools and materials. They use paper and canvas and many types of paint: acrylics and even industrial paints have replaced their traditional colours. They are no longer restricted to the four traditional colours of white, red, yellow and black, and it is now rare to see this older, traditional form of bark painting.

Mick dipped his grass brush into the white powder, then patiently drew tight parallel lines across the crocodile figure, which he then crossed with another set of lines to form an ordered pattern, a traditional in-fill called 'racks'. To fill a big area with these dense criss-cross lines takes much patience and perseverance.

Watching Mick carefully constructing his racks made me think that he must be getting tired. I asked if he would let me try. Smiling, he threw me his brush. I thought he must have confidence in me. Is it because I am also a painter? I was used to Chinese brushes, but this grass stalk brush felt different: it was so light and slender. My first lines came out in varied thicknesses. It was hard to get the speed of the brushwork right. I had to re-dip the colour to make each short line. But after a while, I got used to it and my lines became smoother.

In fact, the technique of bark painting is not difficult to master. The greater difficulty is what to paint: an issue for any artist. I really had to grapple with this difficulty when trying to paint with Aboriginal artists. Even today, not many people in Australia fully understand Aboriginal painting. Often the viewer sees only a series of symbols which may be accompanied by a brief sentence or two of explanation. These are usually very general, saying for example that the painting is about a 'waterhole'. Yet a 'waterhole' is closely related to the life of the land and is a place of critical importance for people living in the desert. Around each waterhole, stories have developed, and these stories are an important part of the painting. Only by knowing these stories and understanding them can you approach the true meaning of the special symbolic language of the painting.

Mick was a typical bush artist. His paintings all related to his land and the stories that had been handed down to him. Many of these stories took place in the Dreamtime, the time of creation, at a place both far away on the horizon and just in front of him. Mick believed in everything that happened in each story.

'This is a story about the moon and the stars', Mick said as he straightened up. Raising one finger and pointing into the distance, he told the story in native language. I didn't understand, but his body language told me that this story came from this place and belonged only to him.

He asked if I had seen a hill, 'rocks… mountain'.

There was a small hill near our camp. In the middle of the piled-up rocks, there was a hole shaped a little like the moon. 'Do you mean the mountain we pass every time we go out?', I asked.

'Yes. Do you think the shape of the hole in the mountain is a little like the moon?' Then he told me, 'It was made by the Rainbow Snake digging into the stones'.

Mick explained: a long time ago, the moon used to be a man. One day, the Moon-man met his friend, and the two of them had a dispute about what happened after death. The Moon-man's friend believed that death was the end. But the Moon-man said that after he died, he was sure he would be resurrected. To prove this, he flew into the sky where he became the moon. So, every month, the moon would die, and a few days later, it would be resurrected, and reappear in the sky. This proved that what the ancient Moon-man had said was true. Today, the place where the moon rises again is revered as sacred by Aboriginal people. It is located near Kakadu National Park Nature Reserve in the Northern Territory.

'What does this hill have to do with the sacred place?', I asked.

Looking mysterious, Mick answered, 'Of course, it is a continuation of the sacred place'.

'Are we living in a mysterious place?', I asked in surprise. Looking around, it did not seem that different from any other place. Yet the rocky hill did look very strange, although I couldn't explain why I thought this. Every time we went hunting, we always passed near it.

Mick said, 'Once in a dream, I saw my father who had died not long before. He took me to a place where there was nothing around, not even a tree, just a pile of rocks. My father asked me to sit in front of him, and then he quietly told me a secret about something that had happened in my family. Only I could hear what he said. Finally, he sighed and, raising his voice, said, "My boy, from now on, these stones are no longer ordinary stones piled together, but they are your father's sustenance. You need to take good care of them because they will become my 'dream'". After telling me this, my father disappeared. When I woke up the next day, I found the place just as I had seen it in my dream. The rocks lie one on top of another like a sculpture. After I had that dream, I would often visit this place to live there for a few days. Then later, I moved to the place where we are now. I have had endless whispers from it. Today I drew these stories on the bark so that I could pass them on to my children. Long, long ago, it was only possible to pass on these stories orally.'

I didn't ask Mick about what his father had told him. If he didn't say, then I knew I shouldn't ask about it. He turned this secret story into series of artworks on the theme of 'Moon and Stars'. He told me that this was his dream story, and that no one could paint it as he does. If they did, there would be trouble.

'What kind of trouble?', I asked.

'Big trouble', he replied gazing back at me with a fierce expression. 'They will be punished and finished', he said, making a swift and ferocious cutting gesture. The usually gentle Mick had become very serious. For him, this was the bottom line, and he would always defend it.

Aboriginal artists like Mick hide their secrets in their paintings on rock or tree bark or on paper by using abstract symbols. They draw on their precious and very rich cultural heritage. One day, a deeper knowledge of these symbols may be made public but only if the traditional owners allow it.

'Do you paint other subjects?'

Returning to his usual gentle expression, Mick replied, 'Yes, kangaroos, birds, fish and crocodiles'. Raising a finger, he added, 'I now paint more about my own stories, like about crocodile'.

Mick told me about how he had come to sell his first paintings in the 1970s. Before that, his paintings had often just been given away in exchange for food or tea bags. The market for Aboriginal art then began to flourish in the 1960s and 1970s. Church organisations also began to purchase paintings, sculptures, and ceremonial objects. When Aboriginal people discovered that their traditional art could bring huge economic benefits, their interest soared. In the 1990s, a good bark painting would sell for only a few hundred Australian dollars. Today the price has multiplied, but there are no rich Aboriginal artists, and that says a lot about how the market is being manipulated.

Hundreds of years ago, when there was no contact at all between Chinese and Australian Aboriginal artists, there were some similarities in their work. In both societies, the artists used a few very simple colours to express deep meaning, although the motivation behind their work was different. In the past, most Chinese painters were highly cultured people who not only painted, but also liked to write poems and essays. They were haughty and high-minded and, seeking to achieve elegance in their paintings, they used a colour palette confined to cyan and brown, the white of their paper, and the black from their ink. These artists would express their emotions by drawing landscapes, flowers, birds, animals and plants from nature. Traditional Aboriginal artists were also restricted to the use of four colours – red, yellow, black and white – because these were the only colours available. Nonetheless, they, too, created equally beautiful paintings with their abstract patterns, like Mick's *Crocodile* or *Moon and Stars* that were based on Dreamtime stories. While paintings made with bark and natural pigments are the original and most natural method, it seems that increasingly many other materials are being used because the cost and labour of bark painting is simply too high. Nonetheless, the original, natural and simple artistic characteristics of bark painting, just like rice paper and ink, demonstrate a rich and profound artistic conception in the ethereal. In both cases, materials have been used as a form of language to demonstrate their distinct cultural characteristics.

In the early 1990s, there was a community called Oenpelli in the eastern part of Arnhem Land. About 900 people lived there, and many white people helped to manage it. A police officer stationed there did something controversial by giving high-quality paper to his Aboriginal artist friends. This caused an uproar, because there were many who opposed the move to painting on paper, and this included people from the Community Arts Centre and many art galleries. They thought that bark was an essential part of Aboriginal painting and warned that if Dreamtime stories were not expressed on bark, they would lose their mystery and aura. From cutting the bark, to preparing it and painting, the whole process was an important part of Aboriginal culture. Therefore, it was seen as necessary to advocate that Aboriginal artists jointly resist the practice of replacing tree bark with paper. The initiative received such a response for a short period of time, but gradually some Aboriginal painters started to paint secretly on paper. These works were easier to display and preserve, and they cost much less, and paper was much easier to obtain than bark. Using paper also protected trees, the trees in the bush. After more than ten years debating the issue, Aboriginal artists finally accepted that it was all right to use paper. The famous artist Bardayal Nadjamerrek was one of the first to paint on paper. Aboriginal artists are not conservative; they are happy to accept all kinds of new things. Today, paintings on paper or canvas are quite common in Arnhem Land. Only a few communities are continuing to produce bark paintings, and it is important to maintain and preserve this unique artistic heritage.

After experiencing similar incidents, I found that many people, including those in power, seem to be lagging on issues, but such things can be accepted or discussed.

However, changes in art practice do not always come from artists. The market can also play a key role in promoting change.

'Have a cigarette. Take a rest', Mick said. My legs were so numb I could barely feel them. Stretching, I slowly straightened at the waist, spread my legs, and fell back on the ground with my arms outstretched, 'Oh, my back!', I grumbled. But my nice stretch was cut short. 'Hey, get out!', a voice yelled.

Sitting up, I quickly looked in the direction of the scream. Pigs, both large and small, were ripping into my bag, instant noodles, rice, tinned foods, paper, and bottles of ink were tumbling out in confusion. A terrible scene.

'Oh, ink!', I yelled, 'Ink, my ink!' I angrily ran towards the foraging animals.

'Get the gun, hurry up!', Mick ordered.

'Oh, sha…', said a woman's voice as a stone flew past me.

'Hey, don't hurt our artist!', shouted someone to the stone thrower. With a gun in his hand, Mick soon arrived running, tagged by a group of children. Still thinking about my painting materials, I was also anxious about Mick shooting from behind me.

The two wild pigs took no notice of our roars, because they were too busy eating my instant noodles. Watching one big defiant beast, I became furious and kicked it hard. It just snorted, glanced up at me and continued chewing up my noodles. Completely exasperated, I picked up a rock and threw it at the pig, and screaming in pain, it ran off. A little wild pig that had been standing to one side, watching timidly, followed the big pig as it ran off. Mick and the children were still all screaming and chasing the pigs. Then a gunshot rang out, and calm descended.

My rice paper was floating everywhere and there was ink scattered all over the place. The big pig had stepped in the ink, then walked on the drawing board and paper, leaving me with a 'wild boar painting'.

Mick and the children looked at me sympathetically and helped me to clean up the mess. Apart from the noodles, paper and ink, almost everything else in the bag had been rummaged through and there were teeth marks everywhere. I picked up a tin. Although it had not been opened, it was quite deformed. The sight of it made at least one person laugh. I remained very unhappy but noticed that some of the mobs had gathered, and heads lowered, were whispering. Someone called out, 'Ink, my ink', in anger and panic, just as I had. Then all the children began to act out my reactions in an exaggerated fashion until everyone was laughing, 'Ink, my ink!'

In a single moment, my peaceful life had been overturned by two wild pigs. In Chinese characters, I wrote on the wall of Mick's cabin: 'The pig licks ink, it's now black inside and outside'. To this day, these characters remain on that shed in Arnhem Land just like a rock painting. Incredibly, news of this little episode spread quickly by walkie-talkie through the bush. This old-fashioned mode of communication was used by many of the outstations. Like Mick's family, many would use the walkie-talkie to exchange news at 8.30 every morning. It was their only link with the outside world. Today, of course, the walkie-talkie has been replaced by mobile phones. The children vividly described what happened to me on the radio walkie-talkie and laughed about the incident for many days. I was the local laughing stock.

A few days later, when I returned to the community school, everyone called out, 'Mr Ink is back!'

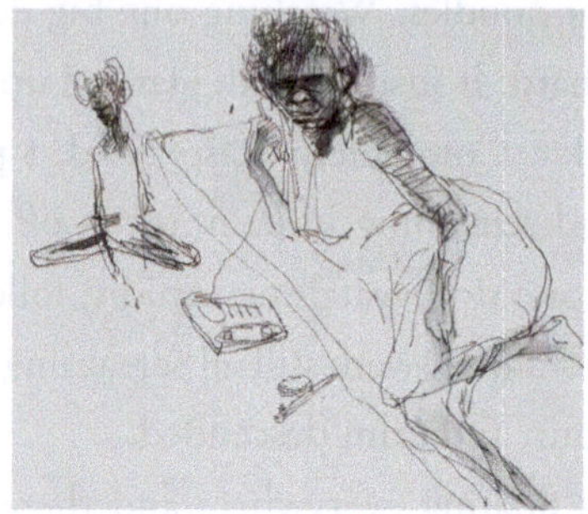

Fishing and resting, in Arnhem Land.

10

The Origin of My Aboriginal Skin Name

On the day that I came back to Maningrida from Yikarrakkal outstation, I heard from far away a deep and wonderful sound. It came from a strange instrument, more than a metre long, as thick as your arm, and made from a hollow tree stick. Aboriginal people call it *yidaki*, while the English name is 'didgeridoo'. It is played by blowing down the tube while keeping the lips loose, creating a vibration that emerges from the tube as a low drone. The *yidaki* is indispensable for Aboriginal dances and ceremonies. It should only be played by men, for its shape is symbolic of male genitalia.

When I drove into Maningrida, I saw a lot of people gathered in the square. I parked the car and walked into the lively crowd, watching a young man playing the *yidaki*. His cheeks were puffed out, and his stomach rose and fell with his breathing. Two elderly men led the crowd singing and rhythmically clapping wooden sticks, and several Aboriginal girls were dancing. Their hands waved around, as they slapped their front, their back, and their upper and lower limbs. The effect was grotesque and funny. I knew this dance, it was the 'Mosquito Dance' about driving away mosquitoes.

Next came the 'Kangaroo Dance': four or five young men stepped out to dance like a kangaroo jumping and running. They looked to the left and to the right, and then took up the alert posture characteristic of kangaroos. Afterwards two young men stepped forward, to play the role of hunters. Listening to the wonderful music and watching this dance, people immediately were drawn into the scene of a kangaroo hunt.

'What day is it today? It's so lively', I asked.

'Graduation ceremony, don't you know?', someone replied.

Oh… I instantly remembered hearing schoolteachers talking about this. I looked around the crowd, and sure enough spotted three Aboriginal graduates, smiling broadly, and wearing dazzling robes. As they were photographed, they held up their exquisitely framed graduation certificates. This was an important and proud moment for the whole community. All three were local Aboriginal people. As small children, they would only have received traditional cultural education. I could imagine just how many difficulties they had overcome to adapt to another culture and way of thinking before they could obtain that special certificate. After receiving it, even more effort would be needed as the whole community would turn to them, looking forward to what they could do for everyone.

Suddenly one of the onlookers in the crowd shouted out, 'Mr Ink, come on'.

'Oh, no, no.' I shook my head and waved my hands repeatedly. Impossible, I can't dance.

'Yeah, come on, Mr Ink', the coaxing continued.

The young man with the *yidaki* came to play right in front of me. The rhythm was so strong, and everyone was so encouraging that I felt a strong impulse to dance, although usually I never do. But now I found that I wanted to try. I started arching my body and bending my legs, stretching my arms to both sides. 'Wow!' When everyone saw this preliminary movement, they immediately applauded.

All right, I would dance! As I rushed out, someone stuffed a handful of branches into my hand. I held them in front of me to suggest that I was hiding behind a tree. From time to time, I peeked my head out, while constantly making steps and moving forward quietly. My dance mimicked the actions of a hunter. Suddenly the rhythm accelerated, and I found my feet following the music, and throwing up a cloud of dust. Soon the music was flying as the dancers all yelled out, 'Yi-yo!' The man who had first played the part of the hunter threw his spear. The others stamped hard on the ground crying, 'Wow!' Another burst of laughter came from the onlookers. The whole dance was very short, only a few minutes, typical of traditional

Aboriginal dance.

'Maynmak!' (Great!), everybody shouted.

'Gojok, Maynmak!', a woman added.

'Gojok, me?' I was surprised.

Then both women and men confirmed what had been said, 'Yes, Gojok'.

An old man waved his hands in the air and announced loudly, 'From now on, Mr Ink is our people. His skin name is Gojok.'

'Yo!', a sound of approval came from all around. Young people came over to shake my hands and hug me. Some called me 'brother', to others I was 'father' or 'son'. From that moment, we became a family.

I now had my Aboriginal skin name: Gojok.

Anyone connected with Aboriginal people will know that non-Aboriginal people can be given an Aboriginal name after they have worked in the community for some time. The name is an honour that indicates that the person has been accepted by Aboriginal people. The giving of a skin name is a public honour from Aboriginal people, but what else did it mean to me? I thought, it means that I have taken a step forward and would now have more opportunities to attend ceremonies, even secret ceremonies. The skin name indicates that I am now regarded as one of their own people, someone they can trust to take proper regard of Aboriginal law and customs. It was as if a door had begun to open and secrets at the heart of Aboriginal culture could now gradually be revealed to me.

'Gojok' is one of eight names used to denote Aboriginal kinship, with each group being further subdivided into male and female. Traditionally, everyone is given a kinship or 'skin' name as well as their individual or personal name. Skin names are very important for determining a person's position in their family and wider society. After a child is born, it naturally belongs to a certain skin type and group according to the position of both parents in the system. Anyone thinking of marriage must strictly abide by this system. Gojok can only marry people of Gamanyjan blood. A Gojok's mother belongs to skin group Galagala, while the mother's brother belongs to Burralug. This means that the brother's wife must come from the Banadejan group. Moreover, no Gojok is allowed to contact or talk with members of his mother-in-law's family. If he does, ominous events will occur. In different regions of Australia, because of the many different languages used, there are many different names for this, but it is all the same system of kinship.

In Arnhem Land, Aborigines are divided into two main groups: Dhuwa and Yirrtja. Each group is then divided into seven sub-groups. If we use a chessboard as an analogy, the river boundary divides the chessboard into two. Beside the river is a public place, and everybody, including women and children, can participate in the ceremonies held here. These public ceremonies are called 'Garma', and people here are elected to form a management team responsible for issuing information and instructions on ceremonies and traditional Aboriginal culture and customs for the younger generation. Their position is that of the river. Above the riverbank is a higher place, called 'Yarra'. The ceremonies held there are not open to the public. The elders belong to that group. They are the people who lay down the rules and make judgments based on traditional law. A very small group of elders constitute yet another group, who make key decisions for the whole community. Their identities may be hidden, as if they had stepped off the chessboard, and ordinary people will not talk about them. When they die, they enter another world, their body and soul transform into their own totem and will live forever.

Since then, everyone in Arnhem Land has called me Gojok.

———≈———

Not long after, I met Michael Wamud, an old man from the Gamudi outstation. He told me something very strange. He said that he could never use the water from Gamudi, otherwise 'I will get sick, very sick'.

'Then how do you manage?', I asked.

'Bring in water from outside.'

'Oh, it will be very troublesome, right?'

'Yo', he shrugged his shoulders to indicate he had no choice. 'That's how I live: on water brought in from outside.'

'So why don't you live in another place?'

'I have tried, but this is my home, I can't leave here.'

Becoming very curious, I asked him how he would react or what would happen if he drank water here.

'Vomiting, my blood pressure suddenly rises… up… and up, dream all the time, can't sleep. I almost died twice.'

'Oh, that's very dangerous. Can't the doctor do anything?'

'No one can help me. I must wait until one day the deity come to summon me.'

I looked at him and saw that he has had a very tough life.

'What's your name? Do you have our name?', he asked.

'Gojok', I replied. 'Wangu-Wangu is my bush name.'

'Maynmak', he said, then turned his attention to the turtle shell in my hand. 'What you want to do with it?'

I said I didn't know, but suddenly I had an idea, 'Maybe you can paint something on it?' At that, he looked at me for a long while without saying anything. I had touched on another strange thing about him. He let me know that while he would have liked to draw something like turtle for me, but he and the turtle were in conflict. He never told me the story. I sensed it was about something sacred. That's how these people were, when you really talk to them, you find many mysterious stories.

Finally, he drew a few small butterflies on paper for me. He said that if I didn't choose a turtle as my totem, I could choose a butterfly. I asked him why? He explained that he could see butterflies flying around my head, and one was falling on to my face. At that, he stretched out his hand as if to catch it.

'Oh, she flew, she flew', he said very emotionally, and I didn't think that what he said was crazy.

At that moment, I was moved by what he was saying and really believed that he saw the butterflies flying over my head. I wanted to hear him explain why he saw only butterflies and not any other things. He smiled and, instead of satisfying my curiosity, he said, 'You will know'. Then he got up and left. Then I heard him say, 'Next time, don't forget to bring some water for me'.

Johnny Bulunbulun was the Aboriginal brother I met in Arnhem Land.

I remember how once, when I was walking past a crowd of people, someone called out, 'Gojok, haven't seen you for a long time, yeah'.

'Yeah, Maynmak', I said as I walked over, 'What are you doing?'

The guy replied that he wasn't doing anything much, just watching Bulunbulun painting.

So, I said hello to Bulunbulun, who was sitting on the ground in front of a small piece of bark. He was humming softly, looking at the bark as if thinking about what to paint.

I sat down with a great deal of interest. Bulunbulun was one of the artists I had on my list of people I wanted to meet. Since that time, many of them have become very famous nationally and internationally.

Bulunbulun began grinding yellow ochre on a flat slate. He was a bush painter who kept to the four traditional colours for bark painting, just like Mick. I asked Bulunbulun if I could help him grind his colours. He was very happy for me to do this, and, pushing the piece of slate towards me, said, 'Good man'. I would often offer this kind of help when I was with Aboriginal artists.

After thinking for a while, Bulunbulun began to draw something very slowly on the bark, using black charcoal mixed with glue. Soon I saw the pattern of a turtle emerge, but I knew that the whole picture would take a few days more to complete.

While drawing, Bulunbulun asked me, as one artist to another, 'Maynmak?'

I kept replying 'Ma!', because I didn't know what else to say.

The people standing around just watched quietly, as no one wanted to interrupt Bulunbulun's thinking and painting.

'When you leaving?', he asked suddenly without looking up at me.

'Maybe next month', I answered. 'My work contract expires next month, but the school told me I could stay on in the community, if I wanted.'

'Oh.'

I watched him straighten up and put his brush down gently. 'Tea, please', he said. His polite request seemed to be aimed at me.

I carefully made him a cup of tea. The others around indicated that he very much enjoyed being served tea by someone like me.

He didn't care what anyone was saying – he just kept looking at his painting. 'Em, maybe you like to come with me?'

Understanding what he meant, I nodded excitedly, 'Maynmak!' In the community, I had become used to this kind of brief verbal exchange. He wanted to take me to his outstation to show me his country. This was great!

While we were chatting, I opened my sketchbook and began to draw him. The people here were accustomed to seeing me do this, and I knew that no one would object. I understood that I was trusted, and this was a great comfort to me. It sprung from mutual respect.

Over the next two or three days, I came to help Bulunbulun by grinding colours as well as painting according to his instructions. He liked to use yellow ochre, which was also my favoured colour. The four different colours he used made the painting harmonious, warm and sharp. It was hard to imagine that it had been painted by the hands of a hunter. A tiny hairbrush, pinched between his thick black thumb and a forefinger, like a needle in a woman's hand, slid skilfully across the painting.

On the fourth day, he finished the small bark painting.

'Gojok, I had a dream last night, saw a big turtle', Bulunbulun said, pointing to the turtle painted on the bark in front of him. 'Just like this.'

'Really?', I exclaimed. 'What a coincidence, because I also had a dream last night, and dreamed of a turtle.' I don't know how likely it is that two people dream of the same thing at the same time, but I felt an inexplicable tacit understanding between us that was verified in our subsequent interactions.

Bulunbulun put down his brush, looked at the painting attentively and affectionately, and said, 'In our culture, everyone should have a totem… Em, from now on, the turtle is your totem. Wanggulu-Wanggulu is your bush name.' Handing me the painting, he announced, 'Now, it belongs to you, bro'.

No formality, no ceremony, just sincere friendship and understanding. From then on, I had my skin name, my totem and my bush name, indicating that now I could really step into their lives. Bulunbulun was older than me, so he was my elder brother.

Not only that, but it reminds me of something that Michael Wamud had said, not too long beforehand: he would like to draw me a turtle. The implication was that my totem should be 'turtle'. His prophecy had been confirmed, and butterflies still have a certain bond with me.

There are many ways to determine a person's totem. For example, before and after the birth of a child, their parents may be inspired by a particular symbol: a child and an animal may appear in a dream at the same time, or a kangaroo may run out in front of a woman and then the woman becomes pregnant. Such coincidences can govern the choice of a child's future totem.

It is believed that in the genesis period, spirits took the forms of various animals and plant species that have come to be the totems of the different Aboriginal clans and moieties. The subjects depicted on this bark are therefore of direct importance to either the artist's birthplace or lineage and they play important roles during various ceremonies when their habits and lifecycles are retold in song and dance. The colour differences between the subjects are apparently not always important, but each colour is sacred nonetheless, with special symbolic significance.

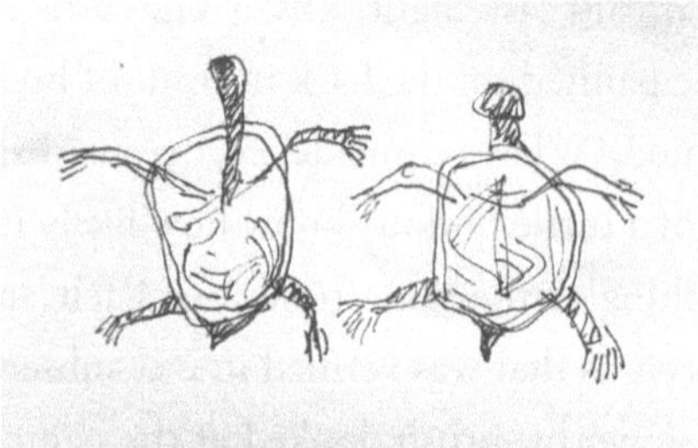

Turtle, my totem.

11

Future of the Children

While I stared at the campfire in a daze, I felt a little hand wrap around my neck from behind, and a small face with snot bubbles under the nose made its appearance.

'What are you doing?', he would ask me almost every day.

I picked up a leaf and grabbed his nose. He had got used to this. After blowing, he would ask if we were going to paint.

I patted his head, 'Do you like painting?'

'Ma [Yes]'.

'Mick will teach you.'

He shook his head.

Mick, sitting beside me added, 'When he grows up, teach him our way'.

I said to the boy, 'Then I will teach you my way now'.

The boy was so happy. Holding my hand, he dragged me to the big shed that was used for class. There were already about a dozen kids there waiting for me.

'Good morning.'

'Good morning, Xiaoping.'

This was how our day started, with a formal greeting.

The crisp voices of the children echoed through the bush and floated off into the cool air. I hadn't heard such sounds since I was an art teacher in China. After so many years, it was incredible to hear these voices in such a remote part of Australia. It seemed unreal. Looking at the cute little Aboriginal faces now before me, I remembered my Chinese students. I used to teach more than two hundred students a day, showing them how to draw, how to observe and express things. Now I wanted to pass on these skills and knowledge to these Aboriginal children. I was really excited by this challenge.

At first, I wasn't at all confident about how to teach these bush kids. Some of them had never seen what the outside world was like. They rarely left their community. But what happened surprised me very much.

I started to draw a line, and they copied me. Then I drew another line, and they again copied me, and so on.

'Bird', Luo-Luo suddenly announced.

'Yes, let's see what it will be next.'

I drew a 'V' shape like a tree fork, and then extended a long line down on both sides, so that a trunk appeared, and the protruding sides became branches. I then extended branches upwards. The kids copied each of my steps.

'Oh, tree. I finished', one of the kids shouted out, holding up his drawing. He was soon followed by others.

Seeing all these drawings, I saw that this was not difficult for them, removing my anxiety that they might be slow to accept art from another culture. I was wrong. This made me realise that many of our self-righteous thoughts are founded in human prejudice, and that 'prejudice' is such an obstacle to establishing 'mutual trust'. Being with these Indigenous children, I often gained new insights.

To arouse their interest, I asked the children to copy what I was doing as I drew a big circle with two small circles inside it. One kid immediately said that it looked like two eyes in a face. I told him to hold the sheet of paper and draw an upturned arc at the bottom of their circle. After I had added two ripples, it looked like a smiling face. The kids all thought it was too easy. Then I asked everyone to turn the arc upside down, and asked, 'What do you see now?'

'Wow, sad face, now.' They all laughed and yelled with surprise.

From then on, becoming more interested, the children added more details to their 'happy' and 'sad' face drawings. One kid drew a bird resting on top of his 'happy' head, to make it look playful. Another child drew three vertical lines beside the head, to represent three small trees. Then he added a few birds and a buffalo. I liked this drawing very much. With the birds flying in the sky and a buffalo on the ground, the drawing was vivid and dynamic. But one thing puzzled me: why was his buffalo tied up with rope? Pictured like this, it looked like a buffalo in rural China rather than like a buffalo running free in the bush. But the kid explained in a forthright manner, 'This is mine, and no one can take it away'. He was worried that someone would take away his buffalo. So, he had put this problem into his picture. No one had ever taught these children how to draw, but this kid did the best pictures of them all. Using bold, immature lines and graphics, children will naturally depict the things around them with an understanding of their own culture in their paintings.

Another boy drew an animal that looked like something between a buffalo and a dog. He added in many details of the side invisible to the eye, just as Picasso might have done. It surprised me, but when I thought about it more carefully, I remembered that traditional Aboriginal painting sometimes included things that are there but can't be seen directly, as for example in their 'X-ray' petroglyphs. I wondered whether Picasso had been

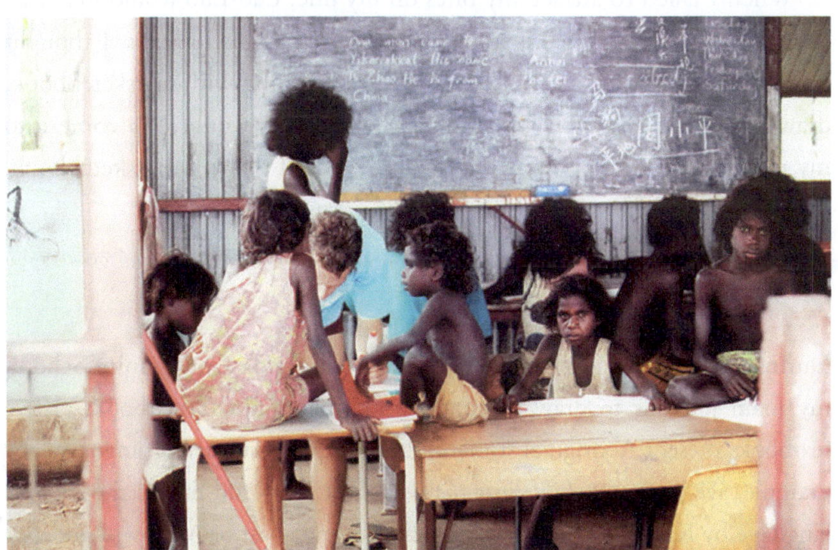

I enjoyed teaching children in Arnhem Land.

inspired by Aboriginal rock art – could this be possible?

People have a similar innate nature but are impacted tremendously by their environment. These kids from the bush, when taught and guided, showed as much talent as anyone. One child drew a big fish, with two small fish in its belly. He explained, 'Baby fish in the tummy'. But another boy broke in, 'Big fish eating small fish'. Surprised, I thought of yet another layer of meaning. You could take the painting as a metaphor for bullying, 'The big and strong taking over the small and weak'.

The Aboriginal children knew a lot about fish and often drew them, because one of the things that everyone did was a lot of was fishing.

In addition to class, painting and sports, we would hunt and fish around the outstation. This was not only for pleasure, but also a necessity. Although these children were usually very lively, whenever they held a fishing line in their hands, they immediately became quiet. They turned instinctively patient, and no longer noisy and mischievous. The outstation was a place of serenity: broad and pure. Sometimes it felt calm like a bowl of clear water, but only those with a generous spirit could live for a long time in this remote spot.

When I failed to attract any bites on my line, Luo-Luo would joke that the smart fish could smell a stranger. Scared off by his remarks, I thought that if I couldn't catch a fish, I could squat beside him with my sketchbook, drawing what I had seen and experienced. Images would also come into my mind while everyone was asleep, and I would sit with my sketchbook, drawing by the light of the fire.

———— ≈ ————

During my time as artist-in-residence at Maningrida Community School, my main job was to draw illustrations for the children's textbooks. These textbooks present Aboriginal stories in both English and native language. For example, *We Took the Children to the Beach* is a story told first in the Burarra language by Katie Fry. It comes from the central coast of Arnhem Land.

Some time ago we took the children for a walk.

We went in a boat and we saw a crocodile.

But we didn't know that the crocodile had caught a turtle.

And then we saw it. 'Hey, what's that over there?'

'Hey, it's a turtle, isn't it?' 'Yes, maybe.'

'Let's hurry and have a look.' 'Yes.'

Then we all went to see it and one person said, 'Hey, it's a turtle for us.'

'Good! We will eat it today and be filled up.'

Then we picked the turtle up and took it up onto the shore and cooked it there.

I drew an illustration to accompany each sentence, and it became a children's textbook. Teachers try to teach Aboriginal children by using familiar subjects as much as possible.

Other stories were about the Dreamtime. One was called *How We Got the Moon and Stars*.

A long time ago, when a pair of sisters went out to pick wild fruits, they put their sleeping child under the shade of a tree. Later, the child was awakened by the sun and cried loudly, but no one heard him. The child was tired of crying, got up slowly, knelt under the big tree, wanted to climb up, but kept falling off after climbing several times. After an unknown period of time the sisters suddenly realized that they had not heard the child's voice, and then realized that they were far away from the tree. They hurried back and found that the child was gone, only the wooden utensils were still left under the tree and many small footprints around the tree. The sisters cried and searched anxiously, thinking they were stolen by kangaroos or wild dogs. At this time, suddenly a voice came from over their heads: I am here. The sisters looked up and saw that the child was climbing on the tree like a little monkey. Mum told him to come down quickly. The child said: I want to go to the sky and become a thing that can emit light, illuminate the darkness, and then you can dance and cry under the light. Your tears will fly into the sky and become countless stars, and I will be the moon. Later, the sisters really recruited many people and did what the child wanted. Everyone danced hand in hand and wept. It didn't take long for the moon to appear in the sky, as well as shining stars. Since then, everyone is no longer afraid of the dark night.

I drew the fourteen pictures for this book mainly at night, because I had to teach children during the day. It was another job I really enjoyed.

In addition to taking care of schoolwork, I tried to visit as many other outstation schools as possible. Even if I could spend only a week with the children at each, it was very important for them. And for the teachers not trained in the arts, it can be regarded as a training session. I would have enjoyed spending even more time at the outstations, in the natural environment and living a contented life close to the earth that is rich in spirituality. But one day I fell ill at an outstation and had to lie down for several days. Headache and diarrhoea were a common occurrence for everyone out there, something we would take pills to get over. This time, the problem arose from damage to my feet. I had hurt my feet while chasing prey and they had become inflamed. This led to a fever, and I could only stagger around holding up one foot, while the other could barely touch the ground without pain.

Being with the children was the happiest time. When this photo was taken, I had an injured foot and could barely walk.

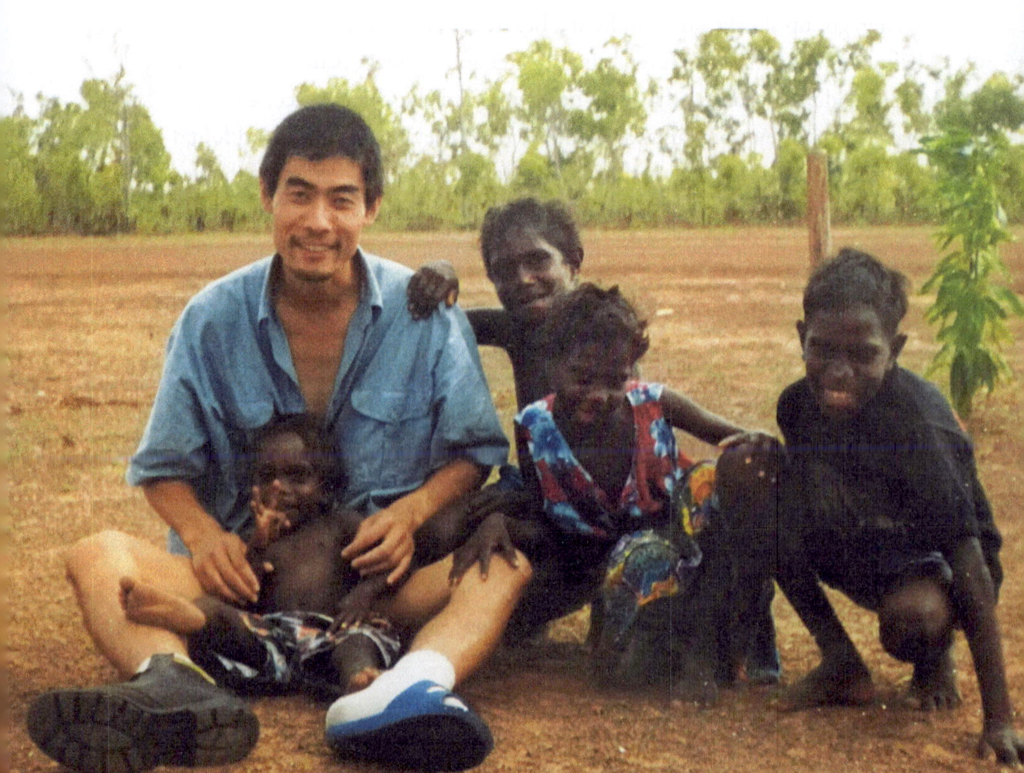

While recovering, I had more time to do what I wanted to do every morning: writing and drawing and looking at my sketchbook for new ideas. One day, I looked at a sketch of an interesting character, a man I had drawn from memory. He had some Oriental features, flat eye sockets, a small, exquisitely made nose neither high nor flat and with a thin bridge. Only his thick lips and dark skin indicated that he was Aboriginal. His hair was pulled back into a short braid. When he saw me, he had said: 'Do you know me? My father was half-Chinese. I want a Chinese girl. Can you help me?'

He spoke to me directly and with familiarity, so joking back I said that he should introduce me to an Aboriginal girl. To my surprise, two days later, he pulled me over in front of two girls, asking which one I liked best. Or would I like both? The girls and I were very embarrassed.

Looking again at his picture, I smiled but once more felt embarrassed, so I quickly flipped the page.

Looking again at these drawings of butterflies, I remembered another story that happened not long ago. I turned the page and there was an even larger butterfly, rendered in beautifully detailed colour. The wings were slightly raised, as if it were about to fly away. It had been painted specially for me by a little girl. During the teaching I had done here, I found that the children needed little guidance, and their works would often surprise me.

A few weeks earlier, I had been at an outstation. After class we set out to go swimming in the nearby river. On the way, we saw several fruit trees. The children picked some fruit and handed it out to everyone. It was sweet, juicy and refreshing. Then a little girl saw a beautiful butterfly. She walked over and gently stretched out her little hand, trying to catch it. Before she could touch it, it flew away, only to stop on the next flower. Again, the little girl stretched out her hand and again the butterfly flew off only to stop on another flower. It was like a game of hide-and-seek. Then just when the girl was ready to give up, the butterfly flew to her and, landing on her shoulder, was finally caught. Holding the butterfly out in front of her, the little girl looked at it very carefully and asked, 'Where else do you want to fly?' To my surprise, she then gently put it back on a flower, saying, 'Fly… fly', while her small hand fanned back and forth. Seeing this, I was quite moved. The little girl told me that she had been trying to catch the butterfly to give me as a gift, but now she wanted to draw a beautiful butterfly for me.

Then, we passed a lotus pond. Two boys jumped in, picked lotus leaves and put them on their heads. They broke off lotus stems and buds to eat. The thoughtful little girl who had chased the butterfly picked a lotus flower and held it in front of me, with a bright smile on her small face. She said, 'Fiona asked me to give it to you'.

'Wow, thank you so much, it's beautiful', I said, very pleased. 'Thank Fiona, too.'

Fiona was a beautiful Aboriginal girl who worked as a tutor at the outstation. We had several good conversations. She told me that she wanted to go to China. After seeing the martial arts videotape, she thought the people over there were so interesting.

I asked her, 'Would you be afraid in a strange country?'

'No, you would take care of me, wouldn't you?', she replied shyly though with some confidence.

'Sure.'

'We're like a family.'

'Thank you for accepting me. I like it here.'

'So, will you still go?', she asked in a low voice.

'Em… Yeah', I said giving a nod.

She let out a soft 'Oh,' as she removed her hopeful gaze from my face and said nothing more. I wanted to try to explain but was afraid she wouldn't understand.

Later, I made several paintings of her. In one, a beautiful black girl holds a white lotus flower, her face lit with a smile. She looks down breathing the faint fragrance of the flower, while a colourful butterfly flies off in the background. It was a picture of a girl full of longing for life.

Because I was with the children every day, I also made drawings of children during this period. The children liked to play in the water. As soon as they see water, they become excited and jump in quickly. Some children would climb up a big tree and dive. Wherever there was children's laughter, there would be vitality and joy. Their laughter alarmed the birds in the surrounding bush, and twittering, they would fly up into the sky. It was a beautiful, vibrant picture. As I took in the scene, a cheeky boy suddenly pushed me from behind into the river. As my head came to the surface, I had little idea about what had happened. A group of children surrounded me, splashing me with water. They were joking with their teacher. As I joined the water battle, I was transported back to my childhood. These children seemed no different from playful children in the city.

I was lying on my sleeping bag in the shade of the tree, flipping through my sketchbook and thinking about what had happened in the past weeks. My eyes fell on my sketches of the children.

'A long time ago, our ancestors travelled from west to east, and they created all kinds of creatures along the way...' I seemed to hear the children's clear voices reading. The sound was coming from a bush shed. It had no walls, and the roof covered only a few tables and chairs and a small blackboard. I slowly closed my eyes. I needed to listen to this sound carefully. While I listened, images came to my mind of the wonderful times I had shared with these children at the outstation. Their story went like this:

I walked quietly into the classroom and watched Fiona hearing everyone read through the last few sentences of the story. Then she told them all with a happy smile, 'Next, it's drawing time.'

'Yeah, Maynmak!' The children were excited to hear that painting was next.

I held out my arms and asked, 'What are you painting today?', thinking about the simple small trees, animals and faces that we had painted already.

Fiona said that whatever I asked them to paint, the children always looked forward to it.

After I had thought for a while, I said, 'Okay, you can start now'.

'What? Paint what? You haven't told us what to paint.' The children laughed and thought I was joking with them.

'What do you see?'

'We don't see anything.'

'What about me? Don't you see me?' This time, I wanted to teach them how to sketch from life. 'What do you see?'

'Yes, but then what?'

'Draw me.'

The children started commenting on my appearance, my height, my clothes and my movements. I pretended to be a model, and the children hit the table with their hands to show their appreciation. But although they were excited by the idea, they still didn't know how to draw. Also, the task was difficult: they were facing a three-dimensional character with complicated details. I asked a child to stand up, and patiently compared the size of various limbs and parts of a person.

After several attempts to get them to understand how to observe a person in this way, slowly but surely, one after another, vivid and interesting pictures finally emerged. This was the first time they had to learn to observe things from this completely new perspective.

Then I noticed a boy sitting with a blank sheet of paper in front of him. He looked up at me with a serious expression. I learned that he had just arrived with his family two days ago from another outstation.

'Why don't you draw?', I asked carefully.

He lowered his head in silence and just looked at the white paper.

I told him not to worry, 'Let's start with the bird'. I drew a circle on the paper, and then a slightly larger semicircle next to it. Then I asked him to draw with me. He carefully picked up his pencil, looked up at me, pursed his small mouth, but the pencil in his small hand stopped still above the paper. He asked what he should draw.

'Anything you like', I said, giving him an encouraging smile.

Summoning up his courage, he drew a twisted circle on the paper. Then came a second line and a third. Finally, he finished his first bird drawing.

It was funny to see how the children drew me. But at a least it proved that they were able to draw very interesting pictures. They were so happy looking at each other's work, even the one with snot bubbles under his nose. The children's cheerful laughter attracted the attention of some of the adults, who came over to see what was going on. Among them was Jack, a man with two wives and six children. He said, 'These little guys have never been so happy as now, what's happened?' I grabbed him, put a pencil into his hand,

and said, 'You will find out, if you sit down and draw with these children'.

'Oh, no, no', he waved his hands in embarrassment.

But the children got even more excited when they heard Jack's protest and almost forced him to sit down. Smiling, he picked up a pencil again, but fiddled with it as if it were a strange magic stick. He was at a loss. The paper before him was dazzling white. When a little bit of black dust fell on it, he carefully blew it away.

'I don't know how to draw. I've never held a pencil before. I'm afraid I will ruin this beautiful paper.' He almost begged, 'Let me go, please'.

I waved him back.

'Oh, what can I do?' He looked at the pencil and his voice dropped, 'I'm just a bushman, you know, but I hope these children can always hold a pen in their hand.'

I was touched and thought I knew what he was trying to say. I held his hand and said, 'I believe it won't be just hope'.

'Maynmak!'

It was a child who couldn't wait anymore and wanted to teach Jack to paint. As Jack remained at a loss, the little guy grabbed the hand holding the pencil and together they drew a line on the snowy white paper. I thought this must have been the first time that Jack had been embarrassed by a small child, but life is like a piece of white paper, and from the first mark, you gradually become enriched. Eventually, Jack's big hand completed a portrait of me, supported throughout by that small hand. The process made everyone laugh. Looking at their smiling faces, I couldn't help thinking that one day, if they could walk out of the bush, with such a big smile, that would be great!

Someone was pulling at the corner of my coat. Looking down, I saw it was the new boy. He held up his picture with a mischievous grin, as if to say: what do you think? My eyes lit up. He had given his image the facial features of a Chinese person.

That night it was very dark, with neither moon nor stars in the sky. It felt hard to breathe. I had made a campfire outside the shed used as a classroom and sat there with Alan, a European man who helped to look after this outstation. Alan threw two large branches on to the fire, making it flame up and crackle as it encountered dead leaves. Soon water was boiling in the billy. I grabbed a handful of tea leaves and threw them in. 'Alan, smell it', I said as I handed the tin of tea to him.

'Well, it's very fragrant. I can smell it', a voice replied out of the darkness. Turning my head sharply, I saw Jack standing behind me.

'You scared me, Jack', I said as I clutched my chest. 'Please make a noise next time you show up in the dark.'

'I'm sorry if I really scared you. But if my feet don't make a sound on these fallen leaves, can you blame me?'

I thought it was not surprising that a man like him, who had lived in the bush all his life, could move so quietly, at one with the trees and the dark night.

'What kind of tea is this?', Jack asked sniffing it hard.

'Green tea, drunk without sugar. It's good for you. Would you like to try it?' I poured him a cup, hoping that he would like it. It would be better for him than the highly sweetened tea that he usually had.

'Not only give up alcohol, but also sugar and salt', he observed wryly. He said that petrol sniffing and gambling were also problems in Aboriginal communities. That was why Jack and his family preferred to live back at the outstation. Sometimes at Maningrida, I heard women quarrelling with their men, telling them, 'You need to go back to the outstation. There's too much alcohol and gambling here'. But people came back to the community to learn and develop their lives, even though they then faced many more problems. What should they do? Stay in the bush or come into the community centre and approach the wider world?

'We will not walk out of the bush', Jack said. 'We belong to the land and the land needs us.'

'What about your children?', I asked. 'Will they think the same way as you?'

In response to this question, Jack remained silent for long while. I believe he was thinking: what will be the future for the new generation? Europeans had already brought a lot of new things into the Maningrida community, so it was becoming more and more like other places, even with things that you could find in the city now right here.

I asked Jack what he thought were the biggest changes he had seen here.

He explained that the community now had clean drinking water from underground, solar power, and better houses. There was more money than in the past, but fewer real hunters.

'Is this what everyone wants?'

Jack said, 'Not everyone wanted this', but the temptation was just too great. 'The white people brought many good things but also some things that we don't want.'

It grew silent around the campfire as we stared into the flames, thinking our own thoughts.

One year I attended a closed-door meeting organised by Indigenous people at Blythe River, which is near Maningrida. During the meeting, Jacky Green spoke of his experience. He had tried to start a small business but found it quite difficult entirely on his own. Different things would prevent him from opening his business on time each day. In his culture, ignoring the time is not a serious matter. But for a business not to open at the correct time is difficult. 'Sometimes we are lazy', he noted, and could not show the same self-discipline as whites. Even so, Jacky had a responsible attitude to work and showed good self-reliance.

The local impact of mining was also a big issue to be discussed.

At this closed-door meeting, many things plunged the participants into deep thought. What is the future for us and our children and grandchildren? Do we want our next generations to maintain our current way of life? Should we walk out of this land? An old man announced that homeland was all-important. 'We are the owner of this land, and we have the responsibility to protect every inch of it for our people, and for the next generations.' His answer was unambiguous: we, and the next generations, will never leave this land.

In fact, both the Aboriginal people's complex relationship with their land and their respect for it have never been widely understood or truly respected by the settlers who came later to this country. Why this has been so is a question worth pondering. In my opinion, the impact of foreign culture is irreversible. Whether willingly or unwillingly, the question now is how to maximise the protection of traditional culture while the nation, as an entity, continues to develop. How can the right balance be achieved? It is an enormous challenge. The government and society in general should be more respectful and inclusive when dealing with Indigenous issues. It is not just a question of money. Long-term planning is needed. In 1974, the city of Darwin was hit by Cyclone Tracy. After complete devastation, the city has undergone decades of reconstruction and is now the newest and most modern of Australian major cities. Thinking boldly, I venture to ask, 'Why should I walk away from this traditional land? Couldn't we dream of building a new type of city in the bush, one that is in tune with the local environment and accords with the wishes of the Aboriginal people?'

The consensus of opinions reached at the closed-door meeting was summarised and submitted to the local government. But they would not include any of my crazy ideas. I hope that one day soon, someone might revisit these ideas from a Chinese artist.

The branches had burned down, and the mosquitoes were coming out. They were biting me through my jeans. There were too many to kill one by one, and I had to wipe them away with a hand.

Looking around, I couldn't see Jack. He had got up and left, as silent as a ghost. The teacher had also moved away, zipping himself into his tent. To avoid the mosquitoes, I hid in my tent, too, even although a few mozzies had got there before me. I tried to pay no attention to them.

Once, I had a terrible cold with a cough and fever. My Aboriginal friends told me to try bush medicine. I was given a bowl of hot water in which two different kinds of green leaves had been cooked together. I put the blanket over my head and buried my face in the steam. Then I drank some of the hot medicinal water. I had two bowls, three times a day. At night I had a very good sleep, the first for a week or so and, by the next day, I was starting to recover.

'It is extremely important that you learn about this', I said seriously to Fiona. The Chinese have used herbal medicines for thousands of years. The

Shen Nong Ben Cao Jing, China's first book of Materia Medica, summarised knowledge of 365 different kinds of medicines used even before the Han Dynasty. I see similarities between Aboriginal and Chinese herbal medicines. It is unfortunate that, because there is no Indigenous written language, Aboriginal medical knowledge is not well documented.

Both the Chinese and the Australian Aborigines are nations with ancient cultures. If there are any similarities between them, one would be their use of herbal medicines. Others are: a strong attachment to the land, an emphasis on family, relatives, and clan relationships.

At the last closed-door meeting, one topic discussed was how best to pass on knowledge of herbal medicine. The number of elderly experts had been declining year by year, so much knowledge is being lost. But while the community wants to preserve and pass on this ancient medical knowledge, there is concern that it would be used inappropriately by white people, by profiteers who just want to steal all their mysteries. Lack of trust in white people has arisen because of many bad cases of exploitation.

'Fiona, you want to leave here?'

'Yes, but I am also scared.'

I nodded to show that I understood. I wanted to tell her that while the outside world is indeed colourful and very interesting, if she doesn't know and accept the rules of survival in that world, she will find life very hard. This choice – of whether to accept or escape – bothers me.

Through Fiona's meticulous care, I recovered fully and was at last able to walk around again. I then took every chance to visit different outstations and succeeded in visiting about fifteen of them around the Maningrida community. Under my guidance, the children drew thousands of pictures, and afterwards I selected more than one hundred for an exhibition in the school library. It was an exhibition that I and the children were extremely proud of.

But after this, my time as artist-in-residence came to an end.

Arnhem Land has been described by some as the most primitive and desolate place in the world today. For the past two hundred years, the people there have lived in a very isolated and closed state. The Aborigines who have lived on this land for generations did not want to be disturbed. This adds to the mystery of this place and the people living there. It is as though the land is shrouded with a veil that is hazy and invisible. Many people might think that this is a truly desolate place, but for me it is very rich. It never displays this wealth to the ignorant but remains mysterious and inaccessible. It is only to those who love it, that it will open its heart.

For me, to see this richness of interaction between nature and culture was fascinating. I benefited greatly, and these experiences have been very important in my life.

Since that time, I began to divide my time between the city, the desert, and Arnhem Land. The difference between these environments proved hard to adapt to and sometimes confused me, even to the point of putting my life in danger.

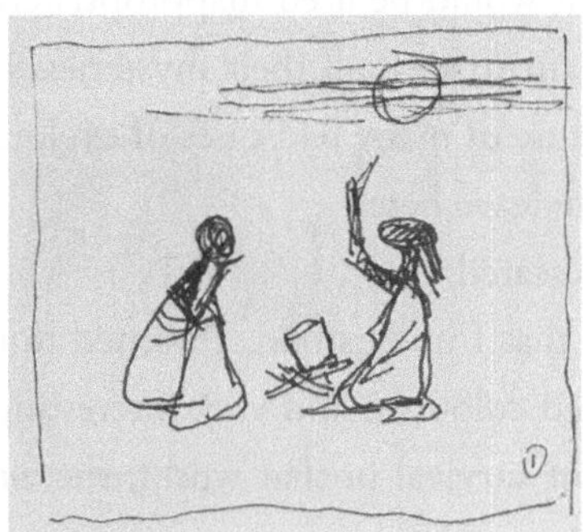

Telling the story of 'How We Got the
Moon and the Stars'.

12

Facing Doubts

After the initial shock, through my sustained efforts I succeeded in achieving some degree of integration with Aboriginal people both in the desert and in Arnhem Land. I had been invited to participate in several ceremonies, and mutual trust and good relationships had been established between us. But this didn't mean that my artworks incorporating Aboriginal themes would be readily accepted by the mainstream Australian public. The more I thought about this, the greater my concern. Frankly speaking, my work grew from intuition. My art was expressed directly, without concern for rules and without prejudice. This statement might appear too straightforward and naive, but I feel that it is based on facts. In my own eyes, I was just like those uninhibited Aboriginal kids I had taught. I painted whatever I saw. However, my representations of reality did not always evoke a positive response, in particular my incisive depictions of striking Indigenous characters clearly impinged on the sensitivities of some people. Emotionally, they found the people in those paintings unacceptable because psychologically they did not want to be confronted by them.

'What will the public think?', my classmates at Darwin University asked me.

'Should I only paint what people want to see?', I naively responded. But having said this I began to think, 'How should I paint?' This question still haunts me to this day. It is a question that raises many issues of public concern – including racial conflict, cultural identity, prejudice within the art world – and many historical problems. This is a sensitive area and one that not many artists are willing to enter. I asked a classmate why he didn't ever address this subject. His answer was candid, 'I don't want to cause trouble'.

'What kind of trouble?' Were there restrictions and forbidden areas for creative artists interested in Indigenous Australia?

'Like the trouble you have right now', he replied.

I was dumbfounded. I stared straight at him for a moment then silently lowered my head. He was right. I was in trouble.

The trouble started in 1995 when I made the decision to study at Charles Darwin University. I chose this university because it was close to Arnhem Land. I thought that this would allow me to stay in contact with Aboriginal people. Also, matters related to Aboriginal people are always hot topics in the locality but seldom talked about in Melbourne or Sydney.

My wife Ke was very supportive of my idea. I must say that she has always been most understanding and supportive of me in my career, especially when we had children and she took on almost all the family duty when I was away from home.

My supervisor was very interested in how I used Chinese paintbrushes and rice paper to express Indigenous themes. He asked me a lot of questions during the painting process, hoping that I could develop each painting more. He maintained that Chinese painting was rather simplistic and quick to complete. However, I recognised that the 'simplicity' in Chinese painting derived from what was initially 'complex' but had been pared back to achieve something ethereal and graceful, energetic and soul stirring. The use of ink-and-wash instead of oils in Chinese art constitutes a remarkable innovation and refinement of line. Ink-and-wash is more than a painting technique: it reflects culture and spirit. As with Aboriginal bark painting, Chinese ink-and-wash painting has evolved from a unique and distinctive culture. In his inability to understand the profundity of Chinese painting, my supervisor was not alone, because Europeans generally find it difficult to understand the Chinese Laozhuang philosophy and Oriental culture on which this genre of painting is based. Moreover, they fail to comprehend the profundity of freehand brushwork. Laozi and Zhuangzi were two of China's most influential Taoist philosophers. Their philosophy explores ideas of personal spiritual freedom that may be gained from letting the mind escape the confines of the real world.

My supervisor and I often talked about non-Indigenous Australian artists who had painted Aboriginal subjects. One example was Russell Drysdale, who explored Aboriginal themes as a major subject during his artistic career. Others had only dabbled in a limited way with these ideas. It seemed to me that, compared with studies of other cultures, especially minority cultures, Australian knowledge of Aboriginal culture was scanty and poorly reflected in the work of non-Indigenous artists. At that time, I found it very hard to understand why more Australian artists did not express interest in these ancient Aboriginal nations with their very rich culture that, from its long living history, provided a wonderful resource for examining the origins of art. Where else in the world can we still find a culture spanning tens of thousands of years that can be studied and observed so closely as it can be in Arnhem Land? This is not just history on display in a museum but a living art history that continues to retain its strong vitality.

I mentioned to my supervisor the work of Ainslie Roberts that depicts Aboriginal Dreamtime stories through surrealistic and fantastical images. He wondered how well Ainslie had understood the Dreamtime stories. If he did not, was he then qualified to paint them? Listening to his argument created a knot in my mind. I immediately thought of myself. Was I qualified to paint this subject?

Sometime later, I learned that the design on the back of the Australian $2 coin had been inspired by a portrait of the Aboriginal man Gwoya Jungarai, drawn by that under-appreciated artist Ainslie Roberts. In 1928, Gwoya Jungarai was the sole survivor of a massacre in Coniston, Central Australia. Almost every Australian has seen his face, yet how many have reflected on the crimes committed by the Australian Government against these Aboriginal people under the White Australia Policy?

After seeing my paintings, my supervisor asked me to give a presentation. I had started my studies with many questions for which I wanted answers. So, I was very pleased to have this opportunity to discuss my work and some of these issues with others. The attendees consisted mainly of postgraduate students from the School of Art on campus. But in the light of what happened next, my thinking was rather too optimistic. When this audience viewed slides of my paintings, their reactions went far beyond anything that I could have imagined. They posed strong, sharp, tough questions that were intolerably harsh.

'I like your Chinese painting techniques, they are very innovative, and the effect of the painting overall is very powerful, but…' And then came what the speaker really wanted to say: 'I don't like the combination of these themes with your painting style. In my view, your works contain an exotic romanticism, especially the people who are depicted as being so intense, ugly and sad'.

This was the first time that anyone had criticised my work so aggressively. In the speaker's view, the unambiguous problem was one of national self-respect.

'Being Chinese, why are you painting these people as subjects?', someone asked.

Were they questioning my motives?

'How much do you know about our Aboriginal people?', another classmate asked.

I thought to myself: more than everyone in this class. However, I didn't dare to say so directly. It was clear to me that this was the first time any of them had seen paintings of this kind done by a Chinese artist. They weren't at all keen to accept them.

I nervously tried to respond to these criticisms by saying that I had just tried to paint my feelings boldly and truthfully. However, my bold and truthful depictions were described as being 'reckless' and 'without historical context'.

Someone else said, 'Aboriginal figures like these were painted in the past by white Australians. Your figures remind me too much of those old "ashtray" paintings. And your painting is too realistic. The subjects seem to be copied from photographs and lack any creativity.'

This was the first time that I had heard of 'ashtray' paintings.

Later, I checked the origin of the word. It turned out that an artist named Eric Jolliffe had visited many Aboriginal communities in Arnhem

Land where he drew many Aboriginal cartoons, some of which were painted on ashtrays. His numerous cartoons often depicted Aboriginal people as objects of ridicule and belittling, and he was criticised by many Australians, especially in academia and the arts. His work was later described as being that of a poster child for racism. But he also found many followers, mostly white supremacists. Most ironically, such a controversial cartoonist was awarded an Order of Australia Medal (OAM) in 1998, for his 'outstanding contribution to the arts as a cartoonist and illustrator'.

One postgraduate student described how some non-Indigenous people would copy Aboriginal rock paintings, and then used them inappropriately without permission, even though these ancient paintings contained secrets of the mysterious history of the Aboriginal people. It was their wealth. In my own painting, I had sometimes drawn images from rock painting, although in a different way and only in the background. Even so, this student found it unacceptable. She thought that it would make some people, like herself, and especially Aboriginal people, embarrassed and angry. She claimed that what I had done was disrespectful to Aboriginal culture.

The students continued with their merciless criticism and attacks. They all spoke frankly in this academic discussion, telling me what I could or couldn't paint, even if I disagreed with them.

An Aboriginal student called Cathy thought that my work might encourage people to pay more attention to Aboriginal culture and dismissed many of the arguments of the others as 'nit-picking'. Nevertheless, she agreed that some important rock art, like the Wandjina painting, must be treated carefully, because of its sacred and symbolic meaning.

'Can you accept the Aboriginal characters in his paintings?', someone asked Cathy.

'I don't see the problem you do', she said.

Hearing this, her questioner shut up. But later, I heard someone say that Cathy could take this view because the image had nothing to do with her. Often people will not refute the person, but will talk behind the person's back, especially when it comes to matters concerning Aboriginals.

All this ruthless criticism made me feel desperate, but it also made me think more deeply about these issues. So, in fact the discussion had left me feeling a little excited.

The story did not end as simply as I had thought, yet the aftermath fully confirmed that the role of art is to make people think. In the more than 200 years since settlers came to Australia, the debate on Aboriginal issues has never stopped.

News of what had happened at my presentation spread across our art colleges and across the university campus, and soon Darwin's wider cultural and art circles began talking about it. One day Steve, a well-regarded figure in the arts and culture field, came to my studio. When he learned about my experiences over the past few years, he couldn't suppress his surprise. It was clear to him that I was not just a tourist or one of the many people who called themselves experts after making a brief visit to one or two Aboriginal communities. Even so, our conversation touched on sensitive topics: why had I chosen this subject? As a Chinese artist, what did I want to tell people? Was I able to grasp the complexities and scale of this sensitive subject?

'Do these works make you uncomfortable?', I asked him directly. After hearing so many accusations, I'd given up expecting to find understanding.

He said that they didn't, really…

'Really?' I looked at him suspiciously. I knew that he had spent years working at the Aboriginal Community Art Centre.

He told me that some people had an emotionally negative response to my work because they had never seen a Chinese artist depict Aboriginal people so vividly and realistically.

I then made the argument that 'real' artistic creation requires action made without too much deliberation. If this is the case, the work will be spontaneous, purer, and freer of the influence of miscellaneous artistic genres. I think that the process of accurate recording is essential and a key factor for creating a work that will impress people. An accurate drawing or painting should not be dismissed as being 'wrong'.

Steve then asked me to think about who would want to unreservedly put their backyard on show in front of strangers. Every argument has at least two sides, so how should my artistic problems best be interpreted? He hoped that I would understand the point that he was making.

He asked, 'Maybe some people will like your painting, but what kind of perspective will they look at it from?'

I didn't know. I really couldn't tell what these white people might think. But his question reminded me of an incident that had happened a few days earlier, during my exhibition in Darwin. A couple came up to me to say that they liked my paintings very much.

The man said, 'Look at this character, it exudes a kind of power. I haven't seen such an exciting painting for a long time.'

The woman said, 'Yes, I was moved by this. Why are these people so unwilling to come out of the bush?'

The man just shrugged his shoulders. The woman continued, 'Honey, they are people just like us. We should give them more care, don't you think?'

The man replied, 'Of course, my dear. It's your compassion that makes me love you so much.' They looked at each other and smiled. Then they turned to me and said a lot of beautiful things about my painting. But to me, their speech and expression seemed so contrived as they talked about Aboriginal people with such elegance. Perhaps they did not realise that their condescension conveyed an inexplicable sense of superiority?

During my time at the Art School in Darwin, one person gave me very pertinent comments about my painting. Like everyone else, he expressed his views bluntly, but they were made in a way that was very useful. Most importantly, he didn't try to change what I was painting.

Mr Smith, from the Art School, didn't raise the problems that so concerned others. His question was different. He wanted to know what impact it would have if I focused on the landscape, particularly the landscape of the outback, instead of on Aboriginal people? The characters I created in my paintings were so powerful. He fully understood that as an artist I wanted to express my individuality, and he saw that as a good thing. However, he added that if the expression of this individuality becomes too confronting, it can be seen as unacceptable and dangerous.

I told him that I hadn't considered what people might think of me and my work. I just wanted to capture my own understanding and feelings for these characters directly and clearly, using line drawing with a strong contrast between black and white. Power, shocking power was what I wanted to express – something that I had felt so strongly at Alice Springs when I saw Aboriginal people for the first time. The power of the painting itself contained everything that I wanted to say and naturally I hoped that viewers would also see it. I was too tired to explain further. But by now I had begun to realise just how sensitive this had all become, simply because I had chosen to explore subject matter related to Aboriginal themes.

'But I can't quite get what you are trying to say', Mr Smith said.

'It's how I want to express myself as an artist', I said, looking at him with some embarrassment. Then I added more ruthlessly, 'You didn't go to see it, did you? Are you afraid to see it?' I was not used to speaking so directly, but there seemed to be no choice. I didn't want him to think that I agreed with his views. I had to drop my usual more polite stance when facing so many harsh accusations.

He stared at me in surprise. My words seemed to have got to him. I sensed that he still wanted to tell me something, something that was bothering or worrying him.

'Think about it. This is not an easy subject', he said finally, as he patted me on the shoulder.

It was more than just 'not easy'. I finally began to understand what my classmate meant about causing trouble.

Long after Mr Smith had left my studio, our conversation remained on my mind. I thought: am I wrong? Why can't I paint the feelings that I have experienced? What kind of problematical messages did I convey in my work? Is my painting so bad that people can't see anything in it?

It was also after my solo exhibition in Darwin that one of the women who had come to view my work told me that she would never hang any of my paintings in her house, because the characters depicted were so strong and unforgettably sad. When she came home to her house after work, she wanted to see much more light-hearted images. But she did add, speaking seriously, 'Your paintings really make me stop, to think and to remember. They are explaining something.'

After facing such severe criticisms, I withdrew into myself. Thoughts went around in my head. Why were there so many forbidden areas when it came to Aboriginal themes? I told myself that I needed to think about this very carefully, but I wasn't going to do it sitting in my studio. I would go back to the bush, live with my Aboriginal friends, and sit by a fire to think about it. When I explained my intentions to my supervisor, he supported me. 'I believe that you will then understand how to paint and what to paint', he said.

This was the real issue.

———≈———

This time I went to Wandawuy outstation, about 80 kilometres southwest of the Yirrkala Aboriginal Community in Arnhem Land. Wandawuy was home to two families and a total of around thirty people. The elder was Djutja Djutja Mununggurr of the Djapu people, and he was also a painter. His wife shared the same skin group as me. I call her Yapa, meaning 'big sister'. Because the two families were connected by blood, I saw them all as one big Arnhem Land family.

Life here was much simpler: mainly hunting and fishing.

One day, we went fishing. On the way there in the car, we were like potatoes stuffed into a jar, swaying together for more than an hour before we reached the riverside. We unloaded some stuff from the car, then Bobby, Djutja's son, asked a boy to go hunting with him, and they drove off together. Meanwhile, the women threw out a fishing line and squatted quietly at the riverbank. The old man Djutja spread out a drop sheet under a shady tree and lay down. Beside him was a small baby looking like a little chubby black ball, sleeping soundly. Djutja crossed his legs, holding a pipe in one hand, from which, from time to time, he took a few puffs. He seemed comfortable and completely relaxed.

After a while, he shouted at the women by the riverbank, 'Caught anything?' Someone showed him a few prawns in a bag from the night before. He reached out, grabbed them, and poured them out. A little girl rushed over. She stretched out her little hand, trying to grab a prawn, but she wasn't quick enough. 'Hey, mine, it's mine', Djutja muttered, quickly putting his hands over the food.

'One, only one', the little girl pleaded.

'Yak [No], go and play.'

But the girl just wouldn't give up and she jumped on him coquettishly. They competed just like children until the little girl managed to snatch a small prawn. Making a funny face at the old man, she jumped away. I looked at Djutja, who was beaming with childlike fun.

Joining the others, I went to throw out a fishing line. I waited, but no fish was willing to take the bait. Losing patience, I returned to Djutja, taking out my sketchbook to draw him.

'Caught anything?', Djutja asked again as he finished eating his prawns.

'Be quiet, old man', an impatient voice rang out.

But not long afterwards, someone came across holding out a piece of bark with several small fish on it.

'Gojok', Djutja said, pointing at the fish.

I knew what he meant. I put down my sketchbook, because it was time to cook the fish. Grabbing a handful of leaves and a few twigs to start making a fire, I put the fish at the edge of the fire to cook. I watched until the skin turned brown and scorched, then put them on some large leaves to present before Djutja.

'Yeah', he snorted with satisfaction, tearing the fish apart with two thick black fingers to reveal the steaming flesh. He then sprinkled a generous amount of salt all over it.

'Not too much salt', I warned.

He ignored me and ate with relish. Before long, only three fish skeletons remained, looking like some fish art by Picasso.

'Gojok', he called to me again, as he picked up the last of the fish with his oily fingers and handed it to me. The pleasure he took in eating made me very happy to accept this morsel. I watched as he licked the last fish juices off the leaves, heaving a long sigh of satisfaction before setting them to one side. A dog that had been lying there quietly, staring at Djutja's every movement, recognised his cue, and picking up the fish bones walked off to enjoy any leftover flavour.

Taking in the scene and tasting and smelling the fragrance of the fish, I pondered about how I could capture all this in a painting.

I took out a blanket from my bag, put it on the ground, and then brought out ink, brushes and rice paper. Djutja looked at me but said nothing. He knew what I wanted to do. He remained as he was, half-lying down, keeping still. Even when the little girl who had come scrambling up to him to grab some prawns grimaced at him, he made no response. I quickly seized this opportunity to paint him, getting down the outline of his shape on my rice paper. I picked up a big brush to paint with ink, adding detail to my initial outlines. Then I used small brushes for even finer effects, especially around the face. The expertise involved in this kind of drawing depends on how thin or thick lines and dry or wet lines are deployed – a special skill that I took delight in.

I looked proudly at my painting. The black body had character, like a solid rock with life and soul. The powerful energy emitted could shock anyone, including those who didn't want to face it.

From the excitement of drawing directly from life like this, I regained my confidence. But at the same time, I asked myself: why do people find it so hard to see the meaning in my painting? I carefully asked Djutja what he thought.

'Yeah, good', he said, keeping it simple as usual.

'Really?' After all the arguments at Charles Darwin University, I still wondered whether my work offended Aboriginal people.

Djutja chatted with Yapa who was sitting beside him, in their own language. Although I couldn't understand, from the tone and their expressions, I felt that whatever it was it was serious.

Seeing me looking so nervous, Djutja asked, 'Why you so worried?' He must have noticed my locked eyebrows and anxious face.

'Because people say I can't paint you like this. It is harmful to your image.'

He shook his head and reassured me, 'It's balanda's [white people's] idea again. Why do we have to pretend to be what they like?'

His words made me think of the Chinese artists who were told to paint propaganda posters during the Cultural Revolution: only positive characters and images were allowed. I used to think that such restrictions were found only in China's authoritarian society, but in Darwin I was encountering something quite similar. It was telling me that freedom of artistic creation cannot exist.

'Balanda – too much thinking', Djutja added, holding up a finger towards his nodding head. 'You alright.'

From that I understood that he thought white people's ideas were just too complicated. He liked my painting. With just a few words, he had restored my confidence.

The women now came back one after another. After a short but busy time, everyone settled down to enjoy their catch. Breathing in the wonderful aroma of freshly cooked fish, I relaxed and let my worries disappear.

Yapa moved a palm-sized fish on to a piece of bark, handed it to the person sitting beside her, and pointed at me. She always took good care of me because she was my Yapa.

'Thank you, Yapa', I said as I took the fish. I picked up bits of the flesh and one by one put them in my mouth. The fish had an extra fragrance, coming from the handful of leaves added when it was grilled, so the aroma was baked into the flesh.

Someone brought up a billy of slightly muddy water from the river.

Djutja began to hum a little tune, then gradually his humming turned to singing. The kids got up to play with pandanus nuts. A couple of the women returned to the riverbank, to catch prawns and some more fish. The kids would quickly grab these when they appeared and throw them into the fire. No matter what outsiders might think, everyone here was living happily together as one big family. Regardless of those I had seen earlier who had suffered great hardship and social injustice, troubles that shocked me and drew my sympathy, here I was seeing the satisfaction and happiness of Indigenous people living freely in their own land. This is how life should be for an Aboriginal family.

I often heard people use the word 'primitive' to describe these Aboriginal people, because they live in the desert or in the bush, in conditions that are very different from those in cities. But there is no need for Aboriginal people to become like city folk if they can return to country and once again care for their land. They still have this knowledge and have never lost it.

Looking around me, I thought: this is life, the harmonious family life of Aboriginal people who live in the bush. Why can't I represent this real life that I have experienced in my work? Yet everyone is telling me to avoid drawing these people and to draw something else.

A few weeks earlier, under supervision, I had completed two paintings representing the scars so often seen on Aboriginal people. My classmates were pleased to see me paint something other than Aboriginal people themselves. As I worked, I became perplexed, because the scars on the Aboriginal people are symbols and not ordinary scars. They are made during various ceremonies, including different men's ceremonies, or during sorry business. The men and women used a razor-sharp knife to cut themselves on the chest or on the back, and then perfunctorily rubbed charcoal ash into the wound, which would eventually form a distinct scar. Each has a profound meaning. For example, in Balgo, Western Australia, I saw scars made during the circumcision of seven young children. In other places, scars were made during other initiation ceremonies carried out as youths became men in accordance with Aboriginal law. It is also a very important process when some people go on to become law men.

There are historical records of such scars and of 'scar art' or 'three-dimensional tattoo art' where scars are formed in orderly shapes for purely aesthetic purposes. In the past, some women's scars looked like a string of beads, protruding like shell necklaces. For Aboriginal people, scars are symbols of adulthood, pride or warrior status.

Aboriginal law is the law of this land. It acts to regulate the daily life and conduct of Aboriginal people and has been formed and continued for hundreds of years. To keep this law alive, Aboriginal people to this day hold ceremonies to impart their traditions to new generations, and to encourage everyone to continue and accept Aboriginal law. But in modern Australia, it follows that they live in two different worlds, each bound by different laws. For the younger generations, opposition and conflict between the two systems can cause great confusion.

For many reasons, the scars evoke many stories that are never told to outsiders. So, artists need to be extremely careful in dealing with this subject matter.

Bobby, the young man who had driven away earlier to hunt, came back with a kangaroo. He also had some flying foxes that he had obtained on the way by bartering with people from his mother's family. While talking of his trip, he began cleaning up the kangaroo, squeezing all the faeces out of its buttocks. I saw Djutja quickly dig out two pieces of kidney fat and throw them in his mouth, as if afraid that someone else would get them first.

Soon we were all busy grilling the kangaroo and then sharing a delicious meal.

'Wow, too full', Djutja said, standing up slowly to indicate that it was now time to go home.

The sun was just setting. In the last rays of warm sunshine, a woman held a jar of leftover kangaroo meat on her head with one hand while clasping a child to her waist in her other hand. The men carried shotguns or spears and the children ran behind fighting playfully as everybody walked towards the car. Here was another very beautiful and moving picture. Walking behind them, I couldn't see any reason why they would ever want to leave this beautiful country.

Even such a painting wouldn't escape criticism, this time because it was too romantic. So, how should I paint? What should I paint? It was not that simple.

———≈———

One day an archaeologist named Fred passed by our station together with his assistant. We chatted that night by the campfire. He said that he had heard about me when he was in Darwin, and the issues that people were talking about.

Quite surprised to hear this, I asked what they were saying.

He told me there were various voices, but those from the mainstream were critical.

Then he told me something quite straightforward, something he had pondered over for some time. He said that whenever an artist displays their work in public, it is also important to explain the message conveyed by the artwork. It is no longer possible just to display the artwork itself. In my case, a drawing of an Aboriginal person must be accompanied by something saying whether Aboriginal people recognise it or not. He gave me the example of the famous Australian artist Russell Drysdale. The Aboriginal images in some of his paintings were criticised by art critics. Aboriginal imagery in Arthur Boyd's paintings had also been controversial. Generally speaking, how artworks will be interpreted at any one time depends on the judgement of art critics and other social and cultural leaders.

He went on to explain that our society is complicated. What may be said often depends on who is seen to have the right to speak. To some extent, the bold behaviour of an outsider, a Chinese like me, may be forgiven or even accepted, because what I show can be something that Australians might themselves see or think, but can't say. He thought that some of the people were criticising me for taking advantage of this contradiction to demonstrate what they saw as compassion, but others might call 'political correctness'. Surprisingly, in doing this they still exhibited a persistent cultural superiority or bias. Even at a time when Aboriginal art is collected, admired and displayed, Aboriginal culture continues to be distorted by the dominant intellectual power of the West.

I was very surprised to hear a balanda put forward such a forthright point of view, saying things that I would not dare to say publicly. If I did, I knew what a storm would arise.

'Do we need a Chinese to tell us what to do?', he asked, before hastily adding that these were not his own words but those of people he had been listening to.

I lapsed into silence. I didn't show surprise or anger, because it wasn't the first time that I'd heard something like this even among my own circle of friends. Instead, I wondered: what did Australians think when facing Aboriginal people? I threw this question back at him.

Just like me, he became silent and thoughtful. We both stared into the campfire. The night once again became quiet, with only the occasional sound of branches falling in the fire.

After quite a while, Fred said that of course, Australians all care about Aboriginal people. But there are also many complaints. He explained a lot of this to me, although he feared that I would misunderstand him. I told him that I could summarise his thoughts with three key words: love, hate and fear. This made him again suddenly fall silent. In the dark, we couldn't easily see each other's expressions. We sat there looking into the fire.

Wanting to break the silence, I looked around for something to do. The branches in the fire had all burned down. Finally, Fred spoke, 'These issues are too big and complicated, and I don't want to discuss them any further'. Then he abruptly changed the topic.

'Why do Aboriginal people accept you? It's my impression that this doesn't happen to many people.'

My answer was simple. 'Respect. If you respect others, you will also be respected and accepted by them.'

'What exactly do you do?'

'We eat, live and share together', I replied. This may sound straightforward, but in truth it is not so simple. It is difficult to do this without sincerity and heartfelt respect.

'It seems that you have become more like a participant, that is, like one of them, rather than remaining just a bystander or someone who studies Aboriginal culture, or even scholars who try to observe without prejudice. This is important. I have noticed that you always use the word "we" when you tell stories about your life in the bush. You don't talk about "them".'

I quickly went over in my head what I had been saying to him to see if this was indeed the case.

'That surprised me. I believe that emotionally you've put yourself together with them.'

I began to admire this man in front of me, a man who was almost a stranger, but who, after only a brief conversation, could see into my inner self.

'I'm still curious', he continued, 'when you say "we" do you think there's any difference between you and them? You're not Aboriginal, even though you're very close.'

'There are lots of differences', I replied, 'but that doesn't stop us from being friends and family. Although in colour and culture we are different, we know how to respect each other.' The more knowledge people have, the more complex their thoughts become, and the further they stray from their original nature. The sense of hierarchy grows stronger and even 'care' given in goodwill can become coercive.

'I heard that you were sick, very sick.'

'Are you talking about my hearing?', I asked, 'Yeah, I thought I'd never hear again.' I explained what had happened.

That day, we were returning in the car from a fishing trip. I was sitting in the front seat feeling drowsy. In my daze, I suddenly seemed to see the movement of animals, 'Kangaroo, kangaroo!', I shouted, awakening from my dream. Bobby, who was driving, quickly stopped the car. I wanted to tell him that I had just been dreaming, but he signalled me not to talk. His sharp eyes searched around and quickly found their target. There really was a kangaroo there. I had to admire his fast reaction. Later, he told me that changes in the environment can often be picked up at a quick glance. But if I wanted to be able to do this, I had to become fully integrated into my surroundings.

Bobby slipped a shotgun out from behind his seat and slowly raised it. Looking in the direction in which the gun was pointed, I finally saw two kangaroos among the trees and bushes, their heads raised and motionless. They seemed to be alert, trying to identify the direction of the sound, before running to save their lives.

Seeing Bobby raise his gun, the people in the car quickly covered their ears with their hands. Someone pointed out the gun to me, but by the time I realised what was happening, it was too late to cover my ears. 'Bang!' a deafening gunshot rang out, like an explosion in a huge, enclosed iron barrel. My head went 'boom' and suddenly I couldn't hear. When I got back to camp, I lay on my bed for several days. Yapa looked after me while Djutja sat humming beside me. I wasn't sure if his prayer saved me, but I miraculously recovered.

After listening to my story, Fred said that I had been lucky. 'You're doing something with your life, but is it worth the risk?'

'I don't think about it that much. If it happens, let it happen', I replied.

Fred and his assistant shook their heads, 'It's incredible. Now we think you're becoming a real bushman.'

Sometimes I think so, too. What's wrong with being a bushman? While others might see this life as 'primitive' it doesn't bother me. It is precisely the rich experience of nature that provides infinite inspiration for my artistic work.

'You never regretted it?', Fred asked.

I thought about it and said, 'Yeah, sometimes, I have'. Because I remembered that once I had been abandoned on a deserted island.

The day, I went to fishing with Ngaritj Uloki, son of Johnny Bulunbulun and his companion from Maningrida.

As our boat gradually moved away from the shore after a while, Ngaritj started shouting, 'Unn, we are here… hope we haven't disturbed you'. He was talking to the spirits– he said that he could feel them all around us. With outstretched arms, we all shouted as loudly as we could, 'We're here'.

As the boat slowed down, we relaxed and just let it move as it would with the small waves. I began to feel nauseous, and my excitement was instantly transformed into the extreme discomfort and misery of seasickness. After we discussed my situation, Ngaritj pointed to a small island in the distance and said that he would leave me there and come back to pick me up later. I agreed, as it seemed to be the only sensible option.

When they left me on the island, as the boat slowly drew away, I waved my hand and with my last bit of strength shouted, 'Don't forget me!'

In the middle of the day, the sun hanging over the equator in northern Australia is extremely hot. I soon realised that it wasn't a good sign not to see a single tall tree under which to shelter.

It is not difficult for readers to imagine what happened next. The fear, the unbearable but necessary exposure, is described in many movies. The thought of regret and even death haunts me.

I took off my shirt to cover my head, praying that I would not collapse before Ngaritj returned.

I picked up the fishing line and a few shrimps that Ngaritj had left behind for me, and a bottle of water, found a suitable place, and threw out the fishing line. I tried to settle myself down as much as I could. But I don't know how long it took, my only bottle of water was almost finished. Only one gulp was left. Every sip I took increased my feelings of anxiety and panic. My hands started to go numb, and I began trembling. My brain was slowly becoming blurred… suddenly, I seemed to hear a voice ringing in my ear, 'Wake up, boy. I heard your shout earlier.' I slowly opened my heavy eyelids, proving to myself that I was still alive. I felt a breeze blowing past me. Was this the immortal energy of the divinity? The sea appeared very green, more emerald, a green with a hint of orange. Moreover, the sun was not as scorching as it had been before. Time marches on…

'Gojok.'

After waiting in anxious silence for what felt like an eternity, I heard a voice suddenly call out to me. 'You're finally here. I'll be tanned like a dead fish', I said, turning toward the voice behind me. It was Ngaritj.

'Oh no.' Ngaritj replied that they would never have left me here. The young man standing beside him gave a knowing smile.

'What?', I asked, thinking that I had some idea of what had gone wrong.

As I continued to question them, Ngaritj at last admitted the truth. 'Because we caught a lot of fish, and so happy… we were almost ashore when suddenly we remembered and then hurried back to pick you up.'

Undoubtedly, I was a 'lunatic' in everyone's eyes. Even the two archaeologists said the same thing. But I don't think it's necessarily a bad thing to have the opportunity to do one or two crazy things in one's life.

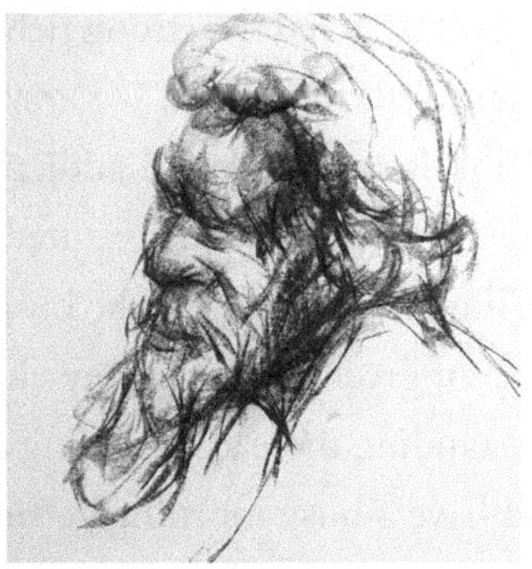

Djutja, Wandawuy outstation, in Arnhem Land.

13

Don't Speak for Me

After around two months, I returned to Art School in Darwin.

Waking up in the morning and finding myself lying in a comfortable bed, where I couldn't see the sky and the familiar bush environment, I felt somewhat lost. For several days, it was like this every morning. I closed my eyes, hoping to recapture feelings of what was happening in the bush. I would take a deep breath, but although beautiful memories flashed into my mind, I couldn't smell the seductive early morning bush air. I needed time to adjust. The sudden dramatic change of environment made me very anxious. As well, my three teachers would be coming to my studio that very morning to examine my progress. I was ready to face another wave of doubt. I knew that in the two months since I had left the school, people had not forgotten all the issues that I had raised. In fact, the discussion had become even more intense.

I got ready and went straight to the studio.

The moment I walked in, I detected the strong rich smell of ink. It was no replacement for the fresh air of the bush, but it too made me feel refreshed. For me, the fragrance of ink is seductive and addictive. After returning to the school, in the previous week or so, I just wanted to lock myself in the studio to work at transferring my feelings for the bush on to canvas.

As I made myself a cup of green tea, Yapa, my eldest sister, appeared in my mind. I imagined her standing there also holding a cup of green tea. She and everybody else would have a busy morning getting ready to go fishing, then they would stay there quietly until sunset, when they would roll up their drop sheets. Thinking of this, I looked at the few paintings I had nailed to the wall. They had been painted with passion over the previous few days. I always like to work on several different paintings at the same time.

I sat down with my cup of tea, to appreciate the paintings on the wall. I felt fulfilled. Whenever I painted something that satisfied me, I would feel this way. The figures in the paintings had been created with strong lines in black ink. Colour was redundant here. Only ink and vigorous lines could properly express my emotions.

I sat facing a large painting about 1.3 metres high and 3 metres wide, with twelve characters portrayed, standing side by side. They were all drawn from life. The first figure, the one with a cross on his chest and a pious look, was a person I had met in Balgo, a man who often held a bible. Next came the card player, who had made me stand behind him to bring him luck. Then there was the *yidaki* player who had tried to teach me how to play this instrument, and then came a footballer, and an artist with a bark painting.

There was another very interesting character, a man wearing a hat and holding a can. His hat was slanted to one side and pressed low on his head, because one of his eyes was wrapped in cloth. This was the artist, David Malangi. Thinking about him, I have another story to tell.

In Ramingining, Arnhem Land, among us was Malangi, a small old man, who I had often seen walking around the community with his hands held behind his back. One time, he approached me with a soup bowl in his hand.

'Where you come from?', he asked.

It seemed that everyone needed to ask the same question, to see if I was a real Chinese, because the likelihood of a Chinese person appearing here was very small.

'China', I told him.

'Welcome here.' He solemnly stretched out his hand towards me. Raising the soup bowl slightly, he said 'very good' in a masterly tone. Then he took out a small cloth bag from his pocket. It was tied so tightly that a lot of effort was needed to get it undone. A silver commemorative coin slipped from the bag into his palm. 'Have you seen this?', he asked in a soft voice, rather mysteriously.

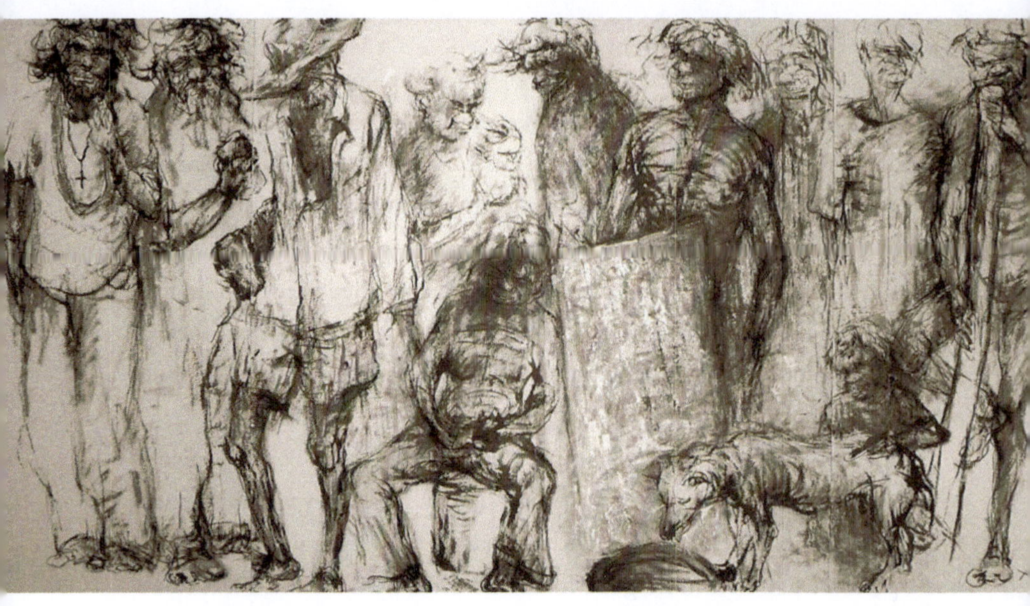

Zhou Xiaoping, *Group Portrait* (1995), ink on rice paper and board, 138 x 272 cm.

'No', I said shaking my head.

'Well, there's a long story here', he said, carefully touching the coin with a meaningful look. 'Do you want to know?'

'Of course.' I wanted to take it to have a closer look, but he just waved it in front of my face, unwilling to let go of it.

Then he briefly told me its story. In April 1964, a panel of experts designed a set of new banknotes and coins for Australia. They included a $1 note featuring several Aboriginal images on one side: a kangaroo, a lizard, a snake, and Mimi spirits – all derived from the rock art of West Arnhem Land. The rest of the design was taken in part from a bark painting by David Malangi, a Yolngu from Arnhem Land. The design team never let Malangi know that they had used his artwork, and they certainly didn't intend to pay him any royalties. Later, 'Nugget' Coombs, the Governor of the Reserve Bank, pointed out that Malangi deserved honour and compensation. So, in 1967 he presented David Malangi with a silver medal, 'in memory of his contribution to the design of the Australian $1 note'. He was also given $1,000 and a fishing kit. As a result, Malangi, proud of his role in designing the $1 note, was dubbed 'Dollar Dave', and honoured as an important Australian artist. In 1996, the Australian National University awarded him an honorary doctorate. He died in 1999 at the age of seventy-two.

To come back to the painting in my studio. All the characters on this painting had been drawn with brush lines in black. But what I didn't expect was that even this painting would draw me into another controversy. The character modelling of David Malangi in the painting was criticised because the tin I had drawn him holding looked like a beer can. This made some white people very angry.

As I was studying my painting, immersed in my memories, I heard someone knocking on the door. Three teachers walked in. They were my supervisor, the Dean of the School of Art, Ray, and Amanda, a lecturer in Art History. I couldn't avoid them. Besides, it can be imagined how much agitated discussion had occurred to bring them all together to see me.

They quickly looked at the paintings in the studio, then almost simultaneously their eyes fell on the large painting. They exchanged uneasy glances. The atmosphere was sombre. I got the impression that our talk would not go well.

My supervisor broke the silence by saying, 'Is this what you want to tell everyone about our Aboriginal people? That this is what they are like? … Especially the character with the beer can.'

I was stunned and slow to react. 'Couldn't it be a soft drink can?', I asked lamely.

He told me that the characters in my painting were clichés. Then, speaking in Chinese, Amanda added, 'Australians don't want to see stereotypical role models like Lei Feng'. She had spent several years living in China and was trying to get me to understand why my paintings were problematical. The soldier Lei Feng, who had died a premature death in his early twenties, was well known for helping other people. During the 1960s and 1970s, he appeared on large billboard posters throughout China as a heroic figure for everyone to emulate.

I told Amanda that I didn't understand the point she was making. What did the propaganda pictures of Lei Feng have to do with my own paintings that were under discussion right now?

She said that my paintings were somewhat similar in presenting stereotype characters, which could, in this case, lead to misunderstanding and even to negative impressions of Indigenous people. 'So, if I were you', she warned, 'I would be very careful'.

Before I had the chance to respond, someone noted that my paintings were like cartoons, and added, 'What exactly are you trying to paint? What is your intention?'

'Intention? It's completely wrong to suggest that my work starts with some specific intention. If you really want an explanation, put it down to the fact that I am purely following my artist's intuition.'

'How much do you know about our Aboriginal people? Are you qualified to paint them?'

It didn't matter now who said what. I clearly heard the message that they were wanting to convey. I understood that they were angry about what I was doing. They had asked about my qualifications, but what criteria were needed for me to be qualified? Was I not qualified to paint? I frowned. Obviously, the tin can that I had pictured in the hand of an Aboriginal person had really upset them.

Ray now pointed to a photo of a group of Aboriginal people that was hanging with some other photos on the wall, 'Where did you get this photo?'

'I took it.'

'How could that happen?', he asked.

My supervisor said, 'I also find it odd that he can go in and out of Arnhem Land so freely and be allowed to take these pictures'.

'It seems that some things we can't do are possible for this Chinese man.'

Listening to them, I wondered: why not? 'Don't they let you take photos?', I asked.

No one answered. I saw them exchange glances.

Ray spoke, 'I can only say that, for whatever reason, you are really very lucky. Not many people have the opportunity like you do. You should cherish it.'

I agreed.

'So, what will you use these photos for?'

'I haven't thought about it yet.'

'You'd better think carefully before showing these photos publicly.'

'Why?'

'It's fine if they're old photos, but obviously they're not. It's inappropriate now to show new photos that don't look much different from the old ones. Won't it give a wrong impression?' Ray added, 'You know what you're doing, don't you?'

I looked at them silently and nodded.

The atmosphere in the studio had become much too serious. I just wanted to grab a beer. To wind things up, Ray looked down at his watch then said to me, 'This is a very special conversation. We all need to think about it, and that means you, too. We will be talking again.'

But before they left, Amanda said to me in Chinese, 'By the way, although I agree with them, as far as my personal preference is concerned, I still appreciate your work'.

After this meeting, I began to think about another question: should there be any restricted or forbidden areas for art?

The artist who, decades ago, painted Aboriginal people as cartoon figures was widely criticised. From that time on, many artists have been very careful to stay away from this bottom line. I asked myself: how was my work anything like the 'ashtray' art of the 1950s?

I recalled the archaeologist's words: when a work is displayed in public, in addition to its nature as a painted object, it will have another meaning, and what kind of information the artwork will convey is very important. Obviously, this was something that I had to think about very seriously.

———— ≋ ————

While painting in the studio one day, I heard someone knocking on the door. On opening the door, I saw a woman standing there. She looked a little serious but was dressed quite casually like most people in Darwin.

'You must be the Chinese artist', she said, and then introduced herself. She was Professor Marcia Langton, who worked in the Department of Aboriginal Studies at the university. Having heard a lot about me, she had come to see for herself what was going on.

Although she had said little so far, her slightly trembling lips showed an inner uneasiness.

She asked if I had known any Aboriginal people before I came to Australia. I told her that I had never heard about them and knew nothing about Australia. Then I briefly described my experience among Aboriginal people, what had happened to me at the Art School and what I thought about when I created my paintings. She mainly listened, occasionally asking one or two questions. Even so, I still felt a powerful aura around us. At the end of our conversation, she announced, 'I like your simplicity, and I don't see anything wrong with you'.

Hearing her say this, I became less nervous and a little excited.

After leaving the studio, she went straight off to find the Dean of the Art School, Ray. They had a long talk behind closed doors.

Two weeks later, the school arranged a seminar to be attended by Masters students together with some lecturers invited by Professor Langton. During the seminar, there was another heated discussion about my paintings. Once again, I explained that my understanding of Aboriginal people was limited to my personal experiences, since I had only arrived in Australia in 1988. My paintings simply expressed what I had experienced. The problem was that these images were not ones that the seminar audience wanted to see, or what they wanted an 'outsider' to see and present to them. Clearly, when an artwork enters the public domain, the message it conveys can be beyond the artist's original intention, but this also depends on the audience's position and perspective.

Art should not constitute someone's ideas of cultural correctness.

At the seminar, some people questioned whether my work contained racially discriminatory content, as the 'ashtray' works had done. To be honest, for a person like me who had just stepped out of a very insular Chinese society, this was all totally unexpected. My mind was like a blank sheet of paper. I was unfamiliar with the words 'racial discrimination' and such thoughts were not in my head when I created my work.

Marcia stated her view that there was nothing in Xiaoping's works that denigrated Aboriginal culture, nor was there any sign of a motive to devalue Aboriginal people. She maintained that my works could not be compared to cartoons. Also, on the contrary, my long-term experience of living with the Aboriginal people had not been achieved by anyone else in the room, 'so, it's ridiculous to accuse him of being a racist'.

When the discussion drew to a close, one of the students commented, 'If we re-examine these works, they are not that bad, and there is evidence that they can be read as a typical case of cross-culturalism. Many artists have been trying to seek creative breakthroughs at the interface of Eastern and Western cultures, or through exposure to different cultural backgrounds. But this is the first time that we have found resonance between Oriental and Aboriginal cultures.'

After the seminar, one of my classmates told me that things were changing. 'No one who was in that room will say that you can't paint along these lines.'

'Why?', I asked.

'Because there are now Aboriginal people standing beside you. No matter how divergent our views are, one thing is important to everyone: the controversy caused by your works will make everyone rethink the issues around using Aboriginal themes.'

Things don't change; what changes is people's minds. Many artists themselves do not have clear answers. Different ideologies lead to different conclusions.

———— ≈ ————

Discussion of my work did not end there.

The following year, in June 1996, a large forum was held in Darwin at the Museum and Art Gallery of the Northern Territory. It was organised by the Northern Territory Centre for Contemporary Art. Professor Marcia Langton, Gawirrin Gumana, Brian Nyinawanga, Djon Mundine, Tracey Moffatt, along with non-Aboriginal artists were invited to come together to discuss a controversial topic: 'How should non-Aboriginal artists represent

Aboriginal subjects?' I only heard about it on the day before the forum. Marcia had told the organiser that the forum was a continuation of the university seminar at which I had been the main protagonist. What was the point of holding such a forum without my presence?

Gawirrin Gumana, a senior artist from Gangan country of northeast Arnhem Land, began the forum by welcoming everyone and making a short keynote speech. He explained to the audience about traditional law and responsibilities laid down in relation to the visual arts. He said, 'We're living in both worlds, Western world, and my own world we live in now… We must be careful ourselves not to be stealing from one another…' Finally, he advised everyone, 'Don't just take "wealth" from our land, but also pay attention to and identify with our culture. Don't deprive our culture, please don't, please.'

Next to speak was Brian Nyinawanga, a senior artist from the Ramingining Centre in Arnhem Land, who told the audience about old ways versus new ways, his own painting, and the obligations of traditional artists to their Aboriginal law.

He was followed by others, then questions were taken from the audience. The atmosphere became very lively. During the discussion, the question of my painting was raised repeatedly. There seemed to be many areas of contention.

First, it was pointed out that my paintings were very skilful, with exquisite brushwork, very Chinese, quite impeccable. Some even seemed a bit romantic. But the more disturbing and embarrassing paintings were too reminiscent of 'ashtray' painting popular in the 1950s, when racist depictions were common, as seen in the work of Eric Jolliffe. But it wasn't clear whether they thought that my work was also racist. Clearly, I had been unaware of Jolliffe's work. In addition to Jolliffe, some of the audience also saw elements of Russell Drysdale and Pro Hart in my paintings, and they wondered: had these shadows all come about simply by coincidence? So, there remained considerable tension in the gathering between admiration for the skilful execution of my artworks and their problematic content – content that reminded people of what Europeans have done in this land.

Second, there was concern about the possible wider impact of this kind of art, and what 'whitefellas' would think when they saw these paintings. Old myths about Aboriginal people's 'primitive' state might be revitalised, leading white people to conclude that this was just how Indigenous people should remain today: wearing no clothes, women's tits flapping everywhere, and men hunting with spears.

A third concern was more broadly about how painting develops from a specific culture. Were Australians too self-centred, blandly accepting long-held views about the history of their settler society? Everyone has their own way of accepting and reading culture. Are we too self-righteous to accept this attempt to use Indigenous themes, just because the artist uses specific ways of Chinese painting and drawing which can look a bit too romantic to us? The way we look at images is always influenced by our own cultural background. There is no overall acceptance of the meaning of various symbols. One speaker brought up the comment that Tracey Moffatt had made about 'ashtray' art and argued that it was 'a very legitimate and interesting remark', because there was a whole history of representation of Indigenous themes by non-Indigenous artists which 'converges with the work that Xiaoping is doing'.

Some people expressed concern about the exoticism of Chinese painting techniques. They felt that the way these paintings were done was being confused with broader attitudes to non-Indigenous use of Aboriginal themes. One person said, 'On the one hand, he's been criticised as being a romantic for simply making things in the bush look fabulous, then he gets shit put on him for doing drawings of Aboriginal people holding green cans. At the same time, he is praised for the exoticism of his Chinese painting techniques.' It was well known that Russell Drysdale had also painted Aboriginal figures. 'Now, by the rules of the art world, these works by Drysdale have no place in art history. His Aboriginal portraits are sympathetic, but ever since Drysdale painted those figures, he hasn't been as popular as before.'

Other people concluded that all the criticism was too much of a fuss. How would people react if Xiaoping depicted white people in same style? Why should he attract all this criticism? Someone argued, 'If we went to

China and painted "chinky ching chong" racist images, like those ashtrays, Chinese people would get offended, too'. A reply came back, 'It's your perception that he's doing that. I don't believe that he's doing that at all.'

Another person disliked what he saw as the romanticism of the paintings, 'If you depict the Aboriginal people sitting on the ground because that's what they do out bush, then that's putting them in a demeaning position, and that's not a good thing. It will be misinterpreted as looking down on the Aboriginal people. How much creative space should an artist have?' Another person chimed in, 'What's wrong with sitting on the ground? We come from the ground, so we do everything from the ground, yeah, and we go back to it. There are more bugs on a carpet than there are on the ground, you know. We sit on the ground in circles, look at and talk to each other; we are all equal. There are no heads, no corners or bends or anything like that involved in the storyline.'

At length, I had to respond to all this discussion. I only made this brief statement: 'First of all, I would like to thank everyone for their comments on my work. It makes me think about all these issues. I have not seen the works of Eric Jolliffe that everyone is talking about, and I do not know who Pro Hart is. Art should stand alone and arise from individual experience. My life in Arnhem Land gave me first-hand creative material. Many of my Aboriginal friends have seen these works, and the feedback I receive has always been: "Maynmak!"

'In my Aboriginal-themed creations, people keep telling me as an artist what to paint and how to paint. Someone told me that I am a Chinese and questioned my qualifications for painting Aboriginal subjects. This really surprised me. I always thought that Australia had a free and open attitude towards creative artists. Narrow and conservative thinking will hinder the development of art in any culture.'

What I wanted to say but didn't dare say at the end of my speech was that some people with love and compassion want to help Aboriginal people, but at the same time they want to move them towards their own way of thinking. It seems there may be nothing wrong with that, but I found that gradually they started taking over decision-making from the

Aboriginal people, sometimes against their will. Australians have never lacked empathy, and each year Australia is one of the world's largest recipients of refugees. But to Aboriginal people, Australians often adopt a condescending attitude, justified by their so-called 'caring' – a noble and civilised word that masks a need to change Aboriginal people. Sadly, this kind of thinking, which I also call 'discrimination', is presented in the guise of introducing 'modern civilisation' to Indigenous people and is widely accepted by Australian society.

I often hear Aboriginal artists say that they don't like whitefellas always telling them what to do. But frustratingly, the voice of power does not belong to those with limited resources, especially in the art world.

In any era, a strong culture will dominate views on art. Whether in China or Australia, the creation of an artist can never be totally free and, although standards may differ, the artist will always be censored or criticised by society.

Later, I created several paintings derived from these thoughts that I hadn't dared to express in public. One was titled *Don't Speak for Me* and was painted on 170 centimetre by 170 centimetre canvas. In the centre was a very common type of white plastic chair, over which was strung a piece of cardboard carrying the words: 'Don't speak for me!' In the background was the desert, with Uluru on the far horizon.

Today, Aboriginal people are still fighting against discrimination for their rights and equal social status.

At the same time, considering the various 'accusations' that I have had to face regarding my work, I am struggling with a social environment that attempts to change and limit an artist's mind.

I finally completed my controversial studies at Charles Darwin University. Later, my classmate who had previously told me that he 'doesn't want to cause trouble' asked, 'Will you continue to paint Aboriginal subjects?' His question demonstrated that he had never understood why I was so persistent with my work, even though he had witnessed the accusations and struggles that I had faced over the previous year.

Of course, I have thought about it a lot; however, the factors of fate and personality are so constructed that I will never give up easily. There is no doubt that this remains a huge challenge in my art career. In the game between individuals and society, my life is a bargaining chip. I am quite aware that while I continue painting in this way, I will always be dogged by controversy, fierce criticism and doubts.

Yet these controversies have helped me to establish my own independent ideas and allowed me to attack old and conservative ways of thinking. I will continue to search for more mature narratives and even better cross-cultural artistic explorations.

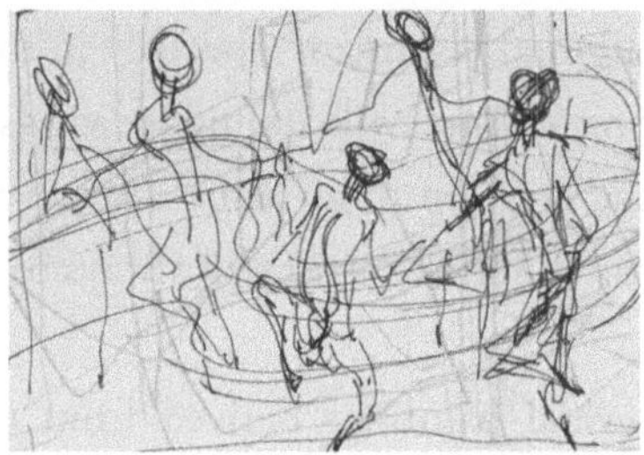

Drawing for a painting.

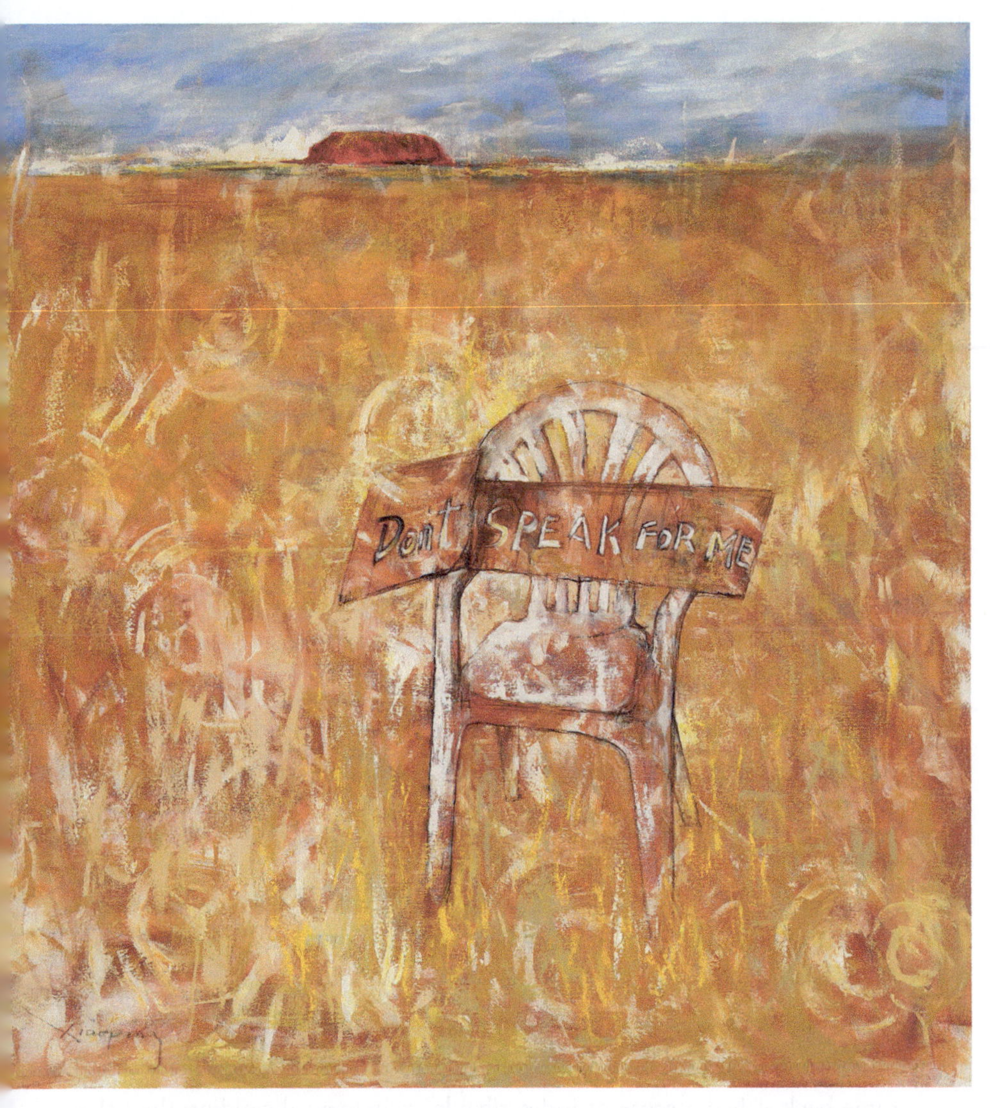

Zhou Xiaoping, *Don't Speak for Me* (2010), acrylic on canvas, 170 x 170 cm.

14

Seeking the Spiritual Tree

'Wamud', Peter shouted to an old man who seemed a little deaf. 'Introduce you to an artist.'

The old man glanced at me, snorted and said, 'Yo'.

Actually, we had met before; maybe he had forgotten.

In 2005, Peter Cooke, who worked for the Northern Territory Aboriginal Land Council, organised an expedition to investigate early Aboriginal settlements in Arnhem Land. The members of the expedition consisted of bushfire experts, anthropologists and several Aboriginal elders including the man standing in front of me. Wamud was his skin name. His full name was Bardayal Nadjamerrek. As an artist, I had also been invited to join the expedition.

From Darwin, our team passed through Jabiru, stopped briefly at the Oenpelli Aboriginal Community where we met Wamud, and then continued towards Arnhem Land.

I wound down the car window, closed my eyes and let the hot wind blow on to my face as I took a few deep breaths of this familiar air. Every time I came back, I had a sense of indescribable excitement, heralding the belief that I was about to learn more about this land and be able to get closer to my emotions. This feeling would persist as I worked on my art.

It was just after the wet season and many areas had been flooded. Our car followed tracks left by another vehicle. The scrub on both sides was more than waist high and indicated that this country had not been burned off for some years, so it was increasingly difficult to control any fires that broke out because they were too fierce. Fire also affected the native animals. Looking around, Wamud sighed, wondering why local people were not taking better care of their country. In his eyes, no part of this land should be forgotten. It also greatly concerned the expedition team.

The road gradually became very poor. Our car swerved about as it crawled and bumped its way along. Often the driver had to avoid fallen trees, and sometimes we had to remove or cut up quite large ones before we could get past.

Suddenly, I yelled out to stop the car. Everyone reacted, asking me what was happening. I felt as if there were countless bugs crawling all over me.

As soon as the car stopped, I jumped out, took off my clothes, and started slapping myself all over my body. Wamud approached me slowly. He put his glasses on the bridge of his nose and, reaching out a hand toward me, said, 'Green ants'. Then he nonchalantly walked away. It turned out that a branch full of ants had hit me through the open car window. These ants were big and fat like a mantis, and hard to distinguish from green leaves.

I scratched my body desperately, as if I wanted to peel my skin off. Wamud reappeared in front of me, holding a leaf carrying many green ants. I thought that he was playing games with me. But I saw in his other hand a plug of hay that he then set alight. He brought the flame close to the ants until they all rolled into small balls to escape the heat and smoke. Wamud then rubbed these ant clumps on to my arms and chest. I felt a burst of heat, which then cooled, relieving the horrible itching. Wamud then picked a few leaves from a tree beside him and told me to boil them and drink the water – bush medicine.

'But be careful about this one. It's poisonous', he warned as he pointed to a very beautiful yellow flower beside him. His people would rub it in the palm of one hand and sprinkle it into a pond to poison the fish.

I asked him if the fish was poisoned like this, could people still eat it?

He said that it poisoned the fish just a little bit. How to use the right amount depends on experience. 'Just be careful', he reminded me, meaning that I should take care if I wasn't sure in the bush.

Before we got back into the car, Wamud instructed the two boys to throw a few sparks into the grass. This looked like something very simple, but Peter said that only Wamud knew how to do it, so that it wouldn't roar up into an uncontrollable fire.

The climate here was divided into dry and wet seasons. From May to October is the dry season, then from November to April of the following year is the wet season, or the monsoon season, often accompanied by big storms.

Fire prevention experts in our inspection team told us that across the year, from May to August is the best time to burn the bush, because at this time the wet season is just over, and all kinds of scrub and flammable grasses are easy to burn as the warmer weather gradually dries them out. When the temperature is at its peak in November and December, it is easy for flammable material to catch alight and start blazing fires. Sometimes spontaneous lightning strikes also cause fires. The most important thing to pay attention to is the wind. Also, fires lit to burn off scrub should only be started in a small area or by the riverside. These controlled burns are used to remove weeds and small trees and shrubs, while the fully formed tall trees in the bush will survive. The experts said that controlled burns should be carried out in the same area only once every three to four years. This protects the local wildlife, as it is important that the bushfires did not destroy their habitat. Otherwise, after a big fire the animals would not return for some time.

While listening to the expert talking, I noticed a look of complacency cross Wamud's face. After decades of experience, Wamud epitomised this ancient practice that respected the land. Aboriginal people believe that if people are to thrive on this land, they must understand and care for it, and this includes caring for all the plants and all the creatures. Only in this way can an interdependence and symbiotic relationship be established and retained.

Wamud began humming a little tune. He made no secret of being relaxed and happy, because we were on the way to his country. Seeing the old man's growing excitement, I was very happy for him. I was also wondering how to extract some stories from this legendary old man.

Wamud mumbled something. Someone asked, 'Can we stop the car?'

'Why?', Peter wanted to know.

'Old man wants to pee.'

'We're nearly there. Just hold for a moment.'

But Wamud said something more which now sounded serious. Everyone laughed. 'He said he is going to pee in his pants', someone else explained.

'Yo, pee in your pants', Peter joked.

'Yeah? You can touch my crotch, wet.'

'Hey, don't pee, I'll stop right now.' Peter immediately said and stopped the car by the river.

Wamud and two other two guys went for a relaxed pee. On their way back, they picked up some branches to make a fire while Wamud looked around. It seemed that we would rest here for a while before we went on our way.

'Want tea?', I asked Wamud as I took out a few cups, a packet of tea, and a jar of sugar from the car.

'Hmm', he replied nonchalantly.

'Don't drink too much, or you'll want me to touch your crotch again', Peter joked. But Wamud just slowly lay down, waiting to be served.

After the water boiled, I made him a cup of black tea, adding two tablespoons of sugar.

'More, and milk', Wamud announced. It seemed that he had been observing my every move.

'Too much sugar, not good', I replied. Nevertheless, I added another flat tablespoon of sugar and two scoops of powdered milk to make the tea just how he wanted it. I put his tea on the ground in front of him. He stirred the tea with a finger that looked like a charred stick, then narrowed his eyes, took a sip, and grinned contentedly.

This made him happy. I asked Peter where we were camping that night.

He glanced at his watch, 'It's almost 6 o'clock now, so it looks like we can't get there before dark'.

I suggested that it would be better to go the following morning. We were all tired and wanted to lie down like Wamud and rest after our long day.

'Yeah, we'll stay if you can cook some delicious food for us tonight', Peter said.

'Is there any rice?', I asked.

Sitting up and squinting his eyes at me, Wamud asked, 'Can you cook it like last time?'

I was pleased to hear this. It meant that he still remembered the fried rice that I had cooked for him the last time we met. I thought he didn't remember me.

'Of course. Without rice, it wouldn't be a Chinese meal', I replied.

'Yo, more', he said, handing me his cup. I filled it up, once again telling him not to have too much sugar.

'Okay', he agreed as he lay down again, humming a little tune.

That night, I did not disappoint him.

'Full, too full', he repeated. Everybody there appreciated my cooking.

After our hard day, we were all tired, so we selected our sleeping spots, spread out our luggage, or set up a small tent to go to bed early.

Although I was tired, I knew that I wouldn't be able to sleep, so I sat staring at the campfire in a daze, as had become my habit.

That night, the bush was very quiet. Very soon there came a faint sound of snoring. I added a few twigs to the fire and set the billy on it, as there was still a little tea left. I then lay on my side on to my swag with a hand supporting my head. Beside me was a sketchbook, because I was always trying to draw or write something.

Looking at the sleeping figure of Wamud, I could see how tall he was. This reminded me that he had an English name, 'Lofty' – a name given to him when he was young by the white owner of the mine where Wamud was working. Not many people knew that Lofty's real name was Badar, but in the bush people still liked to call him Wamud, just like many people liked to call me Gojok.

Wamud was born around 1926 in the Cook Romania area, east of the River Liver, in the wilds of Arnhem Land. When he was a child, he heard about a mining operation that was recruiting people. Apparently, the boss supplied food, and the living conditions were good. So, Wamud and his partner walked hundreds of kilometres to the Maranbe area. In these mines, the Aborigines undertook all the most dangerous and heavy labour, including tree cutting, transport, mining and road building. In return for their blood and sweat, they were given three meals a day. If the boss was kind, they also got a few tobacco leaves or a little sugar. Unable to bear the heavy work, Wamud ran away several times, but was always caught and brought back. He said, 'Since I met these beard officers [white people often grew a beard in those days], I also started to grow a beard. Look at my white hair; it came because I was so worried at that time.' He also learned to speak a little English. Eventually, Wamud escaped and made his way back to his home in Arnhem Land and he never left it again. In the early 1970s, he started painting in exchange for a little food and some tobacco leaves.

He was such an old man now, one who always liked to natter, although no one really understood what he was saying. His friends told me that he had psychic abilities. After living in the bush for some time, exposed to traditional Aboriginal culture, I began to believe this was possible. I had no doubts about the unique powers that Wamud might have.

Gradually, the fire burned down, and my pen slipped from my fingers. Leaves floated in the sky, and fell gently like rain, turning into tall, thin human-like figures. I tried to wave to them, hello… but I couldn't hear my own voice. There was a glow in front of my eyes. I saw many people dancing and singing around the campfire, and one looked like Wamud in full swing. Before I could see them all clearly, they were swept away in a cloud of dust. Then, a gentle breeze dispersed the dust, awakening the flames, and the dancers fluttered like Mimi, sometimes hidden, sometimes present. I raised my hand holding a brush… the night was like a canvas on which I might paint. I couldn't see what I was painting, but I couldn't stop trying to either. I seemed to be half-awake and half in a dream, my painting alternating between reality and fantasy.

When I woke up, it was early morning. Wamud was already sitting there cross-legged with his arms at his side supporting his body. His shoulders were pushed up high towards his head. A pair of glasses with thick lenses hung from his chest. He pursed his raised lips, which seemed tucked closely

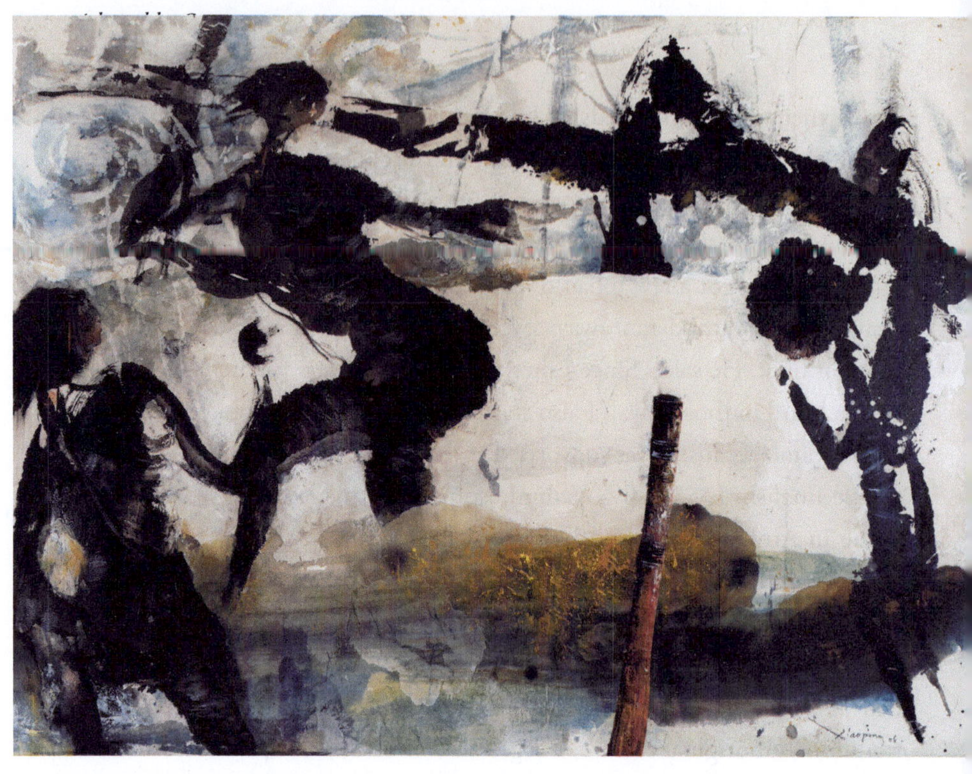

Zhou Xiaoping, *Dancers* (2006), ink, oil on rice paper and canvas, 138 x 175 cm.

under his nose because he had no teeth. On the ground in front of him was my sketchbook, open at some pages where it seemed that I had done drawings of dancers.

Oh, my God! I was stunned. I stared at Wamud in astonishment. Could it be true?

For a while, he said nothing, then pushing the sketchbook toward me, he said, 'Gojok, tea'.

'Yo', I quickly got up and prepared a cup of tea for him.

'Sugar, please.'

Because I was nervous, I had forgotten to add sugar.

'Bread, please.'

'Coming.' I did whatever he asked, like a robot.

Later, as we started to pack up and get ready to move on, I saw him shrugging his shoulders. I was very uneasy as I waited for him to say something about my drawings. His actions and words constantly bemused me. But then Peter brought up the car and, opening the door, said to Wamud, 'Taxi is here, sir'.

Wamud stood up slowly and with just two steps reached the car. He never wasted a bit of energy.

'Thank you', he said solemnly.

Watching this scene, I still felt as if I were dreaming.

When we were in the car, Wamud started mumbling to himself. I wanted to chat with him but couldn't find an opportunity. One problem was that we had to speak very loudly to hear one another. So, we kept quiet in that shaking car for more than an hour.

'Stop!', Wamud suddenly shouted.

'Don't tell me you want me to touch crotch again', laughed Peter.

Wamud ignored him. 'Stop! Out the car!', he shouted more loudly in a commanding tone. Obviously, this time it was not a joke.

When we got out, Wamud raised his voice and said solemnly, 'Here, where you are standing, is my father's country. No balanda [white person] has ever come. I must ask them, before we can go any further.'

He turned around to face the barren bushland, and shouted very loudly in language, then lowered his head to listen.

We all kept quiet. I tried to listen but only heard echoing whistles that sounded like birds far, far away. I looked up to the sky, hoping to spot a few birds flying past, to prove that I was right. But the sky was pure and flawless; nothing else could be seen. Yet as I looked longer, and I heard Wamud's shout turn to singing, strange images came into my mind. I seemed to see another world behind the clouds. Could that be where the whistling had come from?

'You accept them, right?', Wamud asked the spirits of the country, then turning to us he announced, 'They welcome you'. He was acting like a middleman communicating between us and the spirits. 'Forgive me. I haven't come to visit you for a long time. This time I am bringing our grandchildren with me.' He was in dialogue with the earth and its creatures. As he spoke, he again began to sing, spreading his arms wide like wings. He seemed to be flying slowly forward, like some old urchin.

As he chanted, I felt myself brought once again into a wonderful realm. 'Boy, you're back again', I suddenly heard a voice in my ear. Wasn't this the voice that I had heard in Uluru many years ago? It seemed that the message had travelled with me from the desert to Arnhem Land. 'I'm back, I'm back!', I couldn't help myself from shouting out loudly.

'He heard it', Wamud said. 'He's with us.' Having said this, he walked over towards a small creek where we were gathered. He squatted down and scooped up some water, pouring it over his head and body. Scooping again, this time he took a few sips, then walked towards the children, stretched out his neck, and suddenly opened his mouth and sprayed water on them.

Then Wamud told us a story. A long time ago, there was a big river here. Every year when the wet season came, the river flooded this entire area. The crocodiles arrived from upstream and were a big threat to everyone, forcing people to leave their homes. As he remembered it, there used to be a lot of plants here, and mountains formed from piles of stones, not just the flat rocky ground that is here now. There were also many animals, like kangaroos, and he used to like playing with them.

As I listened to him, I looked around but there didn't seem to be any trails or marks from any who had lived here. It was very desolate, but to Wamud that past life was still very vivid.

Fondly he stretched out his arms and touched a big flat rock that seemed to awaken his memories of childhood. He explained that it used to look like a very big bed. He often came here with his companions to play hide-and-seek, and sometimes they stayed overnight. When they did this, they would make a fire to stop their parents getting worried about them.

One time when Wamud was sleeping on this big flat rock with his father, he was awakened during the night by a voice. He saw two people: an old man and a young boy sitting in the dark. He heard the old man telling the boy about the rock: it had been a person before becoming a rock. It was a man who had been killed by a venomous snake. After his death, the man turned into this rock and pressed itself down on top of the venomous snake.

Hearing what Wamud said, we couldn't help touching the rock. I felt a little apprehensive. It was as if I were touching a cold dead corpse.

Wamud continued, 'Before I woke up, I heard the old man tell the boy that he should not talk to anyone about this. But I can tell you', Wamud said, 'because you are all my children'. Then pointing with his fingers, 'Look there…'

When I looked where he was pointing, I saw a mountain in the distance. On the top of the mountain were two strange rocks: one big rock and one small one. I immediately thought of the old man and the boy in Wamud's story. They looked as if they were sitting face-to-face, with the old man's hand pointing up towards the sky, as if he were telling a story to the boy. And Wamud was the boy.

'This is the place where I came the most. Some animals, like wallabies, would play hide-and-seek with me and my companions. They were smart, often it was hard to find them, and they seemed to laugh at us. Here there were also many beautiful flowers and plants, butterflies, river water, um, so beautiful, all things which city-boy, you, like.'

His last few words were directed at me. As he finished speaking, he waved his hand, looking entranced.

Wamud said that sometimes, when he came to this place with his parents to stay a bit longer, they would ask some spirit forms to accompany them. 'Because they can be lonely too, right?'

His humour amused us. 'Did you hear that? I will come back, and take good care of this land', he declared with a voice full of excitement to the spirits. His nostalgia and emotional connection to this place moved everyone deeply.

After this interlude, we kept on walking. Ahead of us was another creek. Wamud walked towards it and took a few sips of water. Turning around, 'Pu…!' – he sprayed a mouthful of water over my face, and it took me a moment to get over the shock. 'They like you and want you to visit them often', he said. Then pointing to my sketchbook, he explained, 'You have already seen them'.

I felt like I had just been baptised. I just stared at him, not knowing what to say.

'Let's go, they [the spirits] are calling us', he said.

I was stunned. I tried to recall how the ethereal images that I had seen in my dreams the night before could have appeared in my sketchbook. Surely, there was no clear explanation.

Thinking this over, we came to a place called Marlkawo. It was still 20 kilometres away from our destination, but it had the advantage of the land around being very open and convenient for helicopters to land. Over the next few days, our expedition would use helicopters because some of the places where we were going were not easily accessible by car.

Peter decided to set up our head camp here.

The first thing we did was to clean up the site and burn off surrounding weeds to keep away any bugs or poisonous snakes that could do us harm. Then we chopped down some trees to build a large tent, more than 30 square metres. This would be our meeting place and kitchen. All kinds of food, mainly in cans, were lined up on simple crude shelves. So behind us was not a map, but a colourful array of product labels on food jars. Various kinds of communication equipment and computers were placed on the long work bench, leaving only a little space free, which was soon occupied by yet more foodstuff. Later, Peter had to put his maps on the ground instead of on the table or the wall.

We then dug a deep pit to use as a toilet. Every day, someone put a few handfuls of lime into it to keep flies away. Later, we also built a shower room surrounded with sackcloth. A big empty rubbish bin was filled up with river water. We used this for washing, so that our soap did not pollute the river water and harm people living downstream. All these arrangements might seem rudimentary, but for us, it made for a luxurious living facility.

In our first two weeks, we mainly inspected places nearby. I asked Wamud how many years it had been since he'd been back – two or three? He just hummed with his finger up, not giving me a specific reply. To him, time was just a number, but the important thing was that he was back.

Aboriginal people accompanied us on each of our inspections. The experts with us made records based on the stories they told us. One question of interest was: why had these Aboriginal people moved from their home? Someone wondered about climate change. Had more severe flooding during the wet season forced them to find better places to live?

One day, the expedition went by helicopter to revisit these abandoned sites. I was carried up into the sky with Wamud and two local Aboriginals. From the air, it was clear after looking at the flat land, the trees and the rivers, that some areas would be easily covered by floodwater. I saw a plume of smoke rising in the distance, indicating that people still lived there. To this day, these small groups remain detached from the outside world, their culture still carrying the secrets of their nation.

For me, this is a place full of spirituality and mystery. I heard an unsubstantiated story, that long ago, many people came to Arnhem Land to search for treasure, hoping to find gold like that found in the southern state of Victoria. These goldseekers came and went, leaving empty-handed. The harsh living conditions were too much, and they gave up their dreams of treasure. But the locals claimed that these dreams were not without some foundation. After assessing the geological features of Arnhem Land, both geologists and geomantic (fengshui) masters have expressed the view that this land could contain the world's largest cache of unexploited minerals. Legend has it that someone once saw a golden light extending over the dense bush for more than ten minutes. The amazing thing was that, thirty years later, this spectacle occurred again. Were science and the supernatural reaching the same conclusion at the same time, adding to the mystery of this land?

I heard Wamud telling the pilot to go down.

'Yes, it's here', a young man named Shane shouted.

After landing, everyone, including the old man, jumped out happy and excited, as if they were returning home. They opened their arms out wide and ran around shouting like loved ones who had been away for a very long time.

Yet here, to my eyes, apart from trees, rocks and a small, dry pond, there were no traces of past life. There were only memories which would never be erased.

'I'm back', shouted Shane running towards me, happy and excited and breaking into native language. 'I'm back, you know.' Grabbing my hand, he tried eagerly to describe everything around us. 'There's still a cracked riverbed over there. Come on, I want to show it to you.'

This was his mother's country. The last time he had come here with his Mum, he was only ten years old. In the past there was plenty of rain, and the fishing and hunting were good, providing the main means of survival. Later, a crocodile came from upstream and took a fancy to the place. Soon the river became home to several small crocodiles. One day some children were playing in the water when they encountered a crocodile, and they all fled in terror. At first, the grown-ups tried to fight against these little crocodiles, but then decided not to mess with them. For some years, they were fine, but since that time, everyone became afraid of the crocodiles. Adults would often use the crocodile to scare their crying children, saying, 'Cry again, and the crocodiles will come out'.

Shane said, 'But we were still scared, worried that they would get angry and hurt us. So, in the end, we were forced to give up the place to the crocodiles.'

But Wamud didn't see things as simply as Shane did. He explained that there are some places that his people cannot and should not occupy – an important statement that can be explored for its very deep meaning.

Wamud was an elder, a wise man. He believed that human beings are just visitors to the world. If the world were without people, everything else – the air, the land, the water and the sky – would continue to live on as nature with all its life and beauty. However, human existence would be meaningless without these.

Years later, in 2019, Wamud's ideas seemed to have assumed greater meaning than ever. During the global coronavirus epidemic, New York fell silent, Melbourne became a ghost town, hugs and kisses were suddenly turned into weapons that could hurt someone, and not visiting one's parents and friends became an act of love. Power, beauty and money cannot buy air for human survival. We are not the masters of the world.

Back then in the bush, we found the original riverbed dry and cracked. It was almost impossible to distinguish the boundary between the land and the river. The crocodiles had gone elsewhere to play. Even so, Wamud's words reminded us that sometimes these crocodiles could be spirit incarnations, and human beings might well be too weak to fight against them.

———————≈———————

Wamud's wife arrived two weeks later and was accompanied by a group of children. Our camp suddenly became very lively. Every night, we needed three or four people to cook in the kitchen, and a second group to do the washing up. Sometimes neighbours from other outstations came to stay for a few days. At its peak, our camp held about forty people. With so many there, our stores of food began to run low. Wamud told Roger to take the bigger boys out to hunt.

Roger came from another outstation. He had seen our fire and came to join us.

'Gojok, you go too', Wamud commanded, throwing me a shotgun.

'Yeah, sir.' I went along with Roger.

'You don't treat him as an outsider, yeah?', I heard someone say behind my back. Everyone laughed.

We thought that we didn't want to walk too far, and before long, we were lucky to come across two wild pigs. It seemed that we would have a pretty good day, but things often turn out in ways that are unexpected.

'Gojok, yo!' I realised that Roger was giving me the chance to shoot a wild pig.

I raised my gun and heard the crisp sound of gunfire echo through the bush. I seem to have killed the pig. But Roger wasn't interested in collecting it. He said that we could pick it up on the way back. He also said that wild pig was not very tasty. They killed the animals mainly because pigs liked to dig holes and destroyed the surrounding environment.

Roger told me to keep my eyes open for kangaroos, because that was what he and everyone else really wanted. I think he knew that kangaroos would not be stupid enough to come so close to our camp. If we wanted to hunt them, we would have to go further away. This wasn't a problem. For a time, we talked and laughed in the usual way. But after a while, we became quiet. It was too hot to talk.

I just followed the others, trying not to wear myself out by thinking too much. Thinking always makes me more tired than physical work. I prefer to leave my heavy thoughts behind in my studio.

Further on, we came to a river. Roger suddenly motioned everyone not to make any noise. He walked quietly into the river alone, with his spear raised high above his head, his eyes alert and searching around.

Suddenly, the spear flew swiftly from his hand, struck the water, and next I saw the spear shaft shaking violently. Roger immediately signalled us to keep still. Walking carefully, he reached over to pull up his spear: there was a big fish, 35 centimetres long, hanging there. Once again, he watched the surface of the water for a minute, and his spear flew 4–5 metres before a burst of water splashed. It was another one.

We made a fire on the spot and buried two fish in the hot sand, ready for our next meal. When the fish was cooked, I carefully separated the flesh from the sandy skin and rapidly swallowed it.

I asked Roger how it was that he could see a fish from so far away and cast a spear at it so well. He said that it's done by feeling and experience, nothing else. This was the living skill of a bushman using his highly developed senses of hearing and vision.

As we were enjoying our meal, Roger suddenly stopped talking, holding himself alert to something. Following his gaze, I saw two buffaloes, one big and one small, in the distance – perhaps the smell of fish had attracted them? It seemed that our luck was in. Roger pointed to my gun and made a negative gesture. From this I understood that this time, he wanted to shoot the big buffalo himself.

Bending forward from the waist, Roger moved cautiously towards the animal. When he thought he was close enough, he raised his gun, and the crisp sound of gunfire echoed through the bush. It sent a happy message to the camp. As the big buffalo rushed forward and fell, the younger one fled in desperation.

There was now plenty of work for a skilful hunter to do. Roger first sharpened a knife carefully on a stone, wanting to be well prepared for the task ahead. The knife was then plunged into the neck of the buffalo, causing a stream of blood to gush out. After this bloodletting came the task of peeling off the skin and cutting away the meat. Roger's knife separated bone and flesh without any hesitation. After cutting off the two hind legs and removing meat until the skeleton of the trunk was well exposed, Roger finally opened the abdomen. The knife went in as if bursting a balloon, and an instant later, all the internal organs poured out. Roger removed only the heart and the liver, giving them to another young boy to wrap in leaves. By this time, Roger was gasping a little, for this was heavy work. He then asked two big boys to pry open the buffalo's mouth so that he could take the tongue. Finally, he remembered to cut off the two buffalo horns for me.

I found hunting very exciting, but walking in the bush for a long time without catching anything can be very tedious and exhausting. Then on the other hand, if we were successful with our hunt, we would have to carry the heavy carcass back to camp, which was why we so often took the car. If we had to walk back with our kill, we would cut a hole through the carcass and hang it around our necks. In such a bloody 'meat dress' we would look terrifying, as if we had been flayed alive. Sometimes we would hang the meat up on a branch, but after a while in those warm temperatures, it would give off an awful smell and attract many flies. It didn't take long before the buffalo skeleton was covered with enormous numbers of flies and mosquitoes making a noise like a weaving machine in a textile factory. The strong smell would also soon attract birds, small carnivorous animals, and other bush scavengers like large lizards. Last to arrive would be large families of ants.

Although we removed less than half of the meat from the buffalo, it was enough to last us several days. As we found our way back to camp, I couldn't help thinking about how I would cook slices of buffalo meat with carrots to make a delicious Chinese meal that night. A few young Aborigines helped me with these preparations, washing and slicing vegetables that were not usually eaten in the bush. So that night, I was able to show off my cooking talent again. After this, every few days Wamud would ask me, 'Tonight, you cook?'

————— ≈ —————

It was early morning and soft rays of sun lit up Wamud's face where he was sitting near the campfire. Everyone was busy making coffee for breakfast. I made myself some tea from Chinese tea leaves dropped into an empty jam jar. Part of the reason I did this was to remind myself always to drink boiled water. Over the past few days, some people in the team including myself had suffered some stomach upset. I suspected the water. It was crystal clear, swift-flowing river water, but we couldn't be sure that it hadn't been polluted upstream with rotten food or animal droppings. One of us began to have diarrhoea. Usually, after taking pills and resting for a day or two, the problem would be gone, but this man did not get better. After three days of high fever, his condition deteriorated rapidly, and blood appeared in his stools. A helicopter took him to Darwin Hospital, where he was found to have a severe gastrointestinal infection. Despite treatment with several different medications, he remained ill, and was transferred south to Adelaide where he recovered only after much specialist medical treatment. So, I was aware that water must be boiled before drinking. Even so, it was not an easy task to do every day. The local people, however, seem more able to adapt to the diet and living conditions, although clearly, long-term consumption of spoiled food is not good for anybody, that's for sure.

A big noise suddenly erupted behind me. Two dogs were raising a cloud of dust; they were fighting and biting each other and interrupting my train of thought. 'Sha!', someone drove them away. Our kitchen was a gathering place. I noticed that about a week after we had set the camp here, a layer of fine dust had settled over everything. Whenever a gust of wind blew, it picked up a cloud of sand.

Wamud had been sitting quietly for some time. There was not a word from him, none of his constant nattering. Usually when he saw me get up, he would say 'Good morning' and then 'Tea, please'. What was wrong with him today? It felt strange.

After a while, I heard him ask, 'When we go?'

'Let me finish my coffee, then go', Peter replied. He took his coffee-making seriously.

I looked at Wamud and realised that he was asking Peter why this was important.

Peter explained that the coffee was a special part of his day. It made a big difference to how he started work. So, Peter was very particular about the preparation of his coffee. He used high-quality beans, and his coffee was always freshly brewed on the campfire, taken without milk or sugar. He would sit there sipping his coffee for about twenty minutes, until the caffeine kicked in, and only then did he start his non-stop work. Often, he ate only one proper meal during the day. Everyone in this team worked very hard.

On this day, I watched Peter finish his coffee hurriedly – the only time that I ever saw him do so.

On most days, after Peter had enjoyed his coffee, he made a phone call via satellite to his colleagues in Darwin, to report our location and movements. As expedition leader, he would ask people from several nearby Aboriginal outstations about the local road conditions and any sorry business and things like that we should know about that were happening in their area. If the outside world did not receive our reports for several days, they would start search measures immediately.

Before concluding the call this time, the person at the other end of the phone told Peter that a government minister was visiting Darwin that day. He had heard about our inspection project and hoped to come in to convey his support.

Wamud said, 'Too busy, coming another day'.

Someone else joked that the minister was our boss. We couldn't ignore him.

'He your boss, not mine', Wamud replied, making everyone laugh.

'The real boss is here', Peter announced as he spread a map on the ground.

During the past three weeks, I had watched as this map was gradually annotated with dense marks and text. Our experts discussed things like the approximate year when the last Aboriginal people had left certain places and they asked the reason for such departures. Could these places be rebuilt? Were there any secret places in the surrounding area?

Each morning, Peter would assign tasks for everyone. That day, some people were coming with him and Wamud to find a place with a big tree. It sounded like a very specific spot. We were told repeatedly not to take any pictures there without permission. Clearly, we were going to a secret place. Wamud said that he had been dreaming a lot over the past few days. In his dreams, he was told that our presence might disrupt the usual life of the local spirits. Our cameras and flashes could kill them.

After we had received our instructions, I set off with Wamud.

Our car was driving where nobody had ever driven before. This was evident from the bush and the absence of any car tracks on the soil. After about half an hour, Wamud told Peter to stop the car. He wanted to walk, stand on the land, touch the trees, and talk to the spirits whose presence he could feel. Doing this would help him to find the tree. After a while, he jumped back into the car, and we continued driving. But not long after, Wamud asked Peter to stop the car again. It seemed that he hadn't visited this place for a long time.

'Shh, turn off the engine', he said, putting a hand behind his ear and listening hard.

'Hear it? Water.' The old man shouted in surprise, 'Yes, it's here'.

I was also listening intently, but all I could hear was the sound of leaves falling and dead branches dropping.

Then I saw Wamud suddenly rushing off towards the left, chanting incessantly, louder and faster. He must have found something. No one thought that the old man could run between the trees so quickly. He had the agility of a hunter. We followed closely, careful not to lose him.

'I'm back!', he was shouting. 'Don't reject my friends… they can't hear you and they can't see you, but they know you hide behind trees and rocks.'

He started singing again.

There was no need for a stage. The performance of a real opera was happening right here in the bush, with an audience of spirits that we couldn't see.

Wamud stopped at a small shallow creek that was covered by leaves and wound between a few big trees before disappearing into the depths of the bush. It would have been almost impossible to find, but its presence was what the old man had been looking for. 'Yes, we are here, it's not far', he told us. Then he leaned down, taking up some water before spraying it out of his mouth like a child. We were told to do the same.

It indicated that we were spiritually connected to this land.

Then I heard Wamud saying, 'Don't go, wait for me'. He charged off in pursuit of the spirit 'audiences'.

We followed him closely, but no matter how hard we tried, we couldn't keep up. His figure disappeared into the trees. All we could hear was an occasional sound. These sounds became more and more remote, as if coming from another world. Was the noise coming from the old man or the mysterious 'audiences'? We ran blindly around in different directions, trying to trace it, only to return to our original starting place.

'Don't move', Roger told us, which was exactly what Wamud had said.

Like robots, we stopped and listened intently. I seemed to hear birds calling and pointed my finger in that direction. Roger shook his head.

'Woo, woo', I heard it again. Before I could react, Roger suddenly turned and ran, followed by the others. I didn't know if we were chasing or avoiding the sound. It seemed very strange.

At length, the sound became more and more clear, and then suddenly it stopped. Everything was extraordinarily quiet, except for the gentle soughing of the wind and the falling of the leaves. We moved gently, until a touching scene was revealed. Wamud stood before a great tree about 4 metres tall. The trunk was mutilated and only half the bark remained. It looked like a hollowed-out old man, bowing and leaning over. Many branches were almost dead. It seemed as if only a gentle pat might cause this frail old tree to topple over. I hadn't expected that this tree from the old man's mind would appear in front of us. Wamud, with tears on his cheeks, stretched out his slightly trembling hands and released his inner sadness, 'Waaa…' His long cry echoed in the bush. A flock of birds flew across the sky with cries attracting other birds which hovered above our heads. Wamud's heart-piercing howl resonated among us as he awakened all the spirits to listen to his story.

Wamud continued speaking and listening to the 'big tree'. They were like two persons reunited after a long absence, with endless things to say to each other. We watched Wamud silently, but it felt as if only the 'big tree' could truly understand him at that moment.

I asked a boy named Kevin, who standing beside me, what Wamud was talking about. Kevin explained that the old man was very sad to see the sorry state of the tree and its desolate surroundings. He was going to move back here and never leave the tree again.

Wamud's daughter, Kevin's mother, used to like to play under the tree, and regarded it as a close friend. Whenever she was bullied by other children, she would run to the big tree and cry out her grievances. Later, after she had grown up and then died while only a young mother, the tree became a symbol that made everyone, especially Wamud, very sad. For a long time, he used to sing under the tree every day for his daughter. She and the tree became as one in his heart, and often appeared in his dreams.

Suddenly, my eyes lit up, because I spotted a new leaf sprouting from the top of the decaying tree. 'Look, look, there is a new green leaf', I told Kevin with great excitement.

'He saw it, too, so he was very sad', Kevin replied. He told me that Wamud had told him that when this new leaf had withered, it would be the time for him to leave this world. After that, the 'big tree' would remain as a reminder to his family.

Wamud grabbed a bunch of leafy branches and gently patted the tree with it. His touch was gentle, as though touching a beloved person. Seeing this, we began to cry. Everyone was sad at what had happened to the 'big tree', but their tears were mixed with pride at its tenacity.

Finally, Wamud told me, Kevin and another boy to clean away weeds growing around the tree. Because we all were of the same skin group', and we were the only ones allowed to touch this special spiritual tree.

As we cleared away the weeds, Wamud led everyone around the 'big tree' singing loudly. This was a symphony made by people and spirits, a tribute to the ancestors, and a testimony to the continuing co-existence of life and spirits on this land. It brought together culture, emotions and life.

After that, everyone reluctantly said goodbye.

'Bo… Bo…', we joined Wamud as he said a temporary farewell to the tree, the spirits that gathered here, and all the creatures on this land.

The chant sounded again, accompanied by sounds full of excitement and joy. We waved to our unseen 'audiences' and we shouted again loudly, 'Bo… Bo…'

Before the sound had died away, a deep long sound was suddenly heard in the bush, as if in response to us. I was completely amazed to hear this long, bird-like chirping that swirled around us.

A lot of my artistic inspiration has come from experiences like this.

———≈———

The team's inspection work had been carried out in an orderly manner for more than a month.

On this day, I felt a little tired and stayed behind in the camp to wash myself and my clothes. I had caught a glimpse of a scary face in the rear-view mirror of the car, a face that was dark, starkly bony and bearded. I couldn't help wiping the mirror, giving a wry smile, and telling myself that maybe it was time to fix up this terrible face. So, I took some soap and my razors down to the river. It was only in Melbourne, and not here, that I shaved every day.

I dipped the soap in my water jug, smeared it on my face and looked for somewhere to prop up my broken mirror. Then I saw a little girl standing near me, staring curiously.

'Could you do me a favour?', I asked. 'Hold this mirror for me.'

Without speaking, she held the mirror in front of me with her small hand.

'Where are the other children?'

'Hunting.'

'Why you not go?'

She said nothing, still staring at me with her large eyes in her small black face.

'Have you been to Darwin?'

Again, no reply.

Suddenly, she asked softly, 'Can I touch it?'

'What? My face?' I was stunned but stretched my face towards her. Timidly she reached out her little hand and smiling, touched my face.

'Gojok', came a voice from the distance. Wamud was waving to me, and he must have been there a while. Raising his head, he pointed to his chin, 'Me too'.

I laughed, 'Yo, wait a moment'.

After my careful efforts shaving, my dark thin face didn't look quite so tired and terrible. I looked in the mirror and raised the corner of my mouth in a big smile.

I packed up my things and went over to shave Wamud.

When I bent in front of him, all ready to start, I hesitated, staring at his face unable to proceed.

'Come on, start', he said.

I kept looking at his face not knowing where to start. This was the first time for me to shave someone else.

'What's wrong?', Wamud asked, opening his eyes.

All right, I told him, I was going to start. I rubbed soap on his long wiry beard. Because of his constant runny nose, the beard under his nose was glued together like a sugarcane field. He tilted his head up, opened one eye slightly, hummed a little tune, enjoying the moment.

We heard a plane somewhere above us. Wamud pointed to the sky, saying, 'I will take it back to Jabiru, tomorrow'.

'You're so virile and energetic, you could date a woman tomorrow', I joked.

He grinned, 'Ma, you, too'.

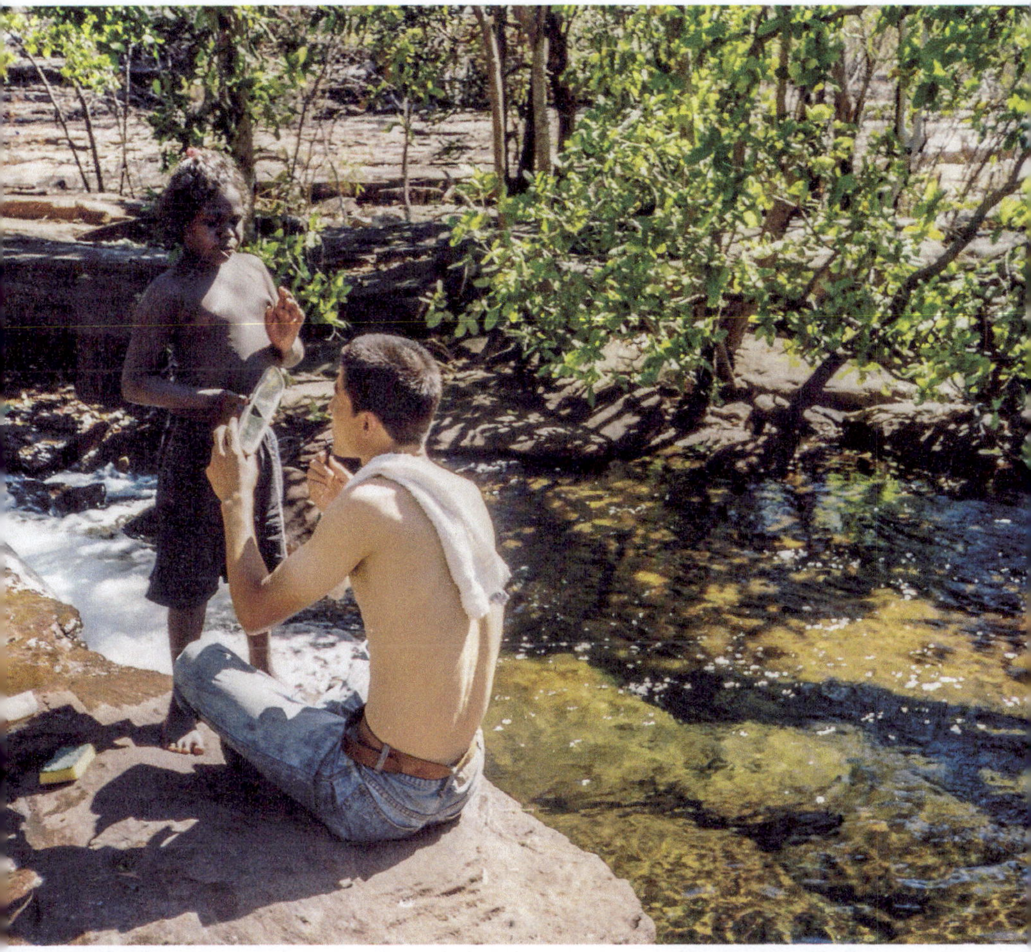

As I shaved by the river, a girl held up a rear-view mirror which we had taken off the car.

Then lowering his voice and speaking in a whisper that even the spirits couldn't hear, he said, 'I'm going to find you a woman'. His mouth was almost touching my ear. 'Yes, tonight', he added seriously.

We laughed.

After his shave, Wamud was not only looking refreshed, but he was also in a much better mood.

'Want tea?', I asked.

'Ma', he replied quite casually.

Every day, most of the time, Wamud was always sitting or lying down.

When he needed anything, he would call me, 'Smoke, Gojok… Toilet paper, Gojok… Hungry, Gojok…' Whenever we had a meal, he was always the first to be served with food. I would present it to him formally, saying in jest, 'Please, my honourable emperor'.

———≈———

I have great respect for Peter, who has been one of the most influential mentors in my journey.

The first part of Peter's study had been completed satisfactorily. The full programme was to be phased out over three years. During the second year, a new outstation was established in Manmoyi that allowed Wamud to settle near his spiritual tree and to live happily, re-imagining the days of his youth.

It touched me that the old man was still talking about me as Gojok. He told the people around him that the next time I came there, he would take me to see some newly discovered rock paintings.

Wamud died in 2010, at the age of eighty-three.

For me, the story of Wamud confirms the real relationships between man, nature and the spirit world. To respect and maintain this interdependence, Aboriginal people celebrate their knowledge and pass it on through the enactment of various ceremonies.

Every time I tell these stories, I feel that I have made a journey back to ancient times. Everything that happened in ancient times is still circulating in this country.

'Dreaming' exists not only in the past, but also in the present and the future. It transcends the constraints of time and space. Therefore, the story of the 'Dreamtime' can be thought of as a kind of 'wealth' that is carefully preserved in the hearts of Aboriginal people. At the same time, it also exists in the divinity of the spiritual world, even if it is difficult for human beings to comprehend and explain this. Divinity is a mysterious energy that transcends rational human thought. The land is the only reality that Aboriginal people have, which is both created and owned by the divinity.

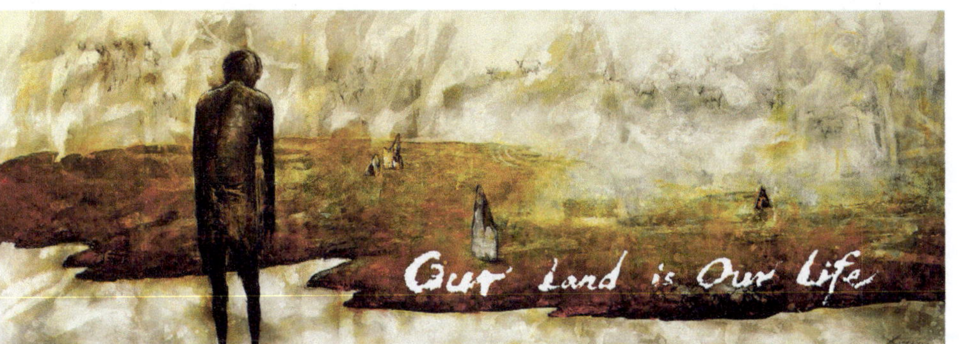

Zhou Xiaoping, *Our Land Is Our Life* (2007), ink, oil on rice paper and canvas, 180 x 540 cm.

Therefore, while people own the land, the land also owns the people. From this, it is not difficult for us to understand how important the meaning of land is to the Aboriginal people.

Our land is our life.

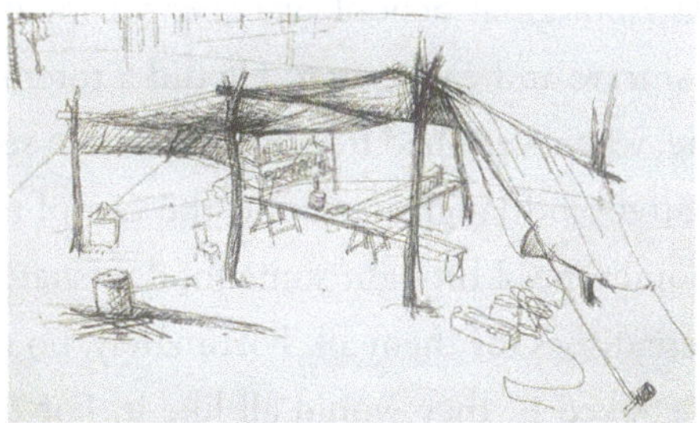

Our camp, Marlkawo outstation, in Arnhem Land.

15

My Brother, Bulunbulun

My story with Johnny Bulunbulun can be told in several parts. Over the years, I formed with him one of the closest relationships that I ever had with an Aboriginal person. As he so often said, 'We are family'. I knew that this was not just politeness. He meant it.

Bulunbulun and I first met back in the early 1990s, when I visited Arnhem Land for the second time. Then later, when I was artist-in-residence at the Maningrida Aboriginal School, we spent a lot of time together. I found him quiet, sincere and easy-going. He did a totem bark painting for me. From that time, whenever I had free time, I went to see Bulunbulun and his family. We chatted and laughed around the campfire like members of the same family. Sometimes I brought some food to share, and sometimes I would cook Chinese dishes for them all. Fortunately, no matter how simple the meal, if I had cooked it, they would all like it. For me, cooking is like painting: I don't like repetition, which meant that I always cooked each dish a little differently. I would cook up a pot of braised fish seasoned with soy sauce and sugar, whereas usually they would just grill their fish on a campfire. If I had any vinegar, I would add this to make this Chinese dish more authentic. Everyone liked to watch me cooking and naturally they would ask me a lot of questions about Chinese meals and things to do with China. After hearing my stories, they said that they wanted me to take them to China. 'We want to go tomorrow.'

Bulunbulun said that he would have to take me to Gamudi outstation for a few days before we could go to China. He mentioned this repeatedly, so one day I took a few days off from teaching at the school and went on a trip with him.

Bush people, like city people, sometimes travel from their home to return to places where they were born and grew up. Chinese people too will go, from time to time, to see their old hometown. This kind of emotional attachment to one's early environment is not just something found among Aboriginal people.

On the morning when I woke up and started to pack for my trip with Bulunbulun, I soon realised that I didn't have much to pack. I needed only my backpack, a change of clothing, my sketchbook and my camera. My swag was neatly tied and lying in the corner, ready to go with me. I always come and go very simply. Travelling like this has become my norm.

'Beep, beep!', a car horn sounded.

I grabbed my cowboy hat, tied it on my head and picked up my backpack and swag. But as I stepped outside, I was shocked by the scene I encountered. Oh, my God, what is this? There were two cars, one with a mattress, three swags and several large travel bags tied on to the roof, while from the front bumper hung a billy, pots and pans and lots of other stuff. It was just like a gypsy caravan that I had once seen in a movie. The second car was even more terrifying. It was completely covered with a layer of white mud, the only clear area being a piece of the windscreen. It was not difficult to imagine what a crazy journey the driver must have been through. I immediately thought that if I could only put these cars in an art gallery, what great artworks they would be. For an artist, anything can be art, when given some thought and perspective. From the open car windows, two dogs barked at me as if telling me to hurry up. I saw that the car was already full of people. They didn't seem surprised; for them, this was all perfectly normal. Relax, life's just like this – it's an attitude that I envy.

Sometimes I wonder what would happen if I chose to live permanently in the bush with these people. I would get this feeling of peace and comfort, but then become uncertain about what I want to do. I would forget that I remain an artist, but can artists ever really disengage from their society? Can I abandon the temptation of fame and fortune to return to being a bushman?

After leaving the community, our artistic car drove along the 'highway'. Bulunbulun didn't dare to drive fast with the car looking like this. However, when we got off the 'highway' and drove along a riverbed where the mud was dried and cracked like giant fish scales, Bulunbulun couldn't help speeding up, and I became quite worried that this great piece of 'car art' would be destroyed.

I kept saying, 'This is crazy. Awesome.'

'You mean the car?'

'Yeah, don't you think?'

'Maybe, we can paint it, together. Yeah?'

'Using acrylic paint on iron instead of ochre on bark, why not? Then will you let me drive the car away?', I asked.

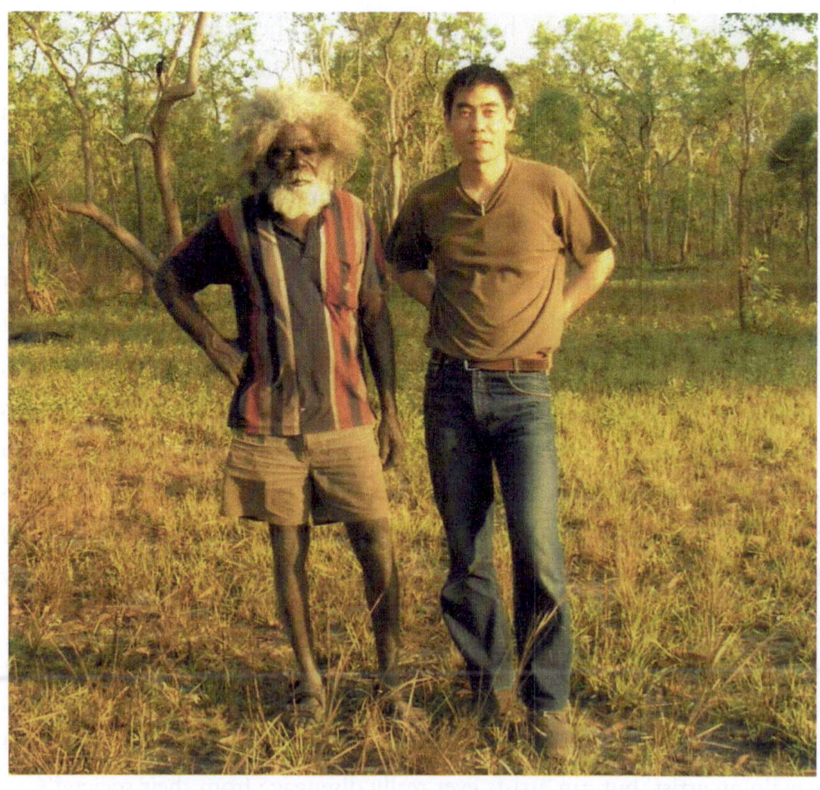

Johnny Bulunbulun and Zhou Xiaoping, Arnhem Land, 2008.

'No, when it becomes scrap metal, then you can have it, like those cars on the side of the road.'

Beside the 'highway' I had seen several abandoned cars. In earlier times this was uncommon, but now derelict cars could be seen everywhere I went, and many outstations were surrounded by them. Obviously, the era of hunting with spears and on foot had long passed.

'You got money?'

'Do you think I'm a rich?'

Listen to me, he has a smile on his face. I remembered a few days ago, a fellow teacher had pinned a notice to the door of the teachers' lounge at the school: 'In order to assist our Chinese artist to continue his journey, those who are interested can buy his sketches for $50 each. Thank you.' Eventually, I sold quite a few drawings, with some teachers buying two or three at a time.

The idea of working with Aboriginal artists had been in my mind for a long time. But how to cooperate on an artwork was a big challenge because of the large differences in cultural and artistic expression, especially for an artist like Bulunbulun. On the other hand, this was potentially a point of great interest. Art for me must probe into areas that other people have not dared to think of, and extend one's thinking into an infinitely vast new space for creativity. To break down old rules and establish new concepts and forms is the never-ending quest of the artist.

I chatted with Bulunbulun while at the same time thinking about all this. Our car reached the end of the dry riverbed where it faced a sea of very tall grass. Bulunbulun didn't stop or turn. He slowed the car and drove straight ahead, and I heard a swishing sound as the grass brushed against the sides of the car. Soon I could see only the sky above, because the car was enveloped in grass. I had the strange feeling that I was in a time tunnel, a mirage-like illusion. It was my luck that I was able to enter such a state of mind.

I wished the car would go a little slower, to make this wonderful moment last longer. Strangely, the car soon slowed almost to a stop. Was Bulunbulun feeling the same as me? Or was I sensing something spiritual? I had no good answer.

It was so quiet around us. If it hadn't been for the call of a kookaburra in the distance, the world would no longer exist.

'So quiet.' Someone in the car made a very small sigh.

I breathed slowly, feeling an ease of body and clarity of mind that I had never felt before.

A slight breeze was blowing, and I could smell the sea. Opening my eyes, I saw a beautiful bay appear before me as our car slipped out of the grass. I took a deep breath and thought: what a wonderful experience, a fusion of man and nature.

I always become excited whenever I see the sea. The surface of the water was like a mirror and reflected the blue sky. I got out of the car, stretched my arms out wide, then walked across this parabolic bay. It was an unforgettable feeling – as if the world were mine.

Bulunbulun threw out a fishing line, then sat on the beach listening to the sound of the waves.

I saw a small island in the distance, where there were many trees. I heard that sometimes the locals went out there after they had caught fish – for them, it was a holiday place. For city people, to experience being in such a peaceful, private, uncontested place would only ever be a fantastic dream.

I heard Bulunbulun's wife, Laurie, call out, 'A big one!' It had not taken her long to catch a really big fish. I helped one of the girls to make a fire, so that we could cook the fish in the hot ashes. Soon, Bulunbulun and the others had also caught fish.

'Too many', I said.

'Not bad', Laurie added, then she dug a piece of damper out of her favourite cloth bag. With some difficulty she tore off a small piece for me. It was old damper, with a skin like leather. I had to dip it in tea for a while before I could eat it.

After having something to eat and drink, we packed away the rest of the fish. The children put out the fire by pissing on it, and we got back into the car. Once we hit the road, Bulunbulun told us that he was making a detour, because there was a place he needed to see. He didn't describe it, and I didn't ask.

It took a few hours to get there. We arrived just before dark. To me, it didn't seem very different from many other places in Arnhem Land, but I believe that evidently for Bulunbulun it was special, a place that held memories. Arnhem Land is extremely mysterious.

We were all tired after a bumpy day driving around. Everyone ate some leftover fish, and then went to sleep. I sat close to the fire, trying to write. As the fire gradually died down, the buzzing of mosquitoes grew louder, and they started biting me like crazy. I rushed to get away from them by diving into my small tent, but some managed to get inside as well. I didn't mind losing a little blood if they eventually left me alone. They were a familiar problem out here. Sometimes I was worried that I would catch some mosquito-borne virus, then I would be in real trouble. However, I pushed aside such anxieties, because they would not help me to live in the bush. Then like everyone else, I soon fell asleep.

In the middle of the night, I was awakened by the sound of dogs barking. In the quiet night, they sounded terrifying. I listened carefully but nothing else happened, and around me the snoring continued. I decided that it must have been the sound of dingoes. They could be very threatening if they attacked as a group. Our camp dogs began barking back fiercely, as if to frighten the dingoes away. These camp dogs were skinny, unprepossessing animals but they had an important task. I got out of the tent, not daring to go far, urinated on our dead fire, then hurriedly got back into my tent. Our dogs walked around outside like patrolmen. Aware of their protection, I slid back into my dream world.

The next morning, I was the last to get up. After I had packed my stuff, I was surprised by a boy holding out a cup of tea for me. Perhaps Laurie, Bulunbulun's wife, had asked him to do this. I patted his head and asked, 'Where's Bulunbulun?', because he didn't seem to be around.

The boy said, 'I don't know'.

'Hey', I signalled to Laurie. She was collecting firewood and held a bundle of twigs in each hand. She signalled with her chin and lips in a particular direction.

'Let's go to find him', I said after returning my teacup. We walked for a while, then saw Bulunbulun standing by himself near a small pond.

As we approached, he asked if I had slept well. I mentioned the dingoes. He hummed as he turned back towards the pond. It seemed we had interrupted him from some deep thought. I just stood quietly waiting. I knew he'd tell me about it if he wanted to, otherwise it was something I shouldn't know.

'There used to be a crocodile in this pond', he said, pointing to the water. I stayed silent. I thought that another crocodile story was coming, one that would make people scared and want to leave here. To my surprise, he told me something quite different.

He told a story briefly and haltingly. 'The white people coming, killed our people, Jimmy's [one of the men on our trip] Dad was killed by the whites. We killed them too, but the whites had guns and horses, and we had only spears. We couldn't beat them. There was blood everywhere. The pond was red. Then he [the crocodile] came along and helped us fight those whites, and eventually drove them away.

'We knew that crocodiles are dangerous, but they can also help people when the spirits call to them. For Aboriginal people, they are totems and the source of strength.'

For the rest of that day, Bulunbulun didn't talk much. He just wandered around humming or talking with the children in language. The children would listen silently to him without asking any questions as he recounted their brutal history, a history where great harm had been done to Aboriginal people.

'We can forgive, but never forget', Bulunbulun told me.

I asked him when he had last come here. He didn't remember. I guess it must have been a long time ago. The scrub had grown so tall. Bulunbulun told the children to light a few fires to burn it off. 'We will be coming back. The country needs looking after.'

I asked Bulunbulun about his dream at this time. Did he have any thoughts about what it meant?

He looked at me but didn't reply. He seemed to be struggling with how to answer my question or whether this was the right time to speak to me of such things. Whatever the reason, one thing was quite clear. The look on his face revealed the turmoil in his heart.

That night the dingoes again threatened to attack us, and great clouds of mosquitoes suddenly descended. Bulunbulun concluded that there must be buffaloes nearby. Buffaloes always brought the mosquitoes. So, in this situation, we tended to be wary, always shooting some buffalo to prevent them from forming a cluster and causing a possible threat to us.

We stayed at this place for three days. Water began to run short as the small pond was about to dry up. Mainly we drank from our two big plastic buckets of water. Bulunbulun sent two young men out to look for kangaroos or to shoot a buffalo. Unfortunately, they returned with nothing.

That night once again we went to bed early. But just before I went to lie down, Bulunbulun said, 'My family was killed here'.

I was stunned; it was my turn to be speechless.

Then he said, 'Go to sleep, we go tomorrow'. With that, he lay down by the fire. I watched as he turned his back to me and lay with his body slightly curled up. If before his face had shown me pain, sadness and anger, now the curled-up back of his body expressed deep grief.

———— ≈ ————

The next day, we left early. After a few hours of tough bush driving, we arrived at Gamudi outstation. Like many of the other outstations, there were only three families here, but according to Aboriginal kinship patterns they all formed one big family.

Soon after we arrived, a girl holding a ball ran up to me. She said, 'Someone is looking for you'.

I laughed. Surely not! I had only just got here, and my butt had hardly touched the ground. She must be joking.

'Go away', Bulunbulun told her. 'Go, get some water.'

'Someone really looking for him', a woman confirmed.

'Really?!' Perhaps they weren't joking. But nobody knew that I was there. I was wondering if it was my wife?

'Who? Call him over', Bulunbulun said.

'The radio, asking. Where he is? When will he go back to the school?'

I recognised this as one of the common 'Missing Person' notices spread throughout the bush. I suddenly realised that I had asked the school for only three days off. I had forgotten the passage of time, which somehow frightened me. It showed how I had changed.

Later, the teacher I worked with told me that he should increase my workload to keep me back at the school.

There was a phone box at the outstation. I immediately called the school, saying that it was raining and the roads were bad. And somehow, there really was a big rain that night.

Of course, I called home, too. 'Everything is fine at home', Ke said. 'Don't worry about us. You take care of yourself… The kids miss you.'

'Me too.' I was gentle, but in a voice from deep within my heart, said, 'Love you all'.

In the middle of that first night, I was woken up by the noise of very heavy rain. Everyone hurried to pick up their pillows and blankets and take shelter. I went to squeeze in with Bulunbulun and the children in the upper level of one of several tree sheds. The ground level was likely to flood if the rain kept up like this. Although my bed now consisted of layers of paperbark, the tree trunks lying underneath hurt my skinny body. Even so, I was glad of the rain, for it gave me an excuse to not drive back to the school immediately.

As I tossed and turned and tried to sleep, all kinds of difficult thoughts came to me. I kept questioning myself: what am I doing here? Was it for my art? So that I could take some unique photos back with me. Was I crazy? I never seemed to settle on a clear answer. Sometimes, when people were curious, I would tell them that a deity was just showing me his world.

I was like a well-behaved, obedient child. I scarcely knew how to rebel. But within my seemingly gentle personality, my one strong trait is persistence. When I was young and very curious, I plunged into Aboriginal life, and willingly accepted all kinds of challenges. The main difficulty I found living in the bush was not the harsh conditions and severe climate, but the ability to endure the loneliness. If you can't be at one with the natural environment and lack respect for the people and land, you will lack a true connection to everything around you, and you won't be able to fully experience the wonders of nature.

The next day, the rain continued. We stayed in the sheds seeking ways to pass the time. Laurie played cards, talking all the time to herself as if playing with others. Bulunbulun was painting. Beside him, young men gathered to chat and drink kava.

In the 1950s, church missions tried to help Aboriginal people address the problem of alcoholism. One solution offered was the introduction of kava. This product is sold legally in powder form at the store. To prepare it, the powder is wrapped in cotton gauze and soaked in water. The powder is then removed, and the kava-rich water can be drunk.

I saw someone pass to Bulunbulun a cup made from half a coke can filled with kava. He quickly gulped it all down.

'Take it easy, yeah', someone warned.

I hesitated when the kava was passed to me. I'd had it before. It was like tasteless mud and made my tongue go numb. Then I got a headache. In medicine, it is sometimes used as an anaesthetic, and it is addictive, and long-term consumption can damage the nervous system.

'Don't drink it if you don't like', Bulunbulun told me. 'But it helps me to sleep.'

This made me wonder if, like me, Bulunbulun had trouble sleeping. 'Er, I just want to taste it', I said.

'Ma', Bulunbulun looked at the painting in front of him. 'Too much work to do… hey… help', he called out to Laurie.

Laurie ignored him. She was engrossed in her cards.

'Hey, help!'

'Yage! [No!]', she replied crossly.

'Let me paint for you', I offered, picking up a long bush brush and starting to draw lines. Bulunbulun didn't object and pushed a plate of white ochre towards me.

This kind of 'help' is very common among Aboriginal artists. Once, when looking closely at some familiar bark paintings in the National Gallery of Victoria, I saw some of my own 'help' there. When artists have painted the same pattern many times, they can readily lose patience. Because Bulunbulun was under pressure to produce, he often had Laurie's help, which then affected his sales. But he always said that he just borrowed Laurie's hands to complete what he wanted to paint. Many contemporary artists borrow the hands and even the ideas of others, especially for installation art, so how should we explain that?

It was still raining. I had told the school principal that I would return as soon as the rain stopped.

I sat there quietly in the shed, hugging my knees, listening to the sound of rain, and staring at the landscape painting in front of me. The bush formed the background, in front were blurred lines of rain. My doze was suddenly interrupted when Bulunbulun said, 'Tomorrow, rain stop, we can go'.

'Go where?', I asked.

'Go back. What are you thinking?'

'No, nothing.'

'You've been sitting like that for a long while.'

'Oh, really?' I wasn't thinking about anything much and just wanted to stay in my daze. It was like being in a void. It was peaceful, a great enjoyable feeling.

'You will end up going back where you came from', Bulunbulun said. He was trying to understand my thoughts.

'Ma', was my only response. My inner self was refusing to return to reality.

Bulunbulun said nothing more to me.

I just let everything take its course. When I walked into the bush, I had warned myself that I must leave the worries and mundane things of the outside world behind and start a new life.

It was not yet the wet season. After a few heavy rains, it was sunny for a few days. On the fourth day after I arrived, the weather cleared up, and Bulunbulun drove me back to the school.

Later, the Bulunbulun family moved to Wudija outstation to live with

Laurie's sister Rhoda. This became my home in Arnhem Land. They are my Aboriginal family.

––––––––––≈––––––––––

Ever since I met Bulunbulun, we kept in touch regularly. In Wudija outstation there was a phone box, which had replaced the old walkie-talkie radio. Later, almost everyone had a mobile phone. Technology in the information age had not completely bypassed this land.

Over the phone, Laurie often liked to complain about some of her daily chores. Once she told me that when they went fishing, they caught a big turtle. She knew that I had been looking for a turtle shell to paint. So, she kept it aside for the next time I went there. She asked when I was coming back. I always said, 'next month'. Then she told me that Bulunbulun had finished a new painting, 'Good one, not rubbish'. She knew that they could sell it to the Art Centre for good money. They wanted to save money to buy a car. Another time she told me that Ricky, one of the boys, had asked for presents for his next birthday. Once I sent her a video player and some CDs. Their old one had broken down. They always liked to watch Chinese Kung Fu and Hollywood action movies.

One day Bulunbulun called me and said that he had been busy taking part in a secret ceremony. From what he said, I understood that the ritual required him each day to lead the singing, so it was apparently a very important occasion.

Towards the end of our conversation, he asked, 'You want to come?'

'Yes, I'd love to', I replied.

'Ma, you should. I'm waiting for you here.'

A few days later, on 1 December 2006, my thirteen-year-old son Joman and I flew from Melbourne to Darwin, then took a small Airnorth plane from Darwin to Maningrida. I still have strong memories of the event that followed. Paul Ngaritj Uloki, Bulunbulun's son, was waiting for us at the airport. He would drive us to the place where the ceremony was being held. At the time, we weren't allowed to say anything about the place while the ceremony was still going on.

We got into his car. I have seen many rundown cars, but this one left me and Joman speechless. The brake and engine oil lights were flashing red; the mileage meter, thermometer and oil gauge were all broken; the dashboard around the steering wheel had been dismantled; the rear mirror was gone, and the seats were cut and revealed pieces of sponge. The car was an entire wreck.

'Why did they make it like this?', Joman asked.

I didn't know how to explain it to him, so I said, 'You like to play with small cars; adults like to play with big cars'.

How much 'attention' does it take for a car owner to produce such a damaged car? The question went unanswered. But that wasn't all. Uloki said that the car was only five years old. We were stunned.

Before we had recovered from our shock, I saw a tornado-like cloud of dust rushing towards us. Surely, it was going to hit us. It seemed to have come from nowhere in this clear and sunny sky. I shouted, 'What the hell is that?'

'Quick, heads down!', Uloki ordered, a note of panic in his voice.

We hurriedly tucked our heads down, but then a strong sense of curiosity made me look up. The dust cloud rolled past us at lightning speed. Looking back, I could vaguely see another car enveloped in dust.

'What was that?'

'Oh, it's not their car', Uloki breathed a sigh of relief that it was not the car bringing several important elders who were coming to host the closing ceremony. According to Aboriginal law, because of their special status as law men, they couldn't be seen by anyone before the closing ceremony.

I took a long breath and patted my chest. Uloki looked at the panicked expression on my face and smiled, adding, 'That was fucking crazy'.

When we arrived at the ceremonial site, Bulunbulun asked if we had been okay getting there. When I told him what had happened, he nodded thoughtfully, before passing me a small ladle of kava to help me get over my shock.

Then Uloki described an encounter he had had with the police back at the community.

'What happened?'

'Nearly got kicked out', Uloki replied.

A few hours earlier, while I was loading up the car with Uloki and other Aboriginal people in Maningrida, a police car stopped right in front of me. A young police officer got out, asked me who I was and where I had come from. He asked Joman and me to show him our permits.

'Oh, shit', I cursed secretly. I had totally forgotten about permits.

Uloki saw that I was embarrassed, so he quickly tried to help us out. He told the policeman, 'They are our people. We are just ready to go to Wudija.'

'Yeah, I know, but they have to show me their permits, you understand?'

'I understand. I'm sorry, but…' What else could I say? In my mind, I thought of this as 'coming home', while ignoring the fact that anyone other than the local Aboriginal people needed a permit to enter Arnhem Land.

Uloki tried to explain that he would act as a guarantor for us.

The police officer asked, 'Are you sure you can guarantee them?'

'Yo, they are our people', Uloki replied with certainty.

The officer hesitated then went off to make a phone call. When he came back, he was smiling, 'Okay, my boss said he knows you. You're all right.' He looked me up and down, and said, 'You know this is the rule, and it's there for your safety'. His tone was now friendly and kind.

I was curious to know why he had checked me. I had gone in and out for years and had never been checked.

'It was because of the two cardboard boxes you just loaded into the car', he said.

His answer made me even more confused.

'There are people selling drugs here', he added.

'Oh, I see. We've got our food in the box, and it's much more important than drugs.' My reply made some of the others laugh.

After listening to my story, Bulunbulun laughed too. He patted the ground beside him, 'Sit down. We just held another meeting to discuss about you. You and the boy can stay with us, but don't walk around casually. No pictures, including the surrounding landscape.' He told us this very seriously then handed me kava in a cut-in-half coke can, 'You not allowed to leave here, bro, before the ceremony finished'.

It was a very strict ceremony going on here. All the surrounding roads were blocked, including all the large and small roads leading off to different communities; no one could approach this place. The ceremony had been going on for about a month and was finally coming to an end. A few important elders would appear to preside over the final part of the ceremony. From the message passed on by the liaison man, the elders estimated that they would arrive during the next few days.

It was the most secret ceremony that I had ever participated in. The reason why I was allowed to be there was, according to Bulunbulun, that 'we are a family'. When I think back to his telephone call asking me to come, I recall that he explained that 'when we get together, you should be here, you are our people, allowed to know some secrets'.

I started drinking my kava and waited for events to unfold.

Kava was not good for me. It gave me a headache. Even so, I drank as much as others to help me to relax. All the events that followed happened at night. I slept or just hung about during the day, and then became immersed in an other-worldly state just like everyone else.

On that first day, I woke up when it was already night. The wind blowing from the sea brought crisp bursts of sand which stuck uncomfortably to my sweaty body. I looked up to see a full moon, which lit up the bush like a lamp in the sky. Bursts of singing whirled about. I knew that these sounds, which seemed like faint bird calls, were sending messages into the far distance and bearing the praise of worshippers to their ancestral spirits. Before long, those spirits were reeling around us.

I seemed to be in a dreamland. People were dancing in the dust as in a mist or a sea of clouds. The long shadows created a very strange atmosphere that pushed towards a climax as the singing became more and more intense. Finally, a frenzied crowd became submerged in swirling dust, and everything suddenly disappeared from my dream. It was such a short dream, so short that it seemed like it had never happened.

All through the night, I wandered about in this dreamlike state.

The next day, two Aboriginal men whose faces and bodies were painted with red and black ochre came to see Bulunbulun, Joman and me. First, they talked to Bulunbulun in language and then they spoke in English mixed with language to me and Joman. Their message was that this was Laurie's country and their country. Here they worshipped the land, and all the creatures of the land. (The more profound meaning cannot be described here.) Last night, accepting the will of the spirits, they had sung and prayed for our safe arrival.

After speaking, the men respectfully shook our hands.

Pointing to me, Bulunbulun said, 'He is Gojok'.

Immediately, they reached out their hands again, now with one hand grasping my wrist. Bowing their heads slightly, and bending over, they told me, 'You are our father'.

In the Aboriginal kinship system, my identity as Gojok – indicating my inclusion in a specific skin group – was very important. It was not just as a polite name.

I felt an incomparably strong aura. Everything happening here was sacred and following Aboriginal law could never be discussed publicly. To protect this heritage from exploitation by other cultures, the ceremony is kept completely secret. Even Aboriginal people from different regions and nations cannot participate unless invited.

After experiencing all this, my relationship with Bulunbulun grew stronger. We regarded each other as family.

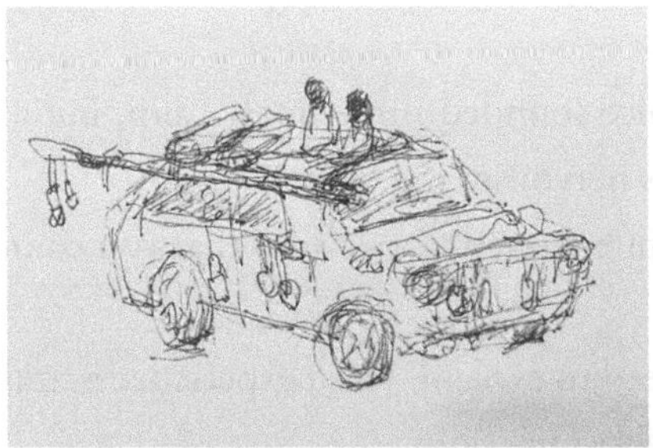

Heading out on a fishing and hunting trip, in Arnhem Land.

16

Bulunbulun in My Studio

Melbourne Airport.

I stood in front of the glass window in the pick-up hall, watching the plane slowly draw up at gate number 5. Soon Bulunbulun and his family would be here. I had not seen them for about three years, although we regularly talked to each other by phone. When I asked him when he was last away from the bush, he couldn't tell me. People in the city regard them as being far away, but they don't see it that way. The bush is the centre of their lives.

At the gate, passengers began to come out in an orderly manner, I was carefully watching out for him. Among all the people rushing forward, one came more slowly, shuffling forward with some timidity in his slippers. He wore sunglasses and his big black T-shirt bearing a picture of a kangaroo was propped up by his round beer belly. The most eye-catching thing about him was his hair. He had a great mass of fluffy, lion-like curly hair that attracted great attention. Behind him I saw his wife Laurie, and then Jennifer and Ricky.

'Gojok.' His voice sounded surprisingly calm, but a little unreal, and it did not disguise his nervousness.

Laurie quickly interrupted, 'I told him that you come, but he frightened of big city'.

There was no need to explain. I also experience a similar feeling of panic, whenever I return from the bush.

I went up to give Laurie a hug. She was dressed as usual in a black vest and a long floral dress. A bag that looked heavy was slung over a shoulder, and in one hand she was carrying a pair of slippers.

As we drove from the airport back to my studio, I asked, 'How is Rhoda?' This was Laurie's sister who lived at the Wudija outstation.

'Maynmak, she says hello to you.'

Knowing that Rhoda liked to weave mats, baskets and fishing nets from pandanus leaves, I asked, 'Has she sold a lot?'

'Yo, not bad. Tom just bought a new car.'

Tom was Rhoda's man. 'Really? He must sell many paintings', I replied. 'You look good, too, Bulunbulun. Are you ready?'

'Yo.'

He knew what I meant. We had this tacit understanding. We stopped at a McDonald's for burgers and chips, Laurie's favourite. She covered her mouth and smiled happily.

Back in my studio, while I made tea for everyone, Bulunbulun sorted things out from Laurie's bag. He brought out three small stones, three plain paintbrushes with worn heads, three long-haired bush brushes, a tobacco tin full of white powder, and a few pieces of crushed charcoal. He lined them up neatly on the floor. Covering her smile, Laurie pulled out a small bottle of latex and then, surprisingly, she took out a large stone the size of my palm with a sunken patch of yellow on it. I recognised this as a stone for grinding ochre. It told me that Bulunbulun had come seriously prepared.

Bulunbulun came to Melbourne this time to create some works for an exhibition I was curating with Professor Marcia Langton about the history of the sea cucumber trade. This trade between the Aboriginal people, the Macassans and the Chinese had taken place in northern Australia since the seventeenth century and was the first international trade known to Australian history.

Bulunbulun was one of the few Aboriginal artists who knew a great deal about this history. In 1993 he had given a three-night performance about it at the Galigo Museum in Sulawesi. Masts and rigging representing a Macassan ship were ornately decorated during the elaborate ceremony. A group of Aboriginal people, their bodies painted, were led by Bulunbulun, as they sang and danced until the ornate mast was completed and presented as a gift. This was a traditional ritual dance detailing a Ganalbingu story that told of separation as their Macassan friends and family departed.

In my studio, a large white canvas was spread across the floor. Bulunbulun and I sat on it while discussing our ideas and making a few sketches. After much discussion, Bulunbulun began to put down a red background colour. He divided this into several areas, drawing a different pattern on each area. He wanted to add two long strong straight lines but, no matter how he tried, they didn't turn out exactly as he intended. I rather liked them because they seemed to be like the lines I had seen in rock paintings. I have a special affinity for lines. Perhaps this has something to do with my training in Chinese brush painting and calligraphy. I find that variations in the strength or clumsiness of lines can create a lot of feeling. Drawing lines transcends culture to create a unique artistic language.

Bulunbulun was not the first Aboriginal artist I have worked with, but certainly our collaboration turned out to be the most challenging. First of all, we were working together on thematic creation; second, on the technical level, we each employ completely different styles of artistic expression. Third, the challenges at the social level were enormous. The various controversies I have experienced in the past still make me somewhat apprehensive. The artistic challenge will be how to re-present a period of history that took place between three different nations hundreds of years ago.

Over the following few days, while Bulunbulun painted, I spliced several sheets of rice paper together on the floor at the other end of the studio and began to draw. The habit of painting on the floor has remained with me from my time in the bush. My work soon attracted Bulunbulun's interest. He would watch me painting, then turn to talk with Laurie about it. Boldly stepping forward, he added a few cut-outs of small figures and dogs to my painting. Even though he clearly understood what I was trying to do, his seemingly casual move still caught me by surprise.

He watched a little enviously, as I walked on and off my painting holding my big, metre-long brush.

'Can you teach me?' he asked.

'You want to try? Come on', I replied.

He took up the brush as I handed it to him, and said, 'Yeah, where to paint?'

Before I could answer, Laurie said excitedly, 'Anywhere you like'.

I said she was quite right, and we all laughed.

Bulunbulun dipped the brush into the ink, and cautiously smeared a stroke on the rice paper just as I had done. But his caution didn't last long, and he was soon laying down strokes very freely.

I was not idle either, starting to add an ink wash. But as soon as Bulunbulun saw me using a bowl to pour out inky water from my bucket on to the painting, he also wanted to try it. Once again, he was unsure of just how to go about it. Once again, Laurie spoke out, 'Just pour it on'.

But Bulunbulun knew that the real question was where exactly to pour it.

Laurie kept gesturing and encouraging him in language. 'More here… and more there', she shouted.

'Laurie, why don't you just jump in?', I asked.

'Oh, no, no', she replied waving her hands, still telling Bulunbulun what to do. But finally seeing him still sitting there, she jumped up, grabbed the bucket from his hand and splashed the inky water over the picture. A fair bit of it landed on me, but she looked at me very me innocently as if this was what I had asked her to do. Seeing my surprise, she quickly covered her mouth with her hand, trying not to laugh. I was speechless.

Bulunbulun started asking me questions: why did I paint those small people and dogs? What did those lines mean? It was hard for me to explain, so in the end, he always said, 'This is your way, yeah?'

'You better paint patiently in your way. Don't try being lazy', Laurie said from the sideline, seeming to take a dim view of Bulunbulun's curiosity.

Whatever Bulunbulun chose to do now, I couldn't imagine what he might do if he developed different painting techniques. What then might he achieve? Sometimes it can be dangerous though for well-established artists to markedly change their style. Some collectors want an Aboriginal artist like Bulunbulun not to change their way of painting, to guarantee the value of the artworks that they have collected.

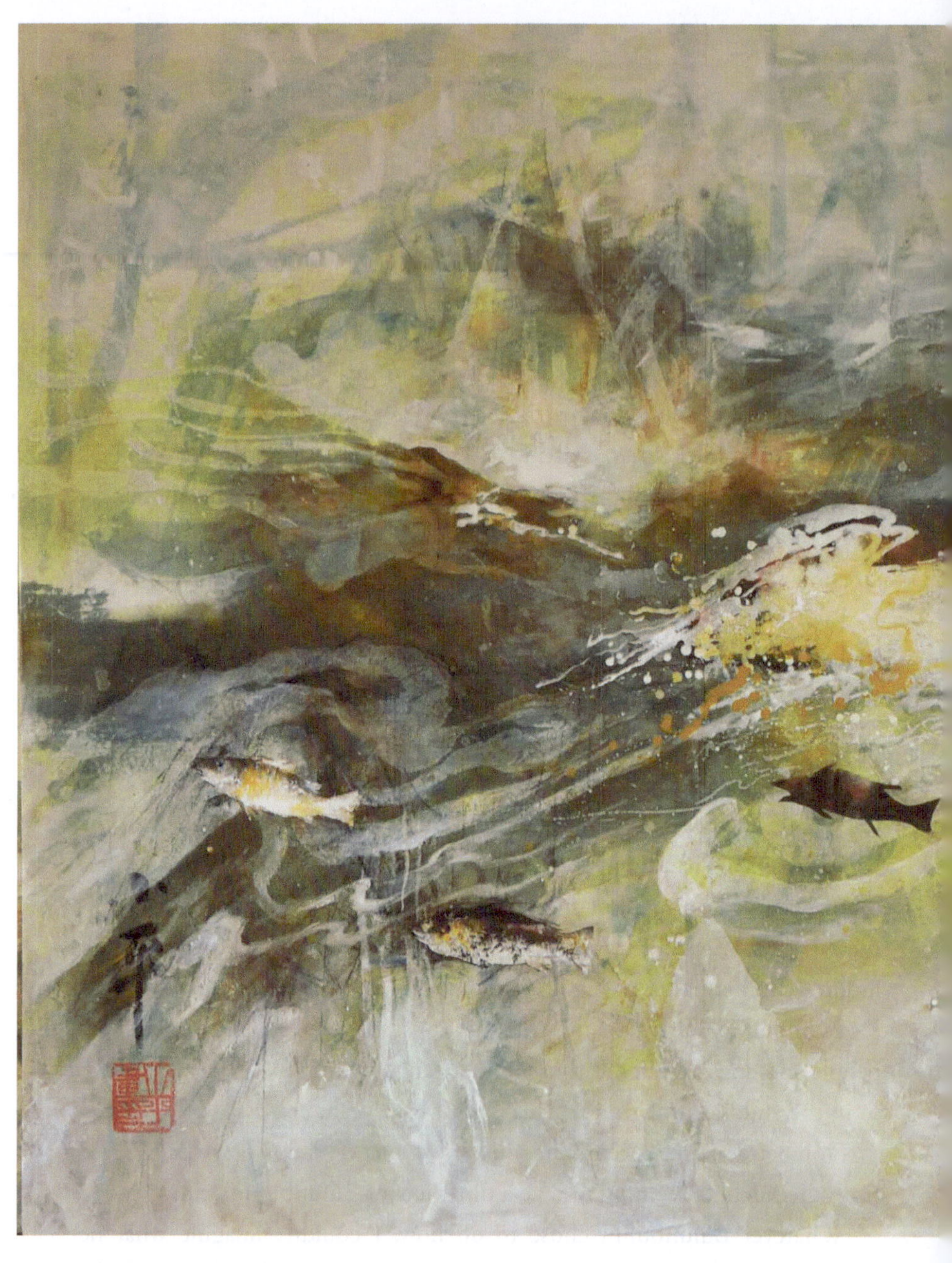

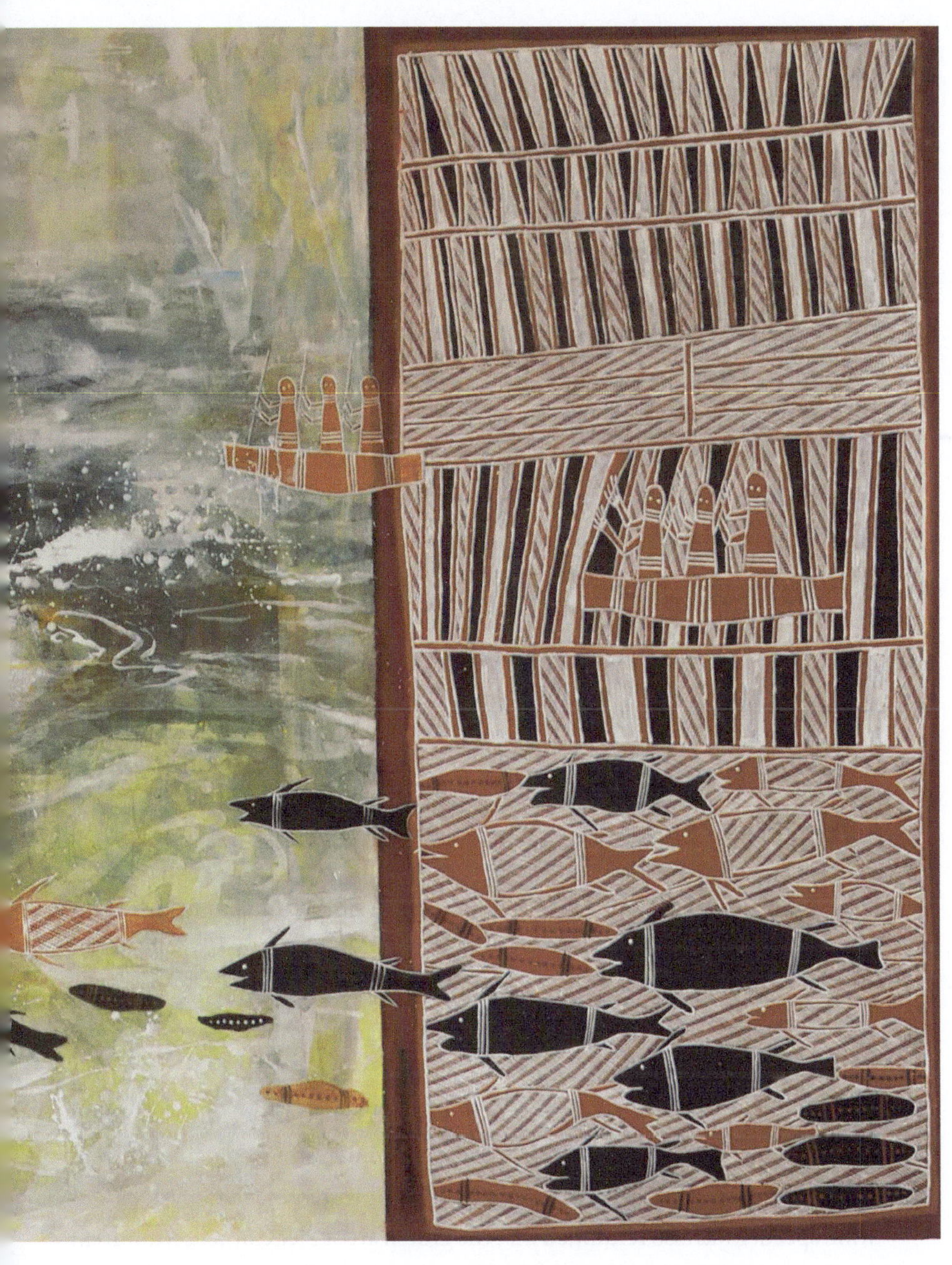

Johnny Bulunbulun and Zhou Xiaoping, *From Art to Life* (2009),
ink, acrylic and ochre on rice paper and canvas, 170 x 285 cm.

In our case, it seemed that we had developed a strong interest in each other's art, and this encouraged us to gradually move towards collaboration. As a result, we painted a large work together that was later named *From Art to Life* (170 x 285 cm). It was started by Bulunbulun. He said that he would paint what he wanted on part of this huge canvas, and then leave me to do the rest. We seemed to be able to work together without much need for discussion. I could see from the first steady line set down by Bulunbulun that he was full of confidence about how things would turn out.

I watched as he drew a triangular symbol, representing wind, clouds and lightning, then added other elements: canoes and sea cucumber motifs. As the work continued, his face showed greater confidence. He was happy and proud of his ideas and creativity. I often react in the same way. If I create a work that I am satisfied with, it makes me happy for quite a long time afterwards. It is common for artists to feel excitement, deep immersion, and both joy and pain during the process of creation.

I was interested to know about why Bulunbulun used triangles to represent the wind and clouds. How did he think about these things?

His answer, as usual, was simple, 'This is our way'.

He explained that when you look at something, you will always habitually draw an image according to the external shape of the thing, and this habit eventually becomes the norm that everyone follows. And he was always overlooking the earth because he comes from the earth, so he has a broader vision. That was how the wind and clouds came to his mind: they were more like certain shapes on the ground.

He added that the shapes of wind and clouds came into his mind and imagination from legends. I noted the interesting coincidence that meteorologists often use a triangle as a symbol to represent the velocity of wind speed. I was also reminded that the Dutch artist Piet Cornelis Mondrian (1872–1944) believed that art should be completely divorced from forms in the real world so that its abstraction could more forcefully express the unity of man and God. Geometric abstraction has long existed in Aboriginal art, but while the forms are abstract, they are drawn from an exploration of life, land and nature. Bulunbulun argues that a lot of things considered by white people to be very precious, are already held by Aboriginal people.

Having finished drawing the main forms in his painting, Bulunbulun started adding detail using bark painting techniques involving fine intersecting cross hatching. This technique is common in Arnhem Land in traditional ceremonial painting and is believed to hold great spiritual power. In the painting appearing on the floor of my studio, there were creatures in the sea, while to the left, three Macassans were rowing a boat. Bulunbulun left it to me to draw the rest of the sea using ink and wash techniques. It took Bulunbulun only a week to complete his part of the artwork, and afterwards I completed it over the next year and a half.

This painting combined two traditional art forms and varied materials: ink, acrylic and natural pigments. It was painted on both rice paper and canvas, allowing us to render the vibrancy and movement of the seascape. However, when I first put the two completely different parts of the work together, the Aboriginal and the Chinese sections failed to harmonise, because there were no linking elements. I thought about it for a long time. Then one day, I fell asleep in the studio and dreamed that the fish and the boat in Bulunbulun's painting were moving. Their dense lines began to twist, reshape and flow. Fish slowly swum out of the painting into the ocean, turning into living fish that were flying and jumping. Not wanting to be left behind, the small boat also took off, plunging happily into the green ocean to look for new partners, splashing water on to me and on to the vast land. When I woke up, I picked up my brush, and painted the fish from Bulunbulun's side on to my side of the artwork. The fish, seen initially as a flat pattern, leapt and gradually came alive. So, the inspiration to complete the painting came from a dream.

When Dr Joe Gumbula, an Aboriginal elder from Elcho Island in northeast Arnhem Land, saw the painting he was very excited and said, 'This painting accurately interprets the Dreamtime. The Dreamtime not only describes the past but continues into the present and the future. It is alive. This is our culture and life. After life has moved to a state of "dream", it is endowed with more powerful vitality, and then returns from the "dream" to life, and the cycle is repeated.' Dr Gumbula believes that the painting provides a more comprehensive and profound explanation for the English word 'Dreamtime'.

'Dreamtime' in English conveys the idea of something happening in the past tense. It does not fully and accurately express this core idea from Aboriginal culture. The idea is a rather complex one that is named differently in different Aboriginal languages but accepted across Australia by most Aboriginal groups. The core concept focuses both on ancestral origins *and* on their ongoing renewal in today's world. According to Aboriginal traditions, in ancient times, the creators made the earth, mountains, rivers, wind, rain, people and all kinds of life. When all these had forms, it was the beginning of the world. The creators became revered as the ancestors. The spirit and soul of the ancestors were handed down into human life. The ancestral spirit was deified and now lives always among people and guides human behaviour.

All nations with a long history have a myth of origin about the formation of the world. The ancient myths of the Chinese describe how, in the beginning, heaven and earth were bound together like an enormous egg surrounded by chaos. A divinity named Pangu used an axe and a chisel to separate heaven and earth, and in doing so, he became a hero and the ancestor of the Chinese nation. Later, a goddess named Nü-Wa appeared, in female form but with a dragon's tail. She travelled around the world that Pangu had created, looking at all the mountains, trees, plants, birds, animals, insects and fish, but saw no higher beings. One day, seeing her own beautiful reflection in a river, she was inspired to mould mud from the riverbed into clay figurines. Nü-Wa blew on to these figures and infused them with life. To some she gave 'yang' energy, the combative male element, and they became men, and to others, she infused 'yin' energy, a gentle female element so they became women. In this way, Nü-Wa became the first ancestor in the creation of humankind.

Australian Aboriginal people do not think of their creation stories simply as myths. They are more like spiritual pillars. They see the change of seasons, the cycle of life back up and the growth of all things, including human beings, as part of an ongoing process of creation by the ancestors. Through wind, water and the sounds of nature, the presence of ancestor spirits can be felt everywhere. The tracks that the ancestors leave behind are reproduced by Aboriginal people in painting and rituals in the form of certain symbols and forms which can be painted on bodies, rocks, bark or canvas. For example, concentric circles are used to represent places where the ancestors have been. They often indicate a specially created environment or a meeting place where people can come together and interact. Likewise, paintings from Arnhem Land often map out specific places of importance where different ceremonies took place or places where special events had happened involving artists and other groups, or places where traces of the ancestors remain. Some of these paintings, especially those from the northern and central regions of Australia, have been used in law courts and land title tribunals to provide evidence of Aboriginal ownership of certain lands.

In our painting *From Art to Life*, the flat symbolic patterns set down by Bulunbulun leap up as three-dimensional forms to submerge themselves into the ocean waters off the Chinese coast. From Aboriginal art forms created with natural pigments, to Chinese carp painted in ink and acrylic, two very different artistic perspectives are integrated into the one painting, fully illustrating our collaborative philosophy. Life is presented in the form of art, and it is endless.

'Gojok, you painted exactly what I thought', Bulunbulun said.

———————≈———————

Ever since Bulunbulun and his family came to Melbourne, we had all been working hard. He always said to me, 'Working first'. This sharply contradicts complaints I have heard about Aboriginal people: that they don't want to work or that they have no sense of work. In fact, the people who say this don't know them. Such prejudices are very hurtful.

Bulunbulun then said, 'I will come back, yeah? You can teach me your way.'

'Yeah, anytime', I agreed. 'But right now, I'm going to buy milk. You want to come?' I like to get out of the studio like this to break the furious pace of work. Sometimes I would go swimming, running, or off to the library to find a romantic novel, or I would watch an episode from a television series. Anything to relax.

At the supermarket, as he often did, Ricky went straight to the freezer for his favourite ice-cream. Laurie would always buy her cigarettes, while Jennifer would select some new snacks that she hadn't yet tried. Bulunbulun would follow one of them and allow the last person to pay.

When we got back into the car, I remembered that Bulunbulun had mentioned the National Gallery of Victoria. So now seemed a good time to take a drive to see the gallery. Everybody was happy with my proposal. The National Gallery is a modern building located in Federation Square in the heart of Melbourne, a unique location. Every year, the gallery exhibits some of the best contemporary art from Australia and across the world. While the gallery attracts many people from Melbourne, it is also an important place where visiting tourists can learn about Australian contemporary culture. A designated gallery has a permanent exhibition of Aboriginal art, and I had seen one of Bulunbulun's paintings there on display. As we walked into the gallery, we passed posters advertising major international exhibitions that were coming to this gallery space. I just glanced at them and led everyone straight to where I wanted to go.

As soon as we entered the hall, Bulunbulun asked, 'Where is it? I could sense the eagerness in his voice. I immediately started looking for his painting. 'It should be there', I said, pointing the way as they all started to follow. But right then, a commanding voice came from behind us, 'Excuse me, but you can't be in here'.

We turned around. It was a member of the gallery security staff.

'What?' I was very surprised. Surely, I had heard wrong.

'He's not wearing shoes. We can't let him in.' The security officer pointed at Bulunbulun's bare feet.

None of them had worn shoes from their very first day in my studio. They seemed to have brought their bush habits with them. Sometimes, Laurie would remind everyone to wear slippers, but inevitably city rules were quickly forgotten.

I said to the guardian, 'This is Johnny Bulunbulun, a famous artist. He has a painting here, we just want to have a look, and then we'll go.'

'I'm sorry', he replied, shaking his head. The refusal was clear despite his polite tone.

'He's from Arnhem Land, a bushman, not used to wearing shoes. We just want to take a quick look. Please.'

The guy listened patiently to my explanation but once again shook his head.

'Can't you be accommodating? We're already here.'

He still shook his head, smiling rather helplessly. Seeing this, my temper began to rise.

Bulunbulun, standing near me, tugged at my shirt then turned to walk out. He understood this man's mind.

'Wait a minute, this is ridiculous! An artist, who rarely comes out of the bush, just wants to see his painting for a minute, okay?', I said loudly.

Turning my head, I wanted to stop Bulunbulun and the others from walking out. All I could see was the back of his slightly hunched figure, walking out trembling, followed in silence by his family, like a bunch of punished children.

Pointing to the small group, I turned to the officer, wanting to slap him down with painful words but my huge anger had left me speechless.

Humans seem to be so weak in the face of bureaucracy. It is hard to understand the mentality and motives of those who implement it. Disappointed and angry, I thought of all those Indigenous artworks by people like Bulunbulun. Here was the artist who had created one of the most beautiful paintings on display, but because of his bare feet he was not allowed to see it hanging there.

'I can't believe this. I want to see your supervisor', I growled.

Unexpectedly, the man still smiled, but spread out his hands, and shrugged his shoulders.

This was not the first time I had met such an obdurate guy – someone who, although you are very angry, still smiles at you, ignoring all your protests and arguments, and acting innocent. In the face of such ignorance and arrogance, I wanted to punch his face. Sadly, none of the other visitors to the gallery came forward to support me. They just stood there and watched, just as people had done so many years ago when I first went to Alice Springs. Once again, I asked myself: what is the attitude of Australians towards Aboriginal people? Jennifer came over and said, 'Let's go', and took my arm to walk me out. Hearing her aggrieved, cautious tone, I sighed heavily, and my anger left me. Lowering my eyes, I could see once again those bushman's feet stepping on the shiny parquet floor. I vividly remember the moment when Bulunbulun turned his head back slowly as he stepped out of the door, glancing one last time at the exhibition hall, still looking for his painting.

'We don't belong here, let's go', Bulunbulun spoke calmly. He spoke as an elder, and no one could object.

Emerging from the gallery, I saw my car being hauled away right in front of my eyes by a tow truck. In my unhappiness, I finally stuck up my arm with a raised middle finger and roared, 'Fuck you!'

Despite our misfortunes we were in the centre of Melbourne, so I thought we should just take a walk or do some shopping to dispel the unpleasantness of what had just happened. Crossing the road from Federation Square, we turned left to walk across the bridge, and then went down to the edge of the Yarra River. Here were many restaurants and cafes where people could sit outside enjoying a drink and a meal. This is a beautiful and scenic city that offers a pleasant life, although sometimes I feel that I can't afford to enjoy so much beauty. Street performers were trying to amuse passers-by and make a little money. Further along the river was Crown Casino, one of the biggest casinos in the southern hemisphere. As we walked along, we continued to draw the attention of bystanders and others around. Not in a good mood like other times, their unbridled gaze and low whispers made us uncomfortable at that moment.

Without thinking, I walked straight into the luxuriously decorated building that houses the Crown Casino. But suddenly the group with me was missing. Turning in a hurry, I couldn't see Bulunbulun and the others. After searching the crowd, I at last spotted him standing in the doorway, his arms outstretched, looking nervous and at a loss. I ran toward them.

'I'm really sorry', I apologised.

'Is it okay to come in?', Laurie said. 'Not blame you, Gojok, but we are afraid'.

This was spoken to me by an Aboriginal woman standing on her land. Her words fell like a heavy stone on my heart. I really regretted that I had let them experience fear once again.

I told them that there is no place in this country they cannot go. 'Come on', I said, 'we should walk here proudly' – just as if we were walking in their country back in the bush.

We found a place to sit in a McDonald's store. I ordered a big pack of burgers and chips, hoping to cheer things up. I picked up a chip, but just as I was about to put it in my mouth a fly flew in and went right down my throat.

It was disgusting, but compared with what had happened at the gallery beforehand, it was nothing.

———≋———

On most days, we would paint, go to a nearby shopping centre, and occasionally hang out with my friends, but Bulunbulun didn't like to be with too many people. He said that there was no sense of security. For their first night in Melbourne, I had organised two rooms where they could stay. But the next morning, I saw the four of them all huddled together in the same room. Laurie told me that they would sleep more easily like this. They felt more comfortable just being with my family and were willing to chat and joke with Ke and the kids, Joman and Danni, and to reassure Ke that they were taking good care of me when I was in the bush. Laurie, particularly, liked Chinese dishes. She said to Ke, 'You should set up a restaurant in our community … make a lot of money'. But when I invited other friends to join us, Johnny became visibly silent. 'They are strangers', he said. The meaning of 'stranger' relates not only to the strangeness of meeting for the first time. Without explanation, I understood what he meant.

One day Laurie, Jennifer and Ricky were watching television, and only

Bulunbulun and I were busy painting.

Suddenly, in the silence Bulunbulun farted.

'Hey', Laurie and Jennifer yelled.

'Excuse me', Bulunbulun said politely.

Glancing back at him, Laurie said, 'You talk like balanda, that gallery guy. He was disgusting.'

Although we never talked about that unpleasant NGV incident again, that didn't mean we could so easily erase it from our minds.

Bulunbulun glanced at me and remained silent. Then at length he said, 'Gojok…'

'Yeah', I replied, without stopping what I was doing. I waited for him to come out with what he wanted to say, but I heard nothing. 'Yeah?', I said glancing back at him wondering why he had become so hesitant.

'Next time you go to China, bring me a Buddha, yeah?'

'Why you want that?', I asked, looking up.

'Lucky. The Buddha can bring me good luck.'

'Why do you believe in Buddha, not others?'

'He looks very happy, and he can help me to win.'

Laurie interrupted to say that she wanted videotapes of Chinese Kung Fu. Bulunbulun erupted with two Kung Fu screams, which stunned us, and then we all immediately burst into laughter. The two women fell to the floor giggling. The atmosphere had suddenly become very lively.

'He never talks like that', Laurie said, imitating Bulunbulun's expression and amusing us all once again. 'We love Kung Fu movies. I want to buy more', Laurie continued.

'You want to buy more?'

The previous day, we had bought four DVDs at Target, so together with the ones we had bought earlier, they now had over a dozen. I remember at the first store, how Bulunbulun had taken two $50 notes out of his pocket and given them to Jennifer so that she could buy DVDs. Then at Kmart, Laurie without hesitation chose a few more. Later, when we passed another store, Laurie couldn't miss the opportunity to get even more, and Bulunbulun paid for them all without comment. Such consumption wasn't because of how rich they were. Rather, it reflected their fragile concept of money.

Laurie joked, 'Money. It's just a piece of paper. You are now painting the money.' Everyone laughed. Then the phone rang. Laurie answered and told me, 'M. wants to come over'.

Ms M. was Bulunbulun's friend who used to work at Maningrida. We had all met by chance on the street the previous week. Excited, she wanted to know why everyone was here. Bulunbulun pointed at me and explained that he had come down to paint with me. Glancing at me quickly, her expression told me that she didn't want to talk to me at all.

'Does Ms C. know about this?', she asked.

Ms C. was the manager of the Maningrida Arts Centre. Bulunbulun nodded and continued chatting warmly to Ms M. It seemed that all she could say was, 'Great to see you all in Melbourne'. But now she had telephoned and was wanting to see them all. Although I could guess her intentions, I reluctantly said, 'Well, if she really wants to come', and agreed to pick her up at the train station with Bulunbulun and Laurie. When they met once again, she said, 'Ha, it's great, it's such a coincidence to see you in Melbourne'. She couldn't wait to inspect my studio, the accommodation I had prepared for them and all the surroundings. I suppressed my unhappiness and answered all her questions one by one. She looked impatient, eager to confirm her suspicions.

It was lunchtime and, after I had made sandwiches for everyone, I asked Ricky to come with me to the local library. The little fella was never shy. He liked to be with me as a helper. Often, he would hold the paint tray for me as I painted and was keen to oblige whenever I asked him to help me do something.

In the library, I got a call from the manager at Maningrida. She asked me about the work environment available for Bulunbulun, saying that she had heard that he felt lonely and worked long hours every day. Finally, she told me that she had no interest in my project. 'I'm not interested in your paintings on canvas either. But Bulunbulun has an agreement, and for any of his bark paintings the sale needs to go through the Maningrida Art Centre.' I explained that I had no intention of buying the two paintings Bulunbulun had done in Melbourne. Anyway, a large part of the two paintings had been done by Laurie, even if they carried the signature of Johnny Bulunbulun. When he left, Bulunbulun took his two paintings with him, but sold them privately to a gallery in Darwin.

When I returned to the studio after visiting the library, I found a taxi parked at the gate. It had come to take Ms M. away. This was the first time I had ever sent a gatekeeper away from my studio. People like this kind of gatekeeper can be seen everywhere in Australia. They always think that Aboriginal people do not have the ability to stand on their own feet and act independently. In this way, they deprive Aboriginal artists of their autonomy and voice. A collaboration between the two artists may seem to have nothing to do with anyone else, but society will still question why a non-Indigenous artist wants to become involved with Aboriginal artists. Such collaborations provoke a big question mark. Australian society is un-usually sensitive to these issues, and I believe that this isn't necessarily what Aboriginal artists want.

This was one of the challenges at the social level mentioned.

———≈———

'Gojok, I want to make a phone call', Bulunbulun said.

He had been restless ever since he was told the news of his nephew's death. Three days earlier, Bulunbulun had had a bad cough. I didn't dare neglect it and rushed him to a clinic. While the doctor found that his lungs were somewhat abnormal, it didn't seem to be anything serious. He was given some antibiotics and we were told to keep an eye on him for a few days. Since they arrived in Melbourne, everything had been fine except that Laurie and Jennifer had had a short spell of diarrhoea. I didn't know what had caused this, as we had all eaten the same food, and the two men and the child didn't have any problem. Bulunbulun thought that it might be because of the new environment, that they had not yet acclimatised.

Driving back to the studio, after seeing the doctor, a call came through for Bulunbulun. While he was staying with me, he used my number as an emergency contact. Taking this call, he seemed different. He listened very quietly, putting his hand up to cover his eyes. Laurie looked serious and gestured to me quietly while trying to follow the telephone conversation. To stop Ricky, a six-year-old, from making a noise, Jennifer pulled up her shirt and stuffed a nipple into his mouth. It seemed that something serious had happened in the bush.

After a while, Bulunbulun hung up the phone, not saying anything, but wiping away tears. A dignified atmosphere quickly filled the car. Everyone held their head down, and even the boy was quietly holding the nipple without taking any milk.

'My nephew is gone', Bulunbulun told me. Laurie and Jennifer already realised what had happened.

Bulunbulun was a very steady and honest man, but also extremely powerful and assertive in his inner world. He told Jennifer to return to Arnhem Land with Ricky, to mourn for the deceased on his behalf.

From then on until he left Melbourne, he would make several phone calls home every day. He constantly worried about his family far away in the bush. 'Big raining over there. I need go back', he said.

When I first heard the news about the death, all I could do was nod without speaking. Laurie muttered a few words in pidgin English – she was concerned that the plane might have been grounded due to the bad weather. Then for a long while, it was extremely quiet in the studio. We were all doing our own thing, but Bulunbulun put down his brush, walked out of the studio and wandered about in the yard. He couldn't paint as he usually did.

Later, he asked me if I would finish up some unfinished parts of his painting. I said that wasn't a problem. But in the end, I didn't. I thought that the unfinished parts documented what had happened in our creative process. Formal incompleteness is also a kind of completion.

Although our artwork was in a good state, it was understandable that Bulunbulun had to leave. He said he'd be back next month, after he had finished family business. He liked working with me.

Jennifer and Ricky had already gone. Before Bulunbulun and Laurie left, we made one last shopping expedition. We went to Westfield shopping centre in Doncaster, where we saw a beautiful floral dress in the window. Bulunbulun wanted to buy it for Laurie. We walked into the shop, where Bulunbulun pointed to the dress in the window and told the seller, 'Want that one'. The woman's eyes swept over us several times. She stared at Laurie without any scruples and with a slight frown. She was not merely curious but vigilant. She didn't answer Bulunbulun, but just watched as Laurie casually looked at these dresses, and from time to time took one out to hold against her. Laurie didn't care about what material the dresses were made of, she was just choosing the colours and big flower patterns she liked.

She held up a long skirt and looked at herself in the mirror. My eyes suddenly lit up: the bright strong colour went well with her dark skin, making her look like a different person. I praised her for having great aesthetic sense. Even the sales assistant standing to the side couldn't help saying, 'It's so beautiful. Which country is she from?' Her question shocked me.

'Hey, look at Laurie', I said to Bulunbulun.

'Maynmak, Maynmak!', he cried in excitement as he looked at her.

'Would you like to try it on?', asked the seller with a reluctant but professional smile on her face. 'It's on special now, let me see the price', and with a very well-manicured finger she began to tap on her calculator. Before she could announce the price, Laurie had taken the dress into the fitting room. I don't think she cared how much it cost.

After a while, laughter came from the fitting room, 'It's too tight'.

'Come out, let us to see it,' I said.

As the curtain was drawn, a coy woman, her face covered by her hands appeared in front of us in a tight-fitting red flower-patterned dress.

I thought: my God, is this our Laurie? So beautiful.

She kept saying, 'Too tight, I can't breathe'. But from her shy laughter, it was not hard to see that she liked herself wearing this dress. It fitted very well on her chubby body, except the bust size was a bit small and her plump breasts were squeezed tight and were partly jumping out of the low-cut top. Really beautiful and sexy. I thought that if she walked down the street in that dress, she would attract even more attention than Bulunbulun's lion-like curly hair and beard.

'Are there any larger sizes?'

'Unfortunately, not anymore. Do you want to try this one? It will be bigger.' The seller took out another dress with dark red flowers in a different style and placed it in front of Laurie. Whether it was to make a sale or whether she thought the dress looked good, the lady became enthusiastic. Her pretty fingers with their red nail polish tapped her calculator a few more times. Before she could read out the price, Laurie said, 'Ma!', and Bulunbulun happily paid for it.

On the way home, we were still talking about how beautiful the dress looked on Laurie. Bulunbulun regretted not buying another one. To my surprise, his attitude was that if she liked it, she should have it.

Often owning something is even more important than wearing something for women, because a women's imagination is more romantic, and the idea of beauty will stay in their memory for a long time.

Not only did I see Laurie's beauty, but I saw the inner romance of a bushman.

The day before they left, Bulunbulun told me that he had had another dream.

'Yeah? What dream?', Laurie asked.

'I'm in China and I sell a lot of paintings', he replied.

'Ha… ha…' Laurie's mouth opened in a wide smile, revealing her few remaining teeth.

'In my dream I saw a lot of Chinese people, and one of them approached me and asked me in English where I came from. I said, "Arnhem Land. And Gojok is my brother."'

'You said you sold a lot of paintings.' This was Laurie's focus.

'Yeah, sold a lot of paintings. Made big money, not rubbish money', he repeated triumphantly.

Laurie couldn't stop laughing, 'You're crazy about money. Ha… ha!'

'Yo, brother, you have gabay?', Bulunbulun asked. 'Gabay' was beer in his language.

'Two bugola', Laurie replied using the pidgin word for beer.

'Yo, pi-jiu', I added, in Chinese.

I had prepared a gift for Bulunbulun, a man who didn't spend even a dollar on himself. It was a pot-bellied jade Buddha that he could hang around his neck. He wanted the Buddha to bring him luck, to win money and to bless him and his family.

After Bulunbulun and Laurie left, I created a series of paintings, among which is one named *How He Sees Me* that is a painting of which I am most proud. In the painting, my self-portrait faces the viewer. My hands are held behind my back, I am looking relaxed, and above my shoulder is a smiling Buddha. Bulunbulun is holding a camera and taking a picture of me.

Every time I see this painting, it reminds me of when Bulunbulun and his family visited my studio. Having these fond memories infused my work with energy and passion as I waited for his return. But in my picture, he seemed to be waving goodbye to me.

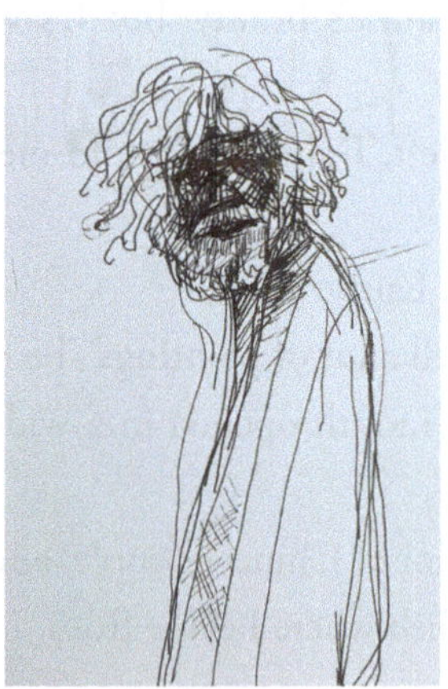

**Johnny Bulunbulun,
drawing for a painting.**

17

Exhibition on Sensitive Frontiers

On Changan Street, one of the major thoroughfares in Beijing, one could see at a distance a huge banner, 25 metres by 5 metres, hung on the outer walls of the Capital Museum. On the left side of the banner was a painting created by Johnny Bulunbulun and me. On the right, the context is explained: 'Trepang: China and the Story of Macassan–Aboriginal Trade, April 1 – June 30, 2011'. Amazingly this huge poster had been hung up by 120 people without using any special machinery or equipment.

An opening ceremony of the exhibition was held at the museum. Laurie Marburru Maarbudug leaned on my shoulder and sobbed, 'He's not here'. It was very sad to hear her say this. I tried to comfort her but couldn't find the right words. All I could do was to hold her hand gently. The person missing was Laurie's man and my brother, Johnny Bulunbulun. His son, Ngaritj, was standing beside us, his eyes downcast. He had just come off the stage and still had two white bars painted on his face. I held Laurie's hand while I told her, 'The Arnhem Landers would be proud of this moment'.

'Maynmak', she whispered as she hugged me. 'They are watching us, Tommy, Rhoda, Jennifer, Rick, everyone, dancing and singing like this…' And ignoring everyone, she began to twist her body in dance. I thought of my Aboriginal family at Wudija, dancing and singing around the campfire, waving to us. Ngaritj seemed to see them as well. He tapped two wooden sticks together and his legs began jumping and turning to the beat of this knocking sound. Then he raised his head and sang. The audience of over three hundred people began to applaud.

The singing and the rising music, as well as the exquisite artwork in the exhibition hall, takes us back to a two-hundred-year history of relations between Australian Aboriginal people and Macassans, linked to the Chinese – a relationship that has never been interrupted. My personal long-term interaction with Indigenous people formed part of this.

Since the eighteenth century, the Macassans regularly visited Arnhem Land, departing from Port Makassar in what is today Sulawesi, Indonesia. In small boats, these fishermen forged a little-known trade route between China and Southeast Asia, bringing not only trade goods but also linguistic, cultural and religious change to the Aboriginal people of the Northern Territory. The traders were mainly Macassans from the Kingdom of Gowa. Every December, following the monsoon, they landed in Arnhem Land and nearby islands in their small boats, fishing in some bays for the precious sea cucumber that is regarded by the Chinese as a gourmet delicacy with aphrodisiac qualities. Then in April–May of the following year, they would return with the turn of the monsoon to sell their catch to merchants who sent it on to ports in China. The Macassans brought tobacco leaves, wine, knives, swords and other iron tools, as well as clothing, to exchange with Aboriginal people. These trade exchanges inevitably had cultural influences on Aboriginal languages, eating habits, music and dance. The trepang trade was the first international commercial trade known to Australian history.

This historical context was presented in our exhibition. In a hall of more than 600 square metres, a large selection of documents, pictures, maps, paintings, sculptures and objects were displayed. The contemporary section contained paintings by either Bulunbulun or me, and there were also some paintings that we had done together. Professor Marcia Langton noted: 'Xiaoping and Bulunbulun bring together their understanding of historical events that entangled their ancestors across cultures and the seas and archipelagos between China and the northern coast of Australia more than two centuries ago. They have illustrated the long reach of this history into present day Aboriginal culture.' In one painting, titled *Journey Starts from Here* (2009), several playing cards float in a dark green sea towards Australia with those Macassan boats. Cards are now an important leisure-time activity in Aboriginal life. In another painting, *String Pulled Across Time: Journey Continues* (2009), a string held by a Chinese fisherman passes to the hands of an Aboriginal man, expressing the relationship held in the span of time and space.

I was very glad to see the audience studying the artworks in our exhibition. I watched a girl who wearing glasses approach a painting called *Source of Life* (2010). The large area of the sea in the painting is like a piece of dark green silk quietly lifted to allow the world to spy on this mysterious nation.

I noticed an old man with a big grey beard, hands held behind his back, standing in front of a painting titled *How He Sees Me* (2009). A few minutes later, he was still standing there, so I stepped forward to say hello to him.

He looked at me and indicated that he was aware the person in the painting was me. The painting showed me standing there while Bulunbulun took my photo.

I wondered what the bearded man thought of the work.

'I'm trying to figure it out because the artist leaves one in suspense', he said. 'What does this Aboriginal man see through the lens? I guess that's an interesting question, isn't it? Maybe that's the key point of this painting.' He added, 'In addition, I think something else that is interesting concerns you'. He pointed at my image to make this clear. 'If I say that you are an artwork, do you understand what I mean? An artwork created in this modern world. When people learn about your story, they must find it incredible, right? You are a cross-cultural ambassador.'

An artist can see anything as art. And anyone can see an artist as an artwork. What the old man said was somewhat unexpected and very wise. I liked what he said, as if I could be shaped into a work of art combining elements from different cultures.

'Young man, may I ask you another question?'

'Of course.'

'The theme of the whole exhibition is very clear, the artworks and all this research help us to re-imagine and delineate the history of the first trade between the Australian Aboriginal people, the Macassans and the Chinese. Was there any direct trade between Chinese and Aboriginal people?'

The old man had asked a very important question, and it is a mystery that historians have been trying to solve. Some have argued that the Chinese admiral Zheng He led his fleet across the Pacific and landed in Australia in the fifteenth century, before the arrival of the first Europeans. But this has been hotly disputed.

I once discussed this issue with Marcia. Her thinking about this was very clear. She believed that there was no direct connection between Aboriginal people and Chinese people in this first Australian trade.

I argued that while there is no direct evidence, there is still ancillary evidence: the boats used by the Macassans were funded and built by Chinese businessmen. Nonetheless Marcia did not find my arguments persuasive.

'Yes', I countered. 'That's for the historians, but we can imagine such contacts through works of art.'

She saw this as complete nonsense. I know her as a very strong personality, with a great memory, often bursting with wisdom when engaging in discussions with others.

I tried to make the point that artistic language is more figurative and more imaginative. Often through it we may glimpse the truth. But my thoughts quickly made Marcia angry.

'Fucken no, no, no! There was never a direct transaction between them', she told me with considerable force. She claimed that I just wasn't listening to her. There simply was no evidence.

I was completely taken aback. These words sound rough, but this was Marcia, an Aboriginal scholar who is extremely rigorous in academic issues. As our relationship was relatively close, there was no need to be too polite.

That was just a small episode in the process of the project.

I briefly talked about our research to the bearded old man, hoping that historians would later find some better evidence to prove my hypothesis to be true.

The old man nodded admiringly, saying, 'It doesn't really matter whether we can find evidence or not. For a piece of art, it's not a commentary on the authenticity of history.'

Hearing serious feedback from the audience at the exhibition was very gratifying. This was the culmination of ten years of unremitting effort, and it made me feel highly emotional. The hard work of our entire project team meant that we had never given up when we faced challenges. The events that happened during the development of the project are worth documenting.

The exhibition also includes several important works co-created by Bulunbulun and myself, which not only tell an important history but also represent crystallisations across cultures.

How does one view these collaborative works? 'Cross-cultural collaboration', what does it mean? I believe that it occurs, in a true sense, when two artists respond to each other's cultural language and establish a certain degree of association. During the process of interaction, new work evolves in which symbols, materials and techniques from both cultures can be incorporated. However, there must be a process of integration in this, as simply grafting together two different symbolic elements is not good enough.

The question of whether a non-Aboriginal artist can collaborate with Aboriginal artists has been highly controversial. Take for example one of my collaborative paintings with Bulunbulun in this exhibition. It is a big painting (240 x 170 cm). Three kangaroos are grouped around a big waterhole, and areas of the painting contain patterns drawn by Bulunbulun. I especially liked how he intertwined orderly white lines across an area of yellow pigment. After seeing this, I used Chinese fine brush techniques to paint a sea with two pieces of blue-and-white porcelain floating on it. In this way, I created a dialogue between Chinese culture and Aboriginal art. The delicate dragon on the porcelain corresponds to the kangaroos drawn in the style of bark painting. The waterhole next to the kangaroos is matched by the blue-and-white porcelain plate. Bulunbulun was very happy with our painting. He made it clear to me that the waterhole he had drawn for this painting had no symbolic or sacred meaning: it was drawn as part of our cross-cultural collaboration. This creative idea that we were so proud of has been opposed, however, by some on the grounds that it undermines the special significance of the waterhole symbol in traditional Aboriginal painting.

Bulunbulun comforted me, telling me not to listen to these ideas from

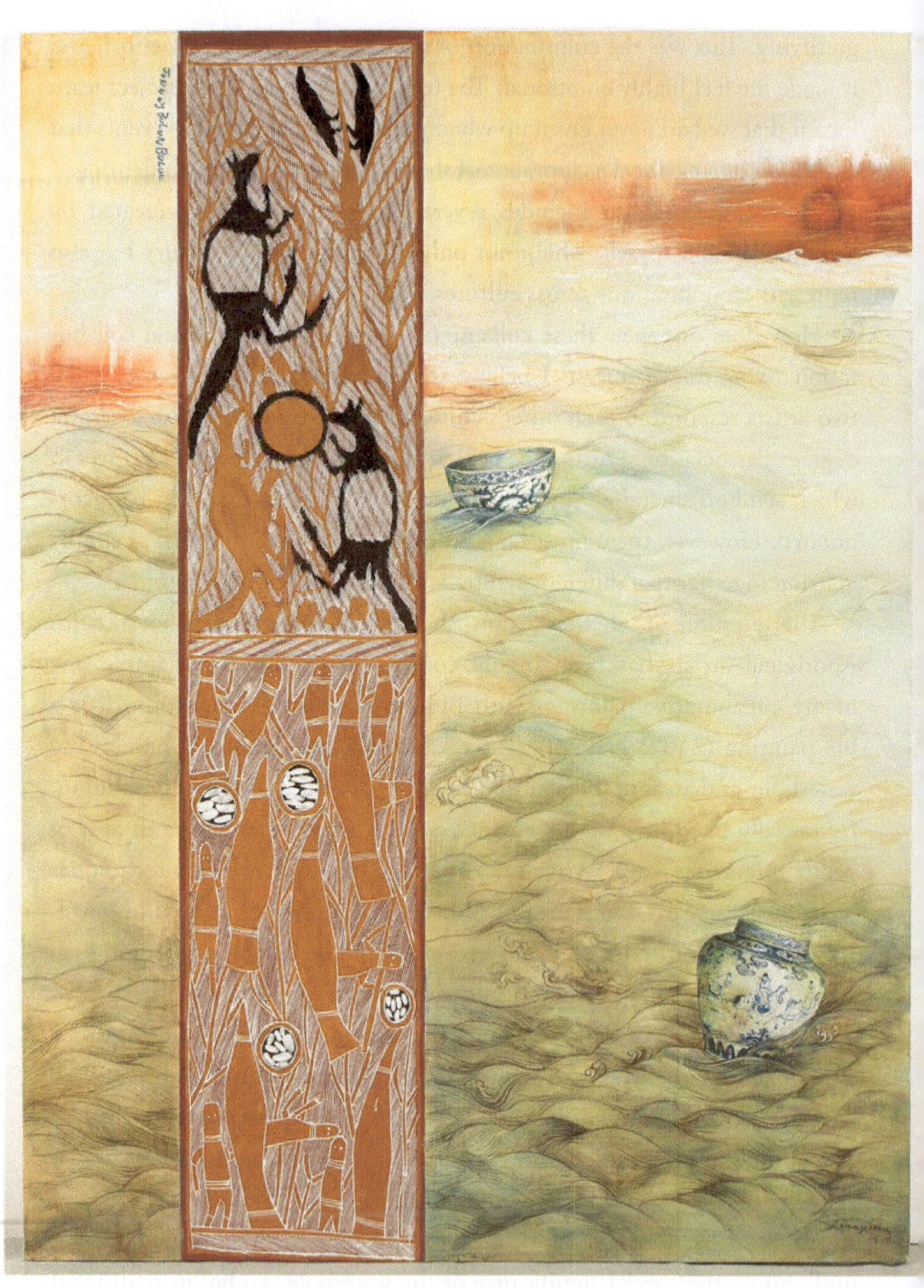

Johnny Bulunbulun and Zhou Xiaoping, *Dialogue* (2009),
acrylic and ochre on canvas, 240 x 170 cm.

white people. Again, he emphasised that not all waterhole symbols are given special meanings: the meaning must be determined according to the story held within the painting.

In the collaboration between myself and Bulunbulun, I thought that we would be able to just ignore other people's opinions. But society will still question the artists, because it involves an Aboriginal artist. Any collaboration with Indigenous artists will receive varying degrees of attention and scrutiny. There is an extraordinary degree of sensitivity to these issues in Australian society, which I believe is not what Aboriginal artists in fact want. Although I have lived in this country for over thirty years, sometimes I have a feeling of not knowing where I am.

Then one day, Bulunbulun called me and said that he had changed his mind about the painting.

'Why? You said you were very happy with our work.'

'Because if I don't change it, they are not going to sell my paintings anymore.'

I was speechless when I heard this.

Over the phone, he tried to explain, but I couldn't take it in. Finally, I just said, 'I'll change it'. I would never yield to any political or cultural coercion or obey anyone's orders about what to paint, but I would never disrespect my collaborator, whatever the circumstances.

I put down the phone, and I looked at the painting for a long time. Finally, my thoughts crystallised as a single question: does an Aboriginal artist have a say in how they represent their own culture?

A very important Australian art gallery once wanted to collect one of my collaborative paintings with Johnny Bulunbulun. But at a certain stage of the negotiations, the plan was dropped. My agent was extremely confused as to why this had happened, because she had often heard the painting being greatly praised. There was no clear answer, until one day she eventually found out. The gallery curator involved was in favour of cross-cultural collaborations, but couldn't accept a collaboration between an Aboriginal and a non-Aboriginal artist, and to be precise, a Chinese artist. So, the gallery preferred to display a painting done entirely by an Aboriginal artist, even if the painting was of a lesser quality.

This brings up another phenomenon. Once at a seminar, I heard an artist speak on the theme of identity. She said quite frankly that as an artist, after facing many difficulties, she was considered unsuccessful. Then one day, when she exhibited as an Aboriginal artist, everything suddenly changed. Her works attracted the attention of curators, and she became highly successful.

It seems that whether it is working with Aboriginal artists or creating Aboriginal-themed artwork, there is always endless controversy surrounding my work. I become frustrated and resentful of this anti-art demand for conformity or 'political correctness' that is imposed on my art but honestly, after thirty-odd years, I am used to it. Nonetheless, as an artist I derive an enormous sense of fulfilment from my artworks, and naturally I want to share my art with others, particularly here in Australia.

I would often lock myself in my studio and let my imagination, my dreams, and even my loneliness assault me from various angles. I would have to confront my own confusion, delusion, helplessness, depression, dilemmas and despair, but on completing a work, I am filled with a sense of elation and achievement, and this drives me to keep on painting.

———— ≈ ————

The initial idea of the 'Trepang' exhibition began from a conversation I had with Marcia. The world was entering the twenty-first century and everyone was celebrating and planning a bright future.

We talked about how Australian art stands out on the world stage. As a multicultural settler society with only two hundred years of history, Australia's mainstream culture has continued to be dominated by European ideas. Multiculturalism now impacts on this in a variety of ways. Newer immigrant groups are encouraged to retain their own cultures while taking part in the wider Australian society. This form of multiculturalism is seen as having been very successful in avoiding many of the tensions existing in other countries. Yet my belief is that the foundation is neither solid nor secure, and I fear that the turmoils of the outside world will at some stage in future stoke conflicts between different ethnic groups. Also, I am uncertain as to what extent this multicultural diversity in fact plays out in the Australian cultural identity.

It is indisputable that Aboriginal art is unique in its distinctive features and representation. Unfortunately, in a world unfamiliar with Aboriginal culture, this Indigenous art was ignored for decades by the art sector until it was discovered that buying Aboriginal art can be highly profitable.

Knowing that I wanted to achieve more than just enriching my personal life, Marcia thought that with my background and experience, I should undertake a cross-cultural project. As we chatted together at Marcia's house, reports were coming through on the television of Chinese jubilation because it had been announced that they would host the 2008 Olympics. The thought suddenly struck me that one way to examine the relationship between Australia and China was through the early trade in sea cucumber. Marcia thought this was a great idea. She told me that historians had done a lot of research in this area.

I replied it was not only academic research that was needed, that history can be presented in other ways, like holding a visual exhibition. Marcia's interest was piqued. If that's the case, she said, we would need to do our own research. Soon, I was going off to China, so I would be able to do some preliminary work.

To this end, I made a special trip to Fujian, to investigate the history of Zheng He's seven voyages to the West and to the South Pacific, and to look for clues that he might have landed in Australia. There are speculations about Zheng He's fleet having done this, but the evidence from various papers and maps is not very convincing. It seems that the first real Aboriginal communication with foreigners began with the Macassan sea cucumber trade that only indirectly involved the Chinese.

After this, we began our project in earnest, forming a project team, carrying out research, collecting data and information, and looking for funding. Several funding applications were unsuccessful – neither the government nor private funding agencies were interested. Even so, Marcia and I did not give up. We believed that this history was significant as the first

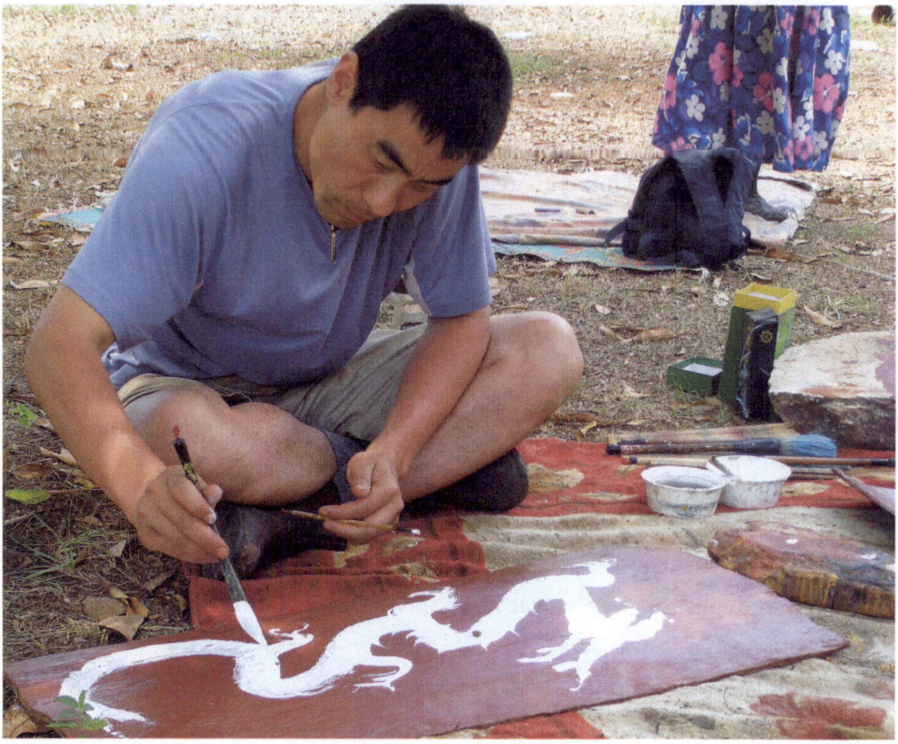

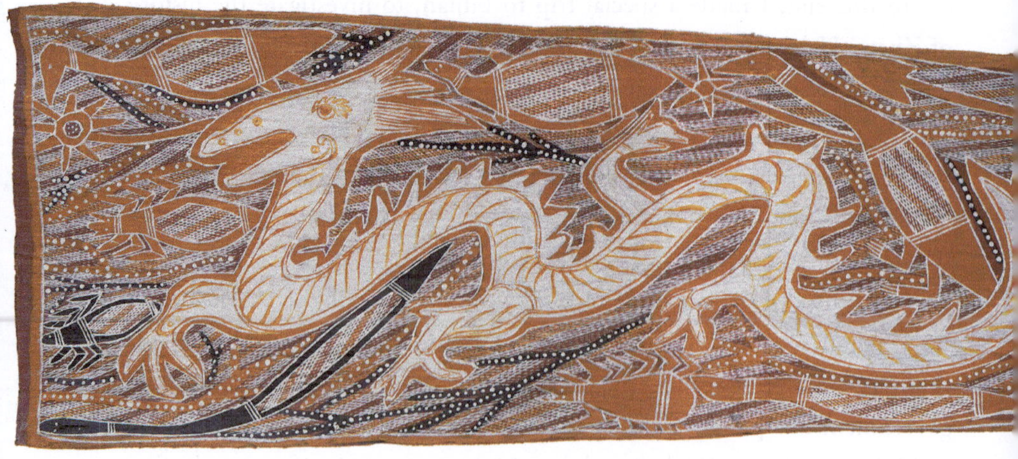

Johnny Bulunbulun, Laurie Maarbudug and Zhou Xiaoping, *Dragon,* ochre on bark, 350 x 850 cm. First, I painted the dragon on bark. Johnny and Laurie later completed the work.

trade exchange in Australian history. Our endeavours continued for eight years until, in 2007, we finally received financial support from Rio Tinto.

We brought together an extremely professional team, and our work progressed smoothly during the following two years: selecting artworks, designing the exhibition, arranging the logistics of transporting objects and art to China, finalising exhibition venues, completing the text and design of the catalogue. Everything was done in an orderly manner.

During this period, the hardest work was finding a high-profile exhibition venue. For this, I went to China several times. In the Chinese art sector, it was important that discussions took place face-to-face. Through my connections, I finally found the Millennium Monument Art Museum in Beijing. They agreed to be a joint organiser, providing the exhibition space for two months free of charge. This was a wonderful opportunity.

As the exhibition date grew near, with just three months to go, a major event occurred that put it on hold indefinitely. I received an unexpected telephone call from Ngaritj. After I greeted him, he fell silent. This was ominous. Something must have happened over there.

After a while, the message I didn't want to hear came through: 'He passed away'.

Ah, I opened my mouth to ask what had happened, but I no words came out.

Ngaritj didn't say anything more. We all needed to digest what the words 'He passed away' meant to us and how we could face this sudden news.

How could it be? Only a few months ago, I had been with the old man at Wudija outstation. We had discussed our plans for the trip to China. He was very excited about it, repeating his dream of selling a lot of paintings for more than 'rubbish' money. He also told me that he had a new idea and wanted to come to Melbourne to paint with me. I was prepared to arrange these trips for him and to apply for his new passport and visa. But now… it was all over. I had not expected that everything would become a memory so early and so quickly.

A voice came from the other end of the phone: 'Laurie wants to talk with you'.

I held the phone and heard Laurie crying… and crying. My heart ached, and any words of comfort seemed so weak. Many scenes were surging through my mind. I remembered most clearly our last meeting at Wudija outstation. I had told Bulunbulun that I wanted to experiment with painting on bark instead of on rice paper. But how would I do this effectively? This really bothered me. I thought of some Chinese elements, like blue-and-white porcelain, dragons, and the figure of Buddha. I asked the crew director, a Torres Strait Island man who was with me making a documentary of my story, what he thought. He didn't like the idea of painting dragons. Yet he believed that there should be no restrictions on what artists drew or painted. This was not the first time that I found Aboriginal and Torres Strait Islander peoples to be quite open-minded in dealing with these issues.

I asked Bulunbulun what the dragon meant in Aboriginal culture. He said that they had no such animal, although perhaps the dragon bore some resemblance to their rainbow snake. He knew that the dragon was a very important symbol to the Chinese, just as the Motj was for him.

'Motj' is a word used only by the Marrangitj people in Arnhem Land. It means the sorcerers and healers. The Motj communicate with people through things in nature, such as wind, clouds and earth, especially on a spiritual level.

So, it seemed that bark painting and dragon symbolism were somewhat incompatible, coming as they did from different cultures. However, I still felt that they could be harmonised via the artist's brush. Bulunbulun told me to paint whatever I liked, then he would finish it afterwards. I picked up a brush and dipped it into the white paint which he had prepared for me, then I drew a dancing dragon on the bark. This was the last painting that we made together. Our collaboration had started with rice paper and ended with bark painting.

Unfortunately, Bulunbulun passed away before the bark painting was completed. And my memory of painting it was interrupted by Laurie's voice on the phone.

'I'm hungry, need food, tobacco', she said in a faint voice.

I told her to go to my gallery in Darwin to get some cash.

After hanging up, I looked up to the sky and seemed to hear the chuckle of a kookaburra from nearby, taking my heart back to country.

Under these circumstances, the exhibition project faced great uncertainty. According to Aboriginal custom, after an Aboriginal person dies, his name is no longer mentioned, and photos of the deceased are not allowed to appear in public places or in the sight of relatives. It is up to the family of the deceased and the local elders to decide when this ban can be lifted, and it often holds for more than a year or two after the death. If the deceased was an artist, all his artworks had to be carefully hidden away.

I called Laurie and explained to her that our exhibition would be held in China and that it would be two years before it returned to Australia. I said that Bulunbulun was a great artist who needed to be remembered and should not disappear from the public eye. Laurie was persuaded by this, as was Professor Marcia Langton. But others dissented. As a sponsor, Rio Tinto was already trying to lessen the negative impact of a recent economic espionage case, concerning Stern Hu, and didn't want to give the impression that they were using our exhibition project to repair relationships during this sensitive period. The executives of the company asked for my opinion. I told them that I believed the death of an Aboriginal artist should not artificially force society to forget him. I thought that this outdated custom needed to be changed, and we should continue to exhibit the work of deceased artists like Johnny Bulunbulun as we would any non-Aboriginal artist.

I told them that hiding something away was a custom, not a law. It was possible for different regions and families to decide for themselves what to do. Curators needed to listen to and respect the wishes of the Aboriginal people of the affected clan. In this case, Laurie and Ngaritj, as immediate family members of the deceased, were very open-minded. They and their family felt that the mourning period did not need to be that long.

A few months later, news of the funeral was broadcast on ABC TV. It was clear to me that while Indigenous people themselves had been changing their thinking, these so-called journalistic experts had not updated their knowledge. They were solemnly announcing that to respect Aboriginal culture, the artworks of Johnny Bulunbulun would be immediately removed from the walls of the art gallery. Incredibly, the wider society also appeared to believe this. There was little effort made to discuss the situation and to confirm that their attitude was well-founded. To me, it seemed that Australians had a complex mindset when it came to Aboriginal issues. I have always found that if issues were treated with sincerity and respect, they would be understood by Aboriginal people. Excessive protection was unnecessary and counterproductive.

Everyone was under tremendous pressure to decide the fate of the exhibition, especially the senior management of Rio Tinto. The situation was complicated and intense. After several difficult and serious discussions, as well as consultation with experts, the company announced that expert advice on Aboriginal law would be respected and, during a twelve-month mourning period, all public activities related to the deceased should cease. I understood and respected the company's decision. They had been – and still were – extremely supportive of this project. I asked everyone, 'On this issue, who should we listen to? The Aboriginal family or those so-called experts?' My question was not raised specifically with our team, but rather was directed to the public who are concerned about this issue.

At around this time, the catalogue designer called me wanting to know whether the catalogue could be published as scheduled without further revision.

I was very hesitant, but said, 'Go ahead, I'll be there tomorrow'. I didn't want to just give up on this exhibition that I'd worked on for eight years. I called the director of the Millennium Monument Art Museum to explain what had happened. He was very disappointed to hear my news and then told me that if the exhibition were to be postponed, it could not be rescheduled for another three years, unless we were prepared to pay a venue fee of A$3,000 per day. For an exhibition lasting sixty days, this would amount to a charge of A$180,000 – an astronomical sum. It would also be nearly impossible to find an alternative venue at such short notice.

During this period, Laurie called me several times a day to tell me, 'I'm going to Maningrida… You come with me… just you and me.' I felt that she was showing signs of a mental breakdown. She wanted me to help her tell the balanda [white people] at Darwin Hospital to send the body back to Maningrida, and not to Ramingining. She kept saying, 'Balanda don't listen to me'. Yet the staff at Darwin Hospital said that they were complying with the family's decision.

I told Laurie that the doctors wouldn't listen to me either. Saying this made me feel completely ignored as well. No one would listen to me.

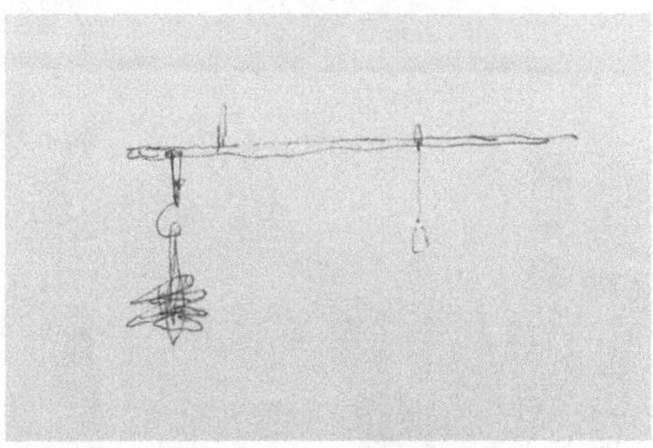

Trade – trepang and Chinese scale.

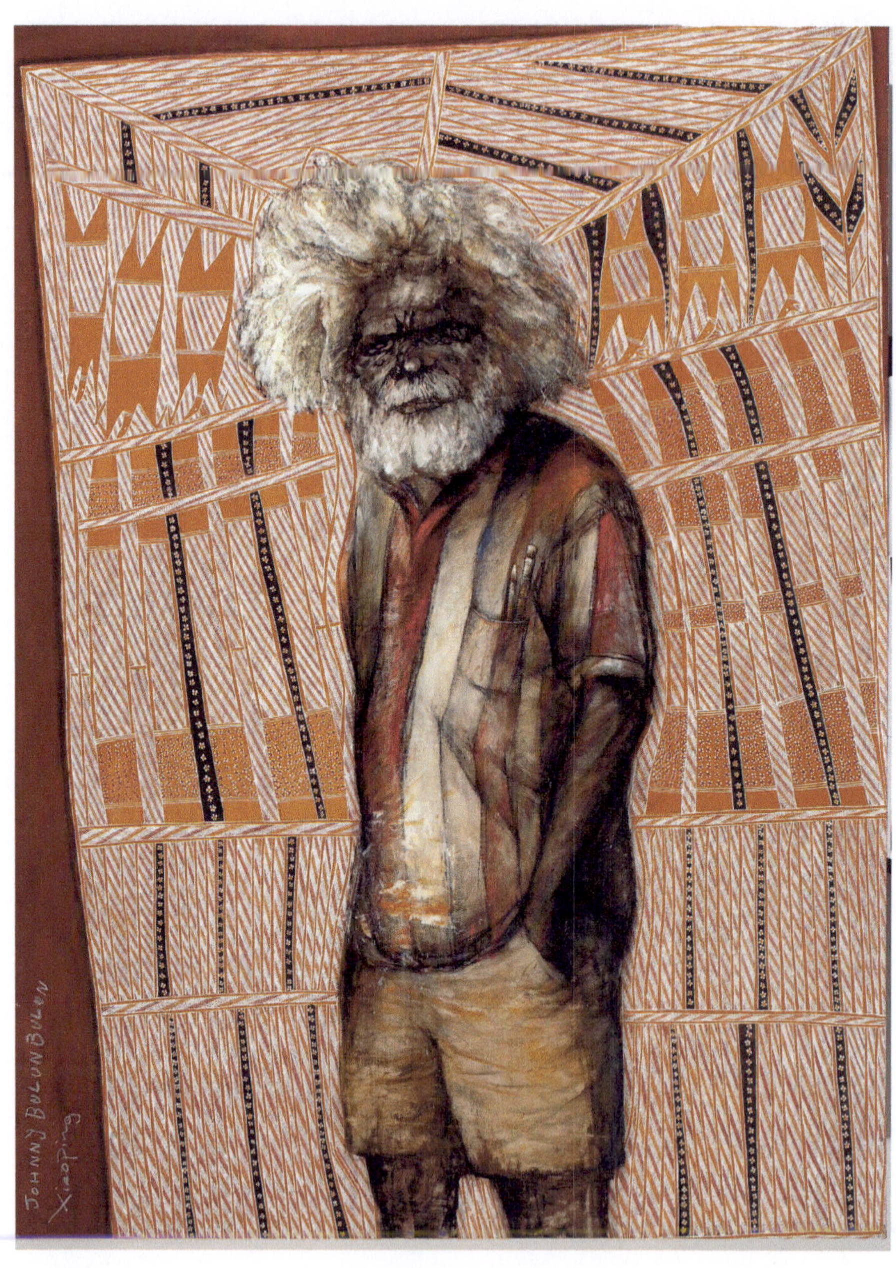

Johnny Bulunbulun and Zhou Xiaoping, *Portrait of Johnny Bulunbulun* (2007), acrylic and ochre on canvas, 200 x 147 cm. The background of the painting was created by Johnny.

18

Bulunbulun's Funeral

All kinds of bad news kept arriving. I wanted to get away from everyone, including our work team. I went back to Ramingining for Bulunbulun's funeral. The family had eventually decided to hold it there. The film crew came with me, as they had followed me about for a couple of years making a documentary of my story. We drove from Darwin to Ramingining, which took us thirteen hours. The day after we got there, I learned that the body had not yet arrived. There was no consensus among relatives on how some things should proceed. While we waited, Ngaritj convened a meeting of more than twenty family members, including Bulunbulun's younger brother Peter Girrirkirri, the Aboriginal elder Richard, and others. Laurie wasn't there because she was very unhappy that the funeral was being held at Ramingining. I brought up the matter of the exhibition. Could it go ahead? Or would it have to be postponed or cancelled?

'Are you really going to postpone? He's a great artist, and we want everyone remembers him', Peter Girrirkirri said.

'Yeah!', the crowd agreed.

But I had to tell them that the project team had taken the advice of experts and were ignoring my and the family's thoughts.

'You know, we don't want people forget him. He is famous artist… try again, please', Ngaritj added, recognising my dilemma.

Hearing this and seeing everyone looking at me, I realised that we were all in accord. Someone muttered, 'Balanda, not be trust'. But I really didn't want to make these grieving relatives even more depressed, so I asked, 'How long we have to wait for?'

'In China, or down the south, you can do now. If in Darwin, after six months. Maynmak?', Peter Girrirkirri told us looking around to see that everyone agreed.

'Yeah', once again came voices of approval.

'Is there a problem for media report?'

'No problem, you can make the catalogue or calendars, postcards… prove he is a great artist', the Aboriginal elder Richard said.

'So, can we make a video?', the director of my documentary asked.

'Yo, you can take pictures at the funeral tomorrow', Ngaritj replied. Then he told me to wait a moment, he wanted to show me something.

He came back with a rolled-up painting. Spreading out a clean cloth on the ground, he laid down the painting and carefully opened it up.

'This is the old man's last painting. It's a secret story painting', Ngaritj said. Then he briefly described the story it told.

There is a full black circle right in the middle of the painting, surrounded by many *gumang* (magpie geese), *guwaynang* (freshwater long-necked turtle) and *garjarr* (water snake) among the lotus in the swamp. While these patterns had often appeared scattered in his other paintings, now they had all been brought together. But I thought that wasn't the main point of this painting. 'Surely', Ngaritj said, 'it emphasises that only women could dance with these lotus and water snakes here. The black circle represents the waterhole, which is still a secret place.' This story was unusual, because this kind of secret story will generally avoid interactions between men and women. It seemed that the simple full black circle was the focus of the painting, and the story behind it couldn't be told in detail in public.

'No one can approach this place, except the grey-haired person', Ngaritj emphasised. 'This was where our ancestors created our homeland, where people and all living things originate.' The elemental symbols used by the old man provided an abstract description of an ancient story in which he and his people still deeply believe. It contains a strong spirituality that is clearly in evidence in the painting. Although Ngaritj's explanation was short, the deeper meaning can only be understood by the artist himself and can only be explained in full to Aboriginal people. Obviously, the painting held extremely profound meaning. I believe that, over time, Aboriginal people will gradually share some of these significant stories with non-Indigenous people, although some secrets will never be known to the world.

Clearly, the old man's painting was not now being withheld from public gaze. 'Why are you sharing this secret story with me?', I asked.

'Old man told me about you. You are one of us, allowed to know it', the elder man called Richard said firmly.

'Yeah…' Once again came approval from the crowd.

'We're also changing', Ngaritj said.

This was the answer that I was looking for. Aboriginal people were changing, but were non-Aboriginal people following this? They did not seem to hear what Aboriginal people were saying, but clung to their outdated understanding, unwilling to accept change, thinking that only in this way could they show respect, care and love for Aboriginal people. But I saw this just as an excuse for lazy thinking.

I said, 'We need to show old man's paintings now, make him more famous!'

'Yo! Maynmak!', Richard took the lead, raising his hand, and there came loud applause from the crowd. To let our project team and our sponsors know what had occurred, I drafted a statement:

> The family members of the deceased JBB agree that the Trepang Exhibition can use the images, artworks, and the full name of JBB in the exhibition, the catalogue and other publications in China and Southern Australia (excludes Northern Territory) at any time from today. After 6 months from today all the above-mentioned items can be publicly shown in the Northern Territory. The family understands that 2 or 3 family members will travel to China for the Exhibition. All travel costs and expenses will be paid by the Exhibition.

This was signed by twelve family members and elders and was given to the project team. They all heaved a sigh of relief.

For the next few days, we waited for the body to be brought back from Darwin Hospital. The waiting was both anxious and emotional.

I have participated in many ceremonies, including some sacred ceremonies that only close relatives or related people can attend, and funerals are also common ceremonies.

Once I attended a funeral in Yirrkala. The man had died of a heart attack while fishing at sea. I saw a boat drawn on the sand in front of his house. Two stones had been placed at either end of the boat and dry tree branches were piled up in the middle. Those attending the funeral sat on the ground all around. People in the front row kept blowing *yidaki*, beating percussive instruments and singing, while a burst of weeping came from the crowd. All their sorrow was expressed in their singing.

After a long while, one of elders stood up and made a short but touching speech, causing the women in the crowd to weep. A young man set the pile of tree branches on fire, then threw the belongings and clothes of the deceased man into the fire. Seeing the fire getting stronger and stronger, accompanied by singing and crying, the sad atmosphere at last reached a climax. A shout came from the elder who was leading the ceremony. At his command, all sounds suddenly ceased, as people prayed silently to

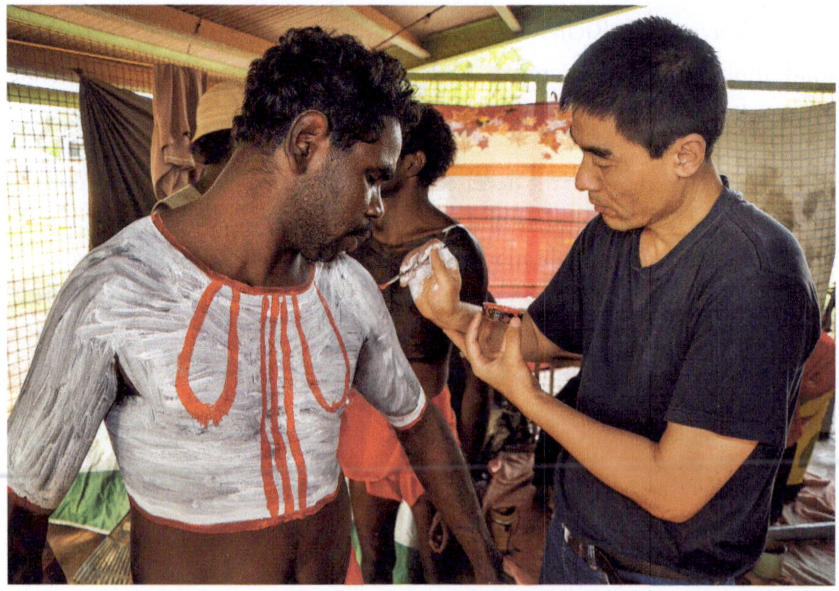

Painting up, in preparation for Johnny Bulunbulun's funeral ceremony.

send the soul to a far place where it could rest. Relatives then began to beat themselves and their children with flaming branches and leaves. They smoked the inside and outside of the house where the deceased had lived, and then extinguished the fire in the sand.

Finally, the coffin containing the body was placed into a small boat, then surrounded with a lot of food and covered with leaves. The boat was then

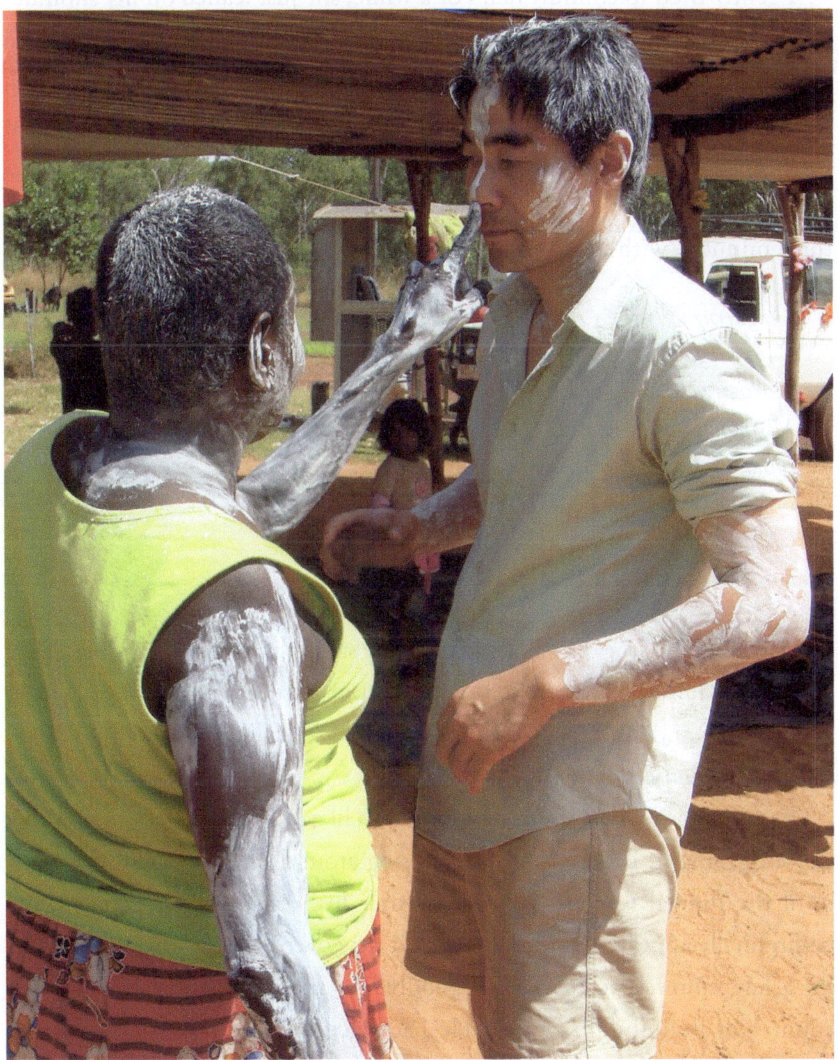

Further painting up, in preparation for Johnny Bulunbulun's funeral ceremony.

gently pushed out to sea. A peaceful start to this journey. After many days, the deceased would be accepted by spirits in the depths of the sea.

Laurie had arrived at Bulunbulun's funeral three days after me. When she saw me, she threw herself on my shoulder and cried bitterly, with no strength left to speak.

'He's gone', she said weakly.

I gently tried to comfort her. For a while, she just leaned on my shoulder and wept softly. The sound slowly subsided until all I heard was the rhythm of her breathing as she fell asleep.

Before dark, several young people had carefully placed a red flagpole at the front left corner of the house. Then at night, there were many sad songs around the campfire, accompanied by *yidaki*. Each segment took two or three minutes, with its meaning in brackets as below:

> *Lungurrng* (Wind)
> *Gapi gungdgalng* (Salt water)
> *Martharga* (Sailing boat)
> *Miringu* (War)
> *Bunapi* (Trepang)
> *Birratha* (Rice)
> *Gadambal* (House)
> *Landjarrnga* (Sleeping).

It was telling the story of Aboriginal people sailing in a boat on the sea. They encountered invaders. The two sides fought. After negotiation, the two sides shook hands and made peace. They exchanged sea cucumber and food. Then life once again became peaceful.

Because this was a story that Bulunbulun liked to paint, they had specially chosen to sing it. People continued to sing around the campfire every night until the funeral was officially held. After five days, a plane carrying the coffin finally appeared in the sky. First, it flew over Yirrkala where it hovered for a few minutes, to say a final goodbye to the loved ones. This was the country of Bulunbulun's father. He had once told me that he would take me to his father's country after our exhibition project had been completed.

Watching the plane, Laurie hugged me and burst into tears.

Bulunbulun's close relatives were staying at the camp, waiting for the body to arrive. They started smearing each other's body and face with white clay. A woman put some on my head, face, arms and finally my legs.

Soon, a faint singing could be heard in the distance, and gradually a group of people appeared singing and dancing around the hearse. The whole camp began to cry, with the voice of one man after another raised in song. Some women slashed themselves in grief. The scene was unbearable.

After the coffin had been placed in the mourning hall in the house, I put a flower on the coffin, and then sat on the ground with other relatives.

A great artist had left us.

My brother had left me.

The exhibition project team and the sponsors finally made the decision to postpone the exhibition for a year. It was clear that if I insisted on it being held any earlier, I would put Rio Tinto in a very embarrassing situation, which no one wanted to see. So, although it was a big disappointment, I had to respect this decision. After eight years of hard work and then to fail at the last minute, you can imagine just how frustrated I was. Even so, I did not forget the project. I still had to deal with our collaborative paintings. I was given two options by Bulunbulun's agent: either to buy each painting at its market value or to cut the painting and return the part that Bulunbulun had painted. In desperation, I felt that I had no choice but to buy the paintings.

Next, I had to find a new venue for the exhibition, believing that somehow it would still happen. Once again, I made a special trip to China. Then I was surprisingly lucky: a new opportunity came from a friend I met at a dinner, who introduced me to people at the Capital Museum. After sending them my proposal, I soon heard back that they would accept the exhibition for a three-month period. My depression suddenly evaporated. Usually, I don't think of myself as a lucky person, but believe it or not, this time luck had indeed found me!

Now all the correspondence had to be started up again. There were many issues, but the most difficult arose from ideological differences. This is the biggest problem that Western countries encounter in the process of cultural exchange with China. I can give an example of the problems we faced. On an old map produced by Britain, Tibet was included as part of India, and the colour of Taiwan was different from that of China. The Capital Museum sent a solemn letter requesting that we remove this map from the exhibition. As expected, this elicited an immediate backlash from some members of the project team, who said that this was Chinese censorship and that they would rather cancel the exhibition than allow this to happen.

Despite the problems arising from ideology, I must emphasise the value that cross-cultural communication and connection brings to the bilateral relationship.

The final thing I had to deal with was the catalogue. We needed to get permission from Laurie and Ngaritj for the images that we wanted to use. When I put these images in front of Laurie and Ngaritj in Darwin, I wasn't sure how they would react to seeing Bulunbulun's photo. They sat on the bed in my hotel room and quietly read each page, occasionally making short comments as I light-heartedly explained the images to them. A smile crept over Laurie's face when she saw a picture of someone holding a long bong (like the one commonly used by Chinese) up to his nose and spewing two thick plumes of smoke from his nostrils. She was amused because this was something that she often does herself. Over the page were several photos, including one of me with Bulunbulun and another of us cutting bark and painting in the bush. I thought that they might have problems with these photos. Beforehand I had imagined what I might do, like turning the book over or closing it immediately, saying: 'Yaka [No]!' I could even get up angrily and walk away. However, I didn't need to do anything like this. Seeing these photos, their expressions remained calm. Laurie pointed to the photo of Bulunbulun and said to Ngaritj, 'This was taken in Wudija. We were cutting the bark, then we drew on the sand.' I saw that she was immersed in her memories. Then, pointing to the next photo of me posing with Bulunbulun, she seemed uncertain: 'This is…' 'It's Wudija, too', I said.

'Oh, yeah, on the way to go fishing', and she began reminiscing about the time we spent together, fishing at the beach, catching crabs, cutting tree bark and painting together.

As they turned the last page, I asked, 'Maynmak?' Both replied at the same time, 'Yo, Maynmak! Maynmak! Time for a drink.'

A year later, all kinds of difficulties were overcome to allow us finally to stand here at the Capital Museum in Beijing.

Laurie opened her arms to me and Ngaritj, and the three of us hugged each other silently. No words were needed, because a gesture or an expression was enough to understand each other's inner world. All our hard work had paid off in this moment.

The exhibition was a huge success. After three months, it had been seen by 300,000 people. To record a memorable moment for myself, I stood in front of my favourite piece, *Untitled History*, in which a piece of blank bark and a piece of blank rice paper stand next to each other – two different materials, each indicating important cultural connotations for two different nations. They hold no words or images but indicate that a new page of history can begin here: 'Trepang: China & the Story of Macassan–Aboriginal Trade'. On 10 September 2011, the exhibition was returned to the Melbourne Museum.

Laurie Marburru Maarbudug passed away in May 2020. Due to Covid-19, I was unable to attend her funeral.

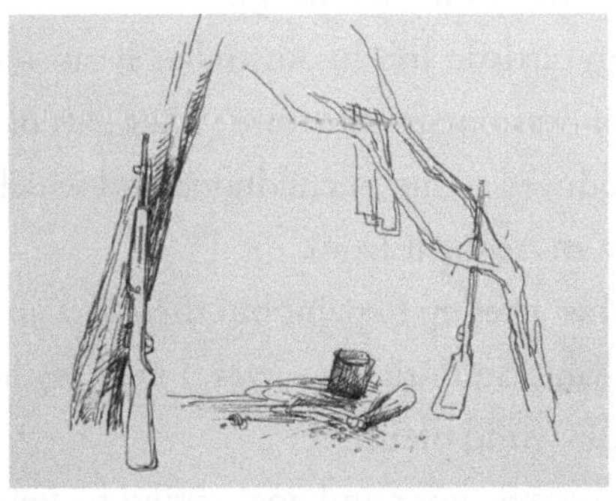

Wudija outstation, the place I once called home,
where I lived with Bulunbulun and Laurie.

19

My Studio in Melbourne

The best way that I can tell the story of my encounter with Aboriginal Australians is through my painting. My art most accurately sums up the profound experiences that span a period of over thirty years.

The studio is a world that I have created for myself, a place where I am never lonely. When I walk into my studio, the first thing I do each morning is to turn on the radio to listen to the news. I find out what is happening in the world, giving me a certain degree of connection with reality. Afterwards, I make myself a cup of tea, and, sitting down on the red revolving chair, I return to a world in which I alone exist. This is my daily routine, where I let myself travel freely between reality and dream, Melbourne and Arnhem Land, while injecting experience and perception into artistic creation.

My works of art are the way in which I tell my story, and making them allows me to include subjects which cannot be described directly but which can be found hidden within my paintings.

Reflecting on my artistic life in Australia, I can see that I have been following the path of 'learning from nature', a key part of traditional Chinese culture, a path introduced to me in childhood and which I have pursued all the way from China to Arnhem Land.

Thinking of all this, I get up to paint but then curl up on my comfortable sofa with a glass of wine. Squinting my eyes, I raise my head slightly, and let myself merge into the world of art.

While my body relaxes, my mind goes racing to some far-off discussion at a campfire in the bush or in the desert. As if in a movie, an image appears:

a drop of black ink falls slowly on to a piece of rice paper, where it gradually spreads. A second drop falls, becoming translucent on touching the paper. As it soaks through on to the hard ground underneath, it breaks into countless crystal-clear beads of water. Flying outwards, these water droplets turn into dots of colour, and transform into a beautiful picture. Beside the picture, two women sit whispering. Suddenly, a hand appears, holding a brush and beginning to draw loose casual lines. It is hard to make out what is being expressed. Is the artist deranged? The brush remains in motion. As more and more coloured dots are put in place, the thoughts of the artist are revealed and hazy insights gradually become clear.

Suddenly as if by magic, a black hand appears, an outstretched index finger draws a circle, while a woman mumbles, '*Kutjupa-Kutjupa Tjuta Utiringanyi Nyangatja*'. She is speaking in her own Pitjantjatjara language, recounting distant memories… silence falls. All that can be heard is the wind blowing across the sand. Responding to far-off music, another black hand very slowly adds a second circle at the bottom of the picture, guided by the first woman. At a gesture from this woman, a few white dots drop down from the brush, representing the tracks of people walking in the desert towards another circle. Clearly, these white dots represent tracks.

Now the two hands turn into two pairs of feet walking in the desert, followed by children and dogs. A woman speaks: 'A long time ago, there was a huge waterhole here, two small homelands near each other. Our people lived happily.' I realise that this is Rene speaking. Beside her walks her daughter, Sharmaine. 'There's a big road leading to these two homelands', Rene says, once again drawing a circle with her finger. She adds a squiggly line extending out to her upper left, then it turns right and continues to the upper right, where there are already two big concentric circles. As she draws, she mutters to herself in language. I am immersed in the process, imagining what will happen next. After a while, a painting seems to emerge from the earth itself: a few straight or curved lines designate a local road, and here and there are dotted patches of brilliant colour like grains of sand in the desert.

'Uwa [No], it should be like this', Rene says tilting her head. 'Later, several important ceremonies took place here.' She continues muttering to Sharmaine in language, confident that I will not understand. But my imagination is rich and fertile, and I can glimpse her meaning.

My eyes move like a lens. I see colours change into bushes and patches of land. Zooming in, some of the dots turn into rocks while the lines stand up and become trees. The birds have just woken up, and they chirp before spreading their wings to fly. A plume of smoke rises behind some bushes and on the horizon a group of strangers appear, their forms as transparent as bubbles. They pass through trees and rocks, then slowly drift away.

'Uwa…', a loud chant drifts across the vast desert, awakening the earth, the different creatures, and the spirits. 'I'm here, I'm here!' Hearing Rene's excited call, I seem to see Wamud himself looking for the tree of souls in Arnhem Land. Running wildly between the trees, he stretches his arms out wide, shouting, 'I'm back, I'm back…' Long chants whirl through the depths of the bush. All remains fresh in my memory.

Finally, after a long whistle ending with 'Uwa … Balya', the singing stops, and the brush sets down a rest symbol. Rene's tribute to the wilderness is complete. A breeze passes by, blowing away the dust, and gently brushing away the footprints. The reddish earth returns to its usual state.

'Continuing from here, there's a big waterhole, too', Rene says suddenly, but it sounds as if something is wrong. She quickly erases her drawing from the ground. 'Waya, waya, we can't draw this.' Whatever happened there cannot be described publicly. Such moments are mysterious. To describe them in language is taboo. Every culture has spiritual elements that uplift the human spirit and are revealed in art. In Aboriginal culture, spiritual stories that are not told to outsiders are often passed down through the generations by means of highly generalised and abstract painting.

Aboriginal people believe that the Divine Spirit created humanity and all other creatures. Under its guidance, people began to live their lives and to build their spiritual and physical environment. Aboriginal people directly express their reverence for the Divine Spirit through their care of the land, the land to which they retain a very close emotional connection. The land embodies their spirit and soul, and it is vital for non-Aboriginal people in Australia to understand this.

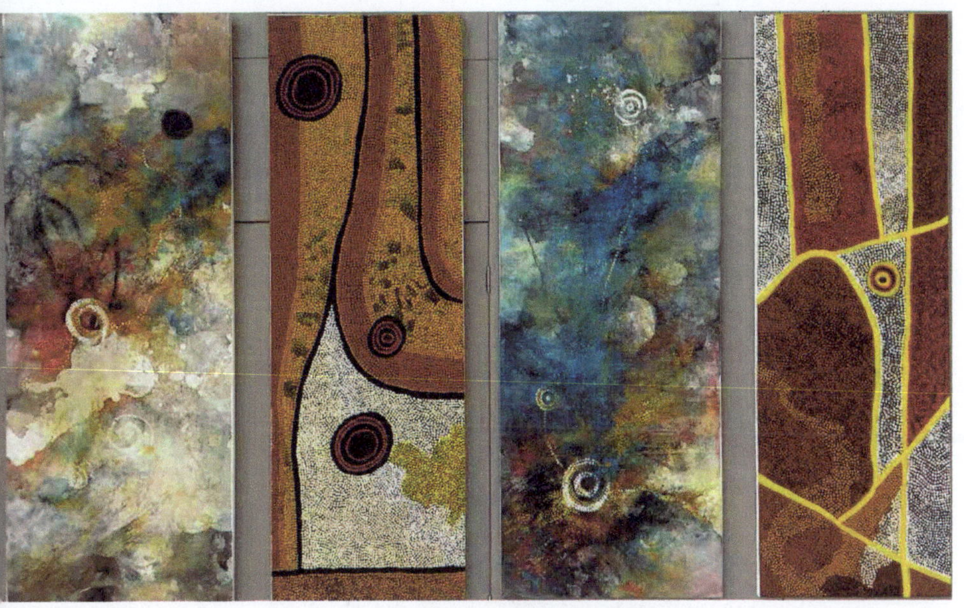

Rene Kulitja, Sharmaine Lesley and Zhou Xiaoping, *One Land, Two Views* (2017), acrylic on canvas, 150 x 90 cm for each panel.

Human beings are mere residents, and not the masters of the physical world as we know it. The Aboriginal people of Arnhem Land have known this truth for a long time. Painting provides a bridge that allows us to learn from the wisdom and spirituality of these ancient cultures that are largely closed to outsiders. The forms of expression employed are highly abstract, but despite lingering adherence to ancient techniques the level of aesthetic achievement is clearly pleasing to discerning modern-day non-Aboriginal viewers.

As Rene quickly scrubbed out her painting, I nodded at her to silently show that I understood why she couldn't draw her story. Bringing her face to my ear, she whispered, 'Because he [the Spirit] will know it'. Rene Kulitja, of the Pitjantjatjara people, grew up in a small homeland in northern South Australia. Later, she moved to the Mutitjulu community near Uluru. In 2002, one of her paintings featured on the outer fuselage of Qantas planes, and this is surely one of the best business cards in Australia.

I have travelled to remote communities, but my Aboriginal artist friends would also come to visit me in Melbourne. In 2017, the artists Rene Kulitja and her daughter Sharmaine came to stay with me for a couple of weeks

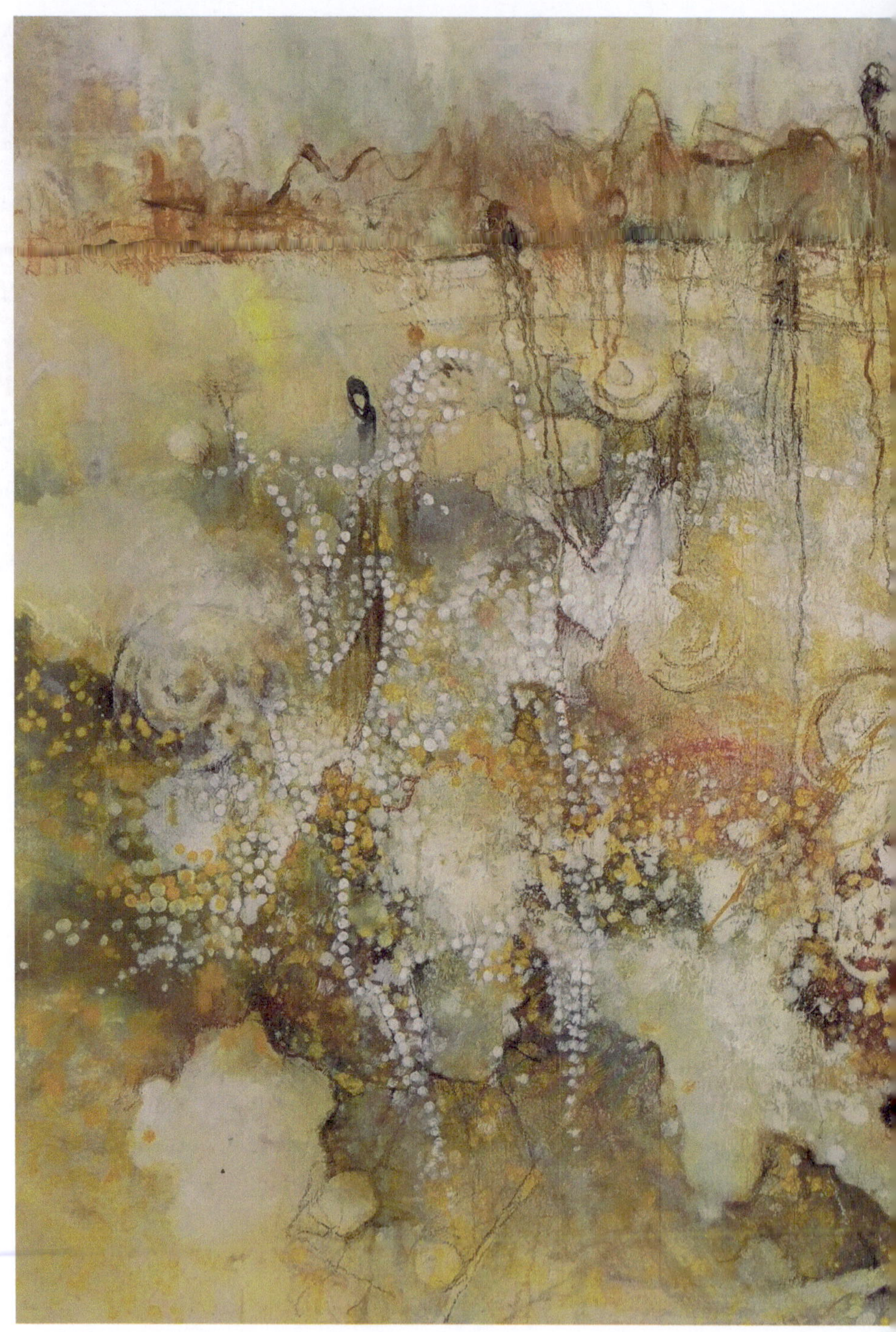

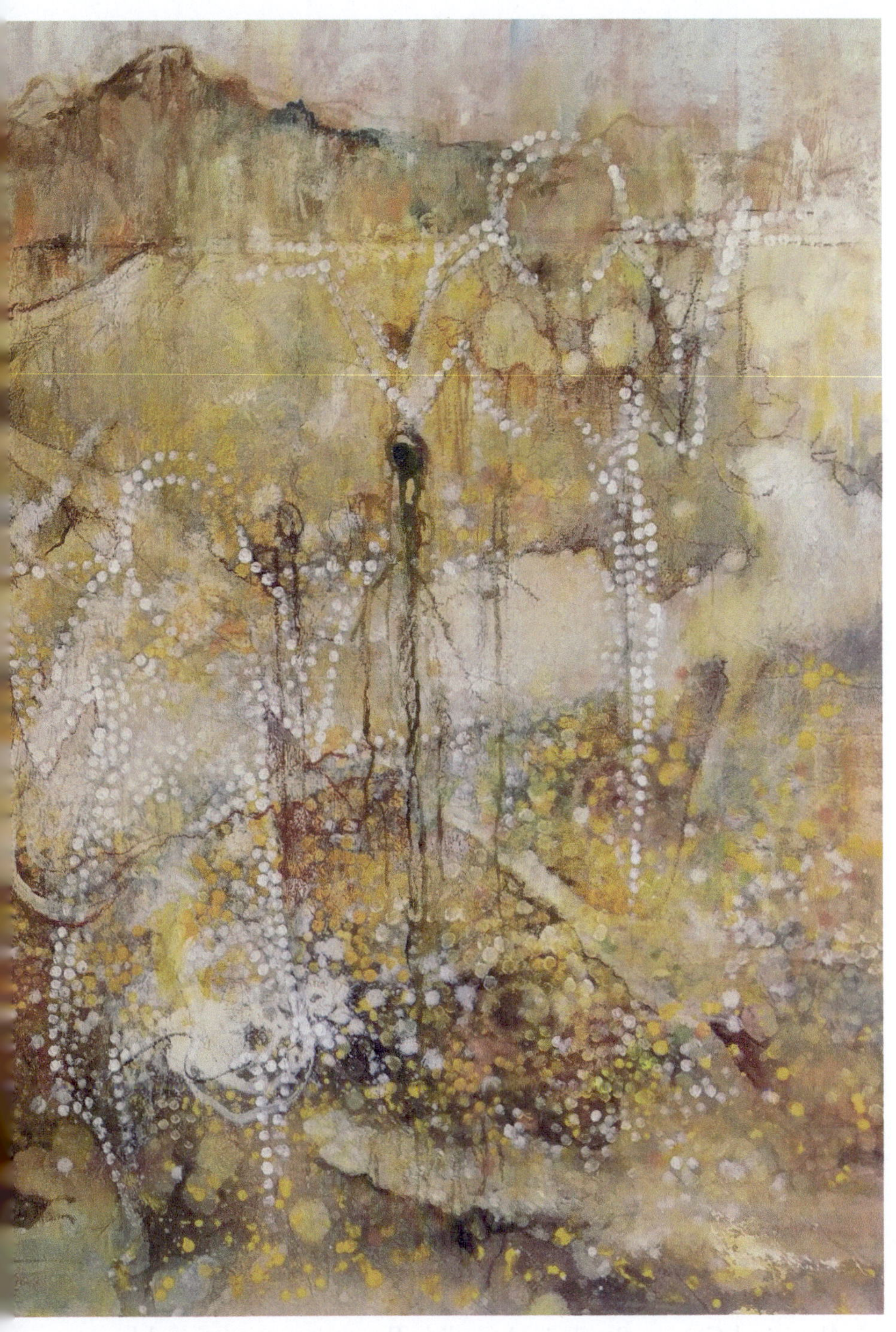

Zhou Xiaoping, *Land of Spirituality* (2018), ink, acrylic and oil on rice paper.

to create works both individually and collaboratively. At the time, I was preparing another exhibition that would go to China featuring the works of several Aboriginal artists including Rene and Sharmaine.

So, let's hide those mysterious stories deep inside the paintings, including the painting we were working on. Taking up my brush again, I asked, 'Should I use white?' Looking up, Rene agreed, 'Uwa, that's what I see'. After a while, I pointed to the painting and asked, 'What about here?' 'I see green, and yellow.'

Eventually, in the guise of abstractions and symbols, a painting representing the landscape as I understood it was completed. Rene considered our work and, pointing, said, 'These look a bit like mine, but they are your circles'. When she said this, Rene was sitting on the ground in the courtyard in front of my studio, but it seemed that to our interior vision, we saw the vast desert, a row of footsteps and slightly raised dust.

On their departure, they left behind wonderful paintings and, looking at them, I was reminded of the desert where I had lived. It is only people who actually live on country that can discover its mysteries. This experience has allowed an artist like myself to re-examine the world in which we live and discover new possibilities for art. Some exponents of 'contemporary art' contend that 'counterculture and subversion' are the main forms for creative expression, but these are not the only avenues. The artist can also be inspired by nature. The richness and greatness of nature are far beyond human imagination and comprehension. The real world is wonderful. The universe of art is also great, and you will find it naturally when you enter it. I am addicted to it, and as in the desert, here I can forget time.

When I walked out of the studio, it was already dark. It had been a long day just like any other day. However, one cannot work so intensely forever. When I feel restless, dissatisfied, or disillusioned, I know that it is time to pack my swag and take to the road again.

In 2020, I brought together a team of historians, artists and Aboriginal people to carry out a research and exhibition project called 'Our Story: Aboriginal Chinese People in Australia'. The project was inspired by my first encounter with the Aboriginal songwriter Jimmy Chi, well known for his musical *Bran Nue Dae*. Later on the same trip I also met Ah Lee and his companions: Aboriginal and Chinese descendants in the desert of Western Australia. These encounters, with Aboriginal people who had some Chinese ancestries, were inspirational and have always stayed with me.

'Our Story' began with three years of research and documentation of the rich and complex interaction between descendants of two of the world's oldest civilisations – an interaction often overlooked in dominant white Australian discourse. The search for this largely unacknowledged history led not only to a book, but also to an exhibition at the National Museum of Australia (10 April 2025 – 27 January 2026). For more information about this project, please visit www.aboriginal-chinese.com.

As an artist, I feel particularly gratified and proud at the completion of this work.

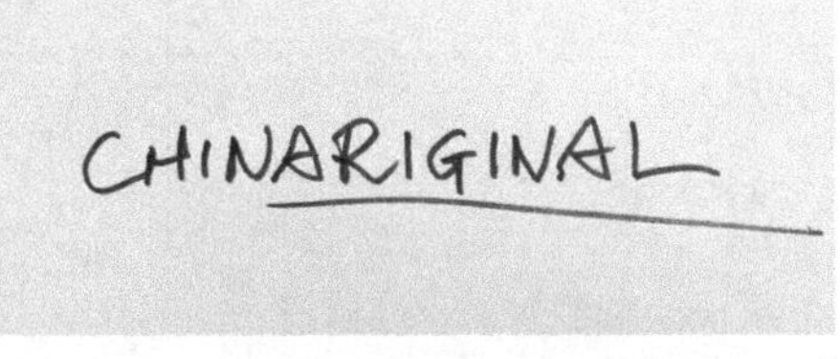

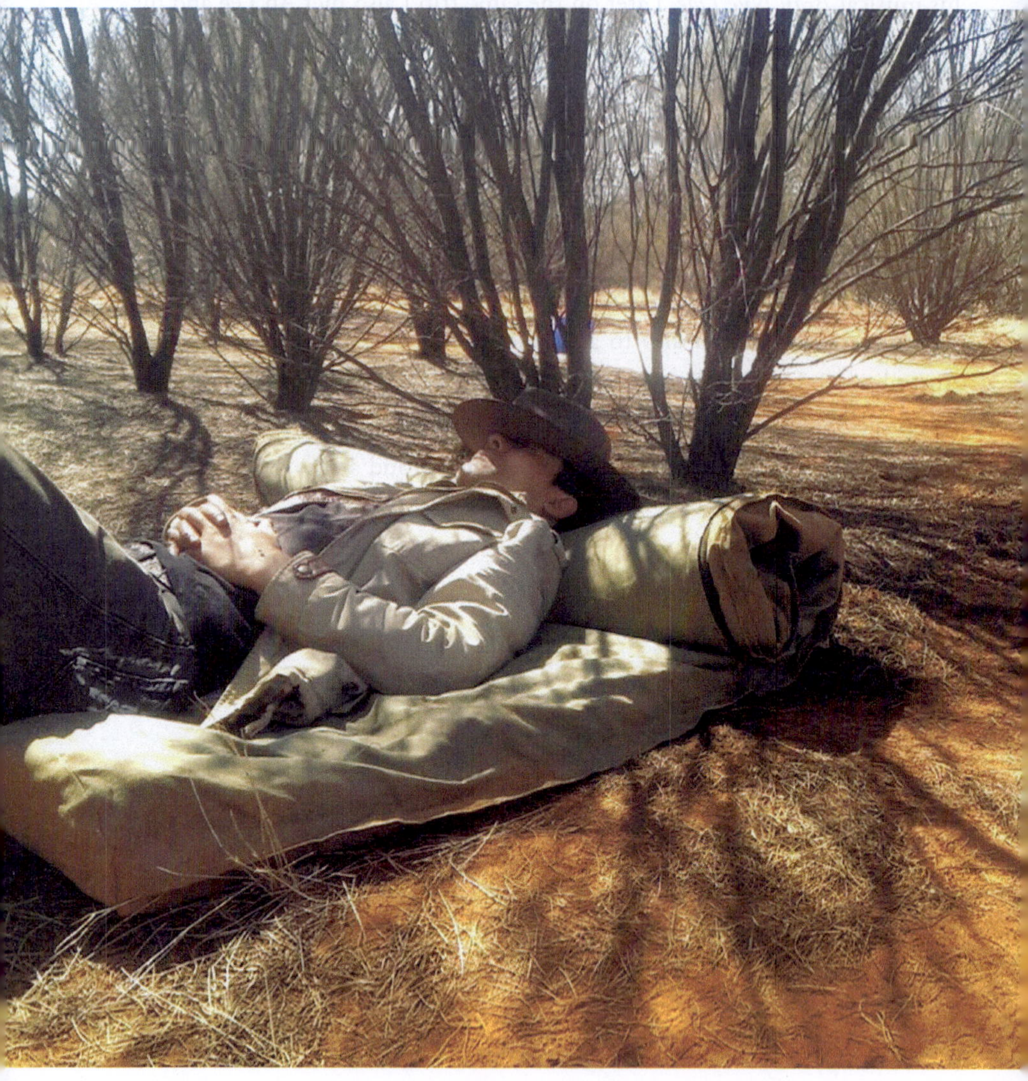

Travel in the bush often requires carrying a swag.

Index

(Page numbers given in italic refer to images/ captions.)

Z

Author Biography

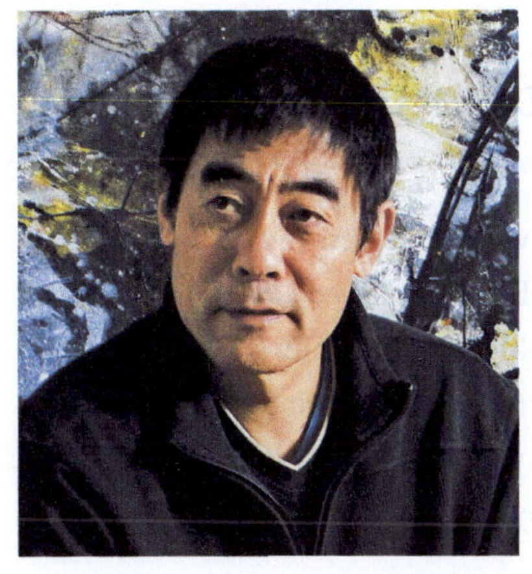

Zhou Xiaoping is a Melbourne-based artist, born and educated in China. Since 1988 he has been actively engaged with Aboriginal communities in Arnhem Land in the Northern Territory and the Kimberley in north-western Australia.

Xiaoping has been instrumental in several key Australian Aboriginal history research and exhibition projects. His collaboration with the late Jimmy Pike resulted in the first exhibition of Aboriginal artwork in China, in 1996. He was the key person in the 2009 'Trepang: China and the Story of Macassan–Aboriginal Trade' project, exhibited at the Capital Museum in Beijing, and at the Melbourne Museum in Australia in 2011. He was also the first to bring NAIDOC to China to celebrate Australia's Aboriginal culture during his exhibition in 2017.

He was Honorary Research Fellow, Asia Institute University of Melbourne in 2019.

Xiaoping has also held fifty-four solo exhibitions worldwide. In 2014, he was invited by the Australian Embassy in Paris to open his solo show at the Embassy, and to undertake a residency at the University of French Polynesia and Museum of Tahiti and its Islands.

In 2023, he participated (as one of three artists) in the exhibition 'Ochre and Sky', presented by the National Museum of Australia, in China.

Currently, he is the leader of the project 'Our Story: Aboriginal Chinese Australia', which has resulted in an important book on Australian history (of which he is the general editor), as well as an exhibition of the same title (of which he is the curator), held at the National Museum of Australia in Canberra from 10 April 2025 to 27 January 2026.

Acknowledgement

In bringing this book to completion, I wish to express my sincere gratitude to all those mentioned within its pages. Each has played a meaningful role in the course of my experience. I am thankful to my family for their constant support. I would also like to thank David Walker, Karen Walker and Mabel Lee for their invaluable assistance, as well as my publisher Nick Walker (no relation) and his team at ASP, copy-editor Diane Carlyle and graphic designer David Morgan.